The

Depression is a Liar

Liar

Series

By Danny Baker

CONTENTS

Depression is a Liar

Book #1 in the *Depression is a Liar* series

PROLOGUE

October, 2013

I picked up the sharpest piece of glass I could find on the side of the road and put it to my throat.

'No!' someone screamed, running towards me.

'Stay back!' I yelled, holding out the glass.

The man froze, raising his hands in the surrender sign.

'Pl-please . . .' he stuttered. 'Please don't do this. Whatever happened . . . it can be fixed.'

'What the fuck do you know?' I yelled. 'You don't know what it's like to be me! You're not crazy! You don't want to kill yourself one week and chase hallucinations the next! What the fuck do you know? What the *fuck* do you know?'

'OK, OK,' he motioned, patting the air. 'I'm sorry. Just please don't do this. *Please.*'

The crowd all tried to talk me into dropping the glass, but once again I brought it to my neck. I pierced the skin, felt hot blood dripping onto my hand.

Death. I craved it, craved it.

It was like a maddening hunger that I wanted to feed so badly. Everything was just so fucked up. Everything had been fucked up for so long and I was sure that this was the only way out. There was nothing I wanted to do but satisfy that craving. Nothing I wanted to do but die. Running that piece of glass over my throat made me feel better, thinking that the craving's about to be fed, thinking that the pain's about to end. So close to the apathy of death. Nothingness! The end! An escape at last!

Plunge it through your throat! Through your fucking throat! Now! Now!

My hand trembled wildly. My whole body shook.

Do it! Kill yourself! End it now!

My hand kept trembling and trembling before finally, the glass slipped through my fingers and fell to the ground. I couldn't do it. I exploded into tears, cried loudly as all my emotions ruptured inside me – in large part because I knew I'd have to keep living and fighting in this crazy fucked up world – but regardless, I knew I couldn't do it. I'm just not a quitter. When it really comes down to it I'm just not a quitter.

A couple of people helped me to my feet, moved me away from the wreckage. I sat hugging my shins on the sidewalk, crying with my head buried in my knees as the crowd watched on silently.

'You're not a quitter,' I kept sobbing to myself. 'You're not a quitter.'

The police arrived. They asked me what happened.

'You're not a quitter,' I kept repeating.

'So fix this.'

Taking a deep breath, I did my best to gather myself before looking up at the officers. And then I told them what happened.

'I'll plead guilty to whatever offence you see fit to charge me with,' I said when I had finished. 'But first, I need to be admitted to a psych ward.'

~~~

The above excerpt is actually the prologue of my as yet unpublished novel *I Will Not Kill Myself, Olivia*.

'What's your book about?' everyone would ask me while I was writing it.

An informative answer might've been that it is a tale of lost innocence, of a boy-going-on-man being sucked so deep into the vortex of depression that he self-destructs almost to the point of death; that it is a book about breakages – both psychological and romantic – yet also one about second chances; and that above all else, it is the story of Jimmy, of Olivia, and of the love that binds them.

But at the time, I didn't want to be informative.

'It's just a messy love story,' I'd mutter before quickly changing the subject.

My novel wasn't something I liked talking about because while I was working on it, I was afraid of being asked the inevitable question:

'What gave you the idea to write about mental illness?'

I don't like lying, and that wasn't a question I was comfortable answering honestly. I wasn't ready to tell anyone that I was just writing what I know – that while my protagonist Jimmy is his own character in his own world, that the apple, so to speak, did not fall far from the tree. I wasn't ready to tell anyone that the only reason I could write authentically about depression – and the alcoholism, drug abuse, medicine-induced psychosis, near-suicide attempts and hospitalisations it can lead to – was because I'd experienced it all myself. I was still in the thick of it. Still trying to get better. I didn't want anyone but the people closest to me knowing what I was going through.

I was gradually able to recover, however, and by the time I'd finished my novel at the end of 2012, I was happy, and ready to be open about my plight to try and help others who were suffering like I had. At the same time I was starting to think about finding a publisher, and that's when I came up with the Depression Is Not Destiny Campaign, to inspire victims of the illness to never give up on happiness. It centres around a video blog following my quest to get *I Will Not Kill Myself, Olivia* published, which will hopefully culminate in the moment when I am offered a contract. Through my blog and this memoir I want everyone to know what I went through, to understand how I recovered, and to be there with me when I hopefully achieve my dream of becoming a published author; if and when it happens, I want everyone to see how overwhelmingly happy I'll be, I want everyone to literally see the tears of joy streaming down my cheeks, because it will show them that depression is beatable, and that even the most severely afflicted can overcome it and go on to live happy, healthy, fulfilling lives. I think seeing me come full-circle – from on the brink of suicide to achieving my dream – will give others hope that they can do the same.

So with that in mind, this is my story – told as candidly as I can possible write it. I hope that after reading it, you'll understand why I'll be so emotional if and when my novel gets published, and I hope you'll be there with me in that wonderful moment of bliss.

PART I

OR

WARNING SIGNS

OR

I DID *NOT* RAPE HER

March, 2007

At the annual Sydney University Scholarship Dinner I got talking to Mr Williams, one of my old high school teachers who'd been invited by the faculty.

'So how've you been, Danny?' he asked.

'Top of the world, Mr W! I'm really happy to be studying Commerce/Law, and I've also started writing my first novel called *Chrysalis* about an orphan's plight in the Great Depression of the 1930s. This year's going to be great! I'm going to get a High Distinction average[1] across all of my subjects and have my novel published by the end of the year! And when I finish my degree, I'm going to become a rich investment banker or management consultant and travel all over the world and live up the high life! It's going to be incredible! I can't wait to jump right into it!'

I kept talking, giddy with excitement as Mr Williams listened indulgently. At some point the mains were served, after which the scholarship holders were called up on stage and presented with awards.

'Congratulations, Danny,' Mr Williams said back at our table. 'You did really well to get such a coveted scholarship. I know you worked hard for it, and you deserve it as much as anyone.'

'Thanks,' I said.

'You've been blessed with so much,' he continued. 'You've been brought up in a wonderful neighbourhood; you're surrounded by a loving, supportive family; and you've got the opportunity and the ability to do anything you want to in life.'

He paused for a moment.

'I hope you use your blessings for good,' he said. 'I hope you always do charity work, and I hope you always try to help people.'

He paused again.

'Remember, Danny: to whom much is given, much is expected.'

---

[1] In the US, this is approximately equivalent to a Grade Point Average equal to or greater than 3.9 out of 4.0.

May, 2007

For all my lofty ambitions, however, it was to my great dismay that my first semester of uni was a struggle from the start. Whenever I studied as much as I needed to in order to get a High Distinction average, I hardly got any writing done. Whenever I stuck to writing – which was most of the time – I fell behind at uni; I'd missed weeks of class and hadn't done even half of the readings for each subject. Playing on the uni basketball team, tutoring high school students and getting smashed on the town two or three nights a week didn't help either, but I was never going to use that as an excuse.

I was so frustrated with myself for being so far behind. I felt so guilty for not working harder. I took pride in being an accomplished person who achieved my goals, so going off the rails like that was completely unacceptable. I hated myself for it.

But the exams were still a few weeks away, so I had time to recover. *If I pull some all-nighters I should be able to catch up and get my High Distinction average,* I thought. *I'll be OK. This is what caffeine is meant for.*

July, 2007

Fucking hell! I swore when I got my exam marks back. *Fuck me dead! An average of 74%! That's fucking terrible! That's 11% off my goal! What a disgrace. What an embarrassment. I fucked up this semester. I failed.*

I was so angry with myself. Once again I felt so guilty for not working harder. And rubbing salt into the wound was the fact that all the other scholarship holders kicked my ass. It made me feel so inadequate. It made me feel so ashamed of myself.

I told Mum how disappointed I was. She couldn't believe it.

'But Danny you were writing so much that you hardly studied!' she exclaimed. 'All things considered you still did really well! How can you possibly be so hard on yourself?'

But that wasn't how my mind worked. The way I saw it, if you set a goal and didn't reach it, then it meant you failed. It was like that when I got 99.6 instead of a perfect 100 for my UAI[2] at the end of school, and it was like that then, too.

I need to work harder next semester, I told myself. *I need to work harder so that I can get my writing done and still have time to study for my exams and get the marks that I want to get. If I work harder, then I won't feel this pain ever again. If I work harder, then I'll end up getting a High Distinction average and writing a great novel of publishable quality and then everything will be fine. It really is that simple. I just need to work harder.*

---

[2] University Admissions Index – equal to the percentile in which one is ranked in the state of New South Wales, as calculated by one's performance in the Higher School Certificate, completed in Year 12.

August, 2007

I met Chanel at the beginning of the next semester. It started how it often does at that age – being introduced, getting to know each other a bit, flirting at uni and then hooking up one Saturday night at a club before jumping straight into a relationship. When it happened I was imbued with a pulsing rush; this was a new world to me – I'd never had a proper girlfriend before – and Chanel was glamorous and beautiful and intelligent and I wanted to be with her.

Our first official date was in the city on a cloudless sunny day. We found ourselves holding hands across the table at lunch, strolling through Hyde Park with our arms around each other, sharing a big bowl of mixed gelato and feeding each other spoonfuls, and then making out beneath the trees at the Royal Botanic Gardens. We just felt so comfortable together, like we'd been a couple for years instead of only a week. In the afternoon we sat hand in hand on the grass and leapt into each other's souls, and I found myself telling her things I'd hardly spoken of before. I told her about how I'd always wanted to be a professional basketball player, and about how gut-wrenchingly devastated I was when my knee blew out in Year 10 and ruined my chances. I told her how that up until then I never bothered studying and always came in the bottom 10% of the year, and that once I'd injured my knee and had no chance of going pro anymore, nearly everyone at my snooty private school (including most of my friends) said that I was washed up and would amount to nothing; I told her that they all looked down on me so much and made me feel so inadequate that I vowed to start studying really hard and kick all their asses in Year 12. I told her that even though high school was ancient history, that the whole experience had ignited this lasting obsession in me to want to beat everyone in everything I did, to always want to be the best, to always want to be the guy that everyone looked up to instead of being the chump that everyone ridiculed and laughed at. Chanel listened, she understood, she shared the tribulations she'd been through. It all just happened so naturally, with an intimacy and tenderness deeper than any I'd ever known.

When night had blanketed the sky, I walked her to her platform at Central Station. We looked into each other's eyes, and for the first time I realised how spectacularly blue hers were, how easy it was for me to lose myself in them. We kissed until her train came, and as I watched her board the carriage and the vehicle grow smaller and smaller in the distance, I remember feeling the tug of love at my heart, a dazed sort of bliss I'd never experienced before. I remember having a really good feeling about her. A really, really good feeling indeed.

September, 2007

It had all started off so sublimely. I was convinced I'd found everything I'd ever wanted in a woman, and that our love would burn brightly for the years to come. But then a sickening notion infected my mind, and began to fill me with an anxious dread.

I think Chanel has something going on with one of my best mates.

She'd keep denying it, but I'd see the way Brad and her would look at each other. I knew they talked on the phone all the time. *And if nothing is going on,* I'd think, *then why does she always invite him to hang out with us? Why does she at other times blow me off to spend time with him?*

We'd fight about it all the time.

'I'm telling you, we're just *friends*,' she'd always say. 'Why do you keep putting me through all this arguing? You're a dickhead for accusing me of liking him. If you really loved me, you'd believe me.'

She'd always manage to guilt me into feeling like an asshole and letting the matter drop, and I'd find myself hanging up the phone thinking I was the bad guy.

She's right, I'd tell myself. *I'm being a jerk for not trusting her. I'm implying that she's a shit person by accusing her of two-timing. How must that make her feel? . . . But still! This just doesn't make sense! The way she's acting, something* must *be going on!*

It was such a maddening situation. Day after day it would persecute my mind. The good times – the Botanic Gardens days – became fewer and farther between, and our relationship gradually disintegrated into one big fight. Instead of being a blessing, I came to view love as a torturous curse.

~~~

I was binge drinking a lot those days, 20 standard drinks a night two or three times a week. I'd always embodied the "work hard, play hard" mantra, and getting wasted was my favourite way to wind down after an intense week of studying and writing. To my parents it was a constant cause of concern, but I was convinced I had everything under control.

'I'm just being an 18 year old,' I'd say whenever they'd reproach me about my drinking. 'Plus I work so hard during the day, so that gives me the right to cut loose at night.'

Not to mention, I'd think, *that all the fighting with Chanel is driving me nuts.* It seemed like that's all we ever did. Non-stop. All the time. Twenty-four/seven.

For fuck's sake, I remember thinking, *I'm studying Commerce/Law, I'm writing a novel, and my girlfriend who I adore is probably fucking my friend. So don't I deserve a bottle of bourbon to relax?*

October, 2007

Chanel and I eventually broke up. She finally admitted she had feelings for Brad, so that was it. I was heartbroken. When I was alone after it happened I burst into tears, cried long and hard into the palms of my hands. I was so overwrought. So shattered. I'd lost the woman I loved and I was absolutely gutted.

'Fuck Chanel,' my mates from school would say. 'She was making you miserable anyway. Just forget about her and that whole uni crowd. Come out with us, meet another chick, have a rebound fling. Start having fun again, man. We've never seen you this unhappy before.'

So I started spending more time with my school friends again, hanging out at their houses and going to parties with them. It was hard-going at first – I was missing Chanel like crazy and I just wanted to be with her. But after a few weeks, I began to turn the corner. I started forgetting about Chanel and got back to enjoying a life of studying, writing, playing basketball and chilling with the boys. I started realising that maybe I didn't need her, that my life was actually better without all the fighting and the drama. I even met another girl at a party and was contemplating asking her out, but then Chanel caught wind of it and hit the roof.

'I can't believe you're going to start dating someone else already!' she yelled into the phone. 'It's only been *three* weeks!'

'Are you kidding me? Chanel, *you're* the one who broke up with me because you said you liked Brad.'

'I didn't think you'd start seeing someone so soon!'

'What did you expect me to do? Spend the rest of my life crying over you?'

'No, but – '

'Why are we even having this conversation? Shouldn't you be off fucking Brad?'

'Don't say that!'

'Why not?'

'Look – I made a mistake, OK?'

'What are you talking about?'

She went on to say that she'd been really confused – that at the time we broke up she wasn't sure what she wanted, but that since then she'd had a chance to figure everything out. She said that she no longer had feelings for Brad – that that was all well and truly over with and was just one big mistake. And then she said she still had feelings for me.

Like a dog that'd been kicked in the morning but then petted at night, I was exhilarated, and had completely forgotten about the way Chanel had previously stomped on my heart. I was a sucker in love, and hearing her say that she still liked me was heavenly music to my ears.

'So do you want to go out again?' I asked excitedly.

'I can't,' she said.

My heart dropped.

'Why not?'

She said she wasn't ready to be in a relationship yet – that she needed some time to focus on herself.

'But I will be ready soon, though, and I want you to wait for me until then.'

I felt uneasy straight away.

'You . . . you want me to . . . *wait* . . . for you?' I asked hesitantly.

'Yes.'

'Well . . . I mean . . . how long for?'

'Not very long. Just until the end of the semester.'

'Why can't we just go out now?'

'I told you – I'm not ready yet.'

'Why not?'

'I don't know. I'm just not.'

I was suspicious. What she was saying just didn't make sense. And I still didn't fully trust her after the Brad fiasco.

She sensed my reservations.

'Danny . . . why are you being so misunderstanding?'

'I'm trying to understand, but – '

'I thought you loved me. Can't you just do this one little thing for the woman you love?'

More guilt trips. More manipulation. With hindsight, I shouldn't have capitulated. I shouldn't have let myself get sucked back into a situation that I didn't feel comfortable in. But I was blinded by love and wanted nothing more than to be with her.

'OK, Chanel,' I said. 'I'll wait for you.'

~~~

As per our "agreement", we weren't together, but we also weren't allowed to be with anyone else, and there was the clear understanding that we'd be a couple again as soon as Chanel was "ready for a relationship".

I hated it.

Breaking up with her was devastating, but at least I had closure and could begin to heal by moving on. Under this new set of circumstances however, I got the worst of both worlds. I was stuck in no man's land. I was miserable.

'I can't stand this, Chanel,' I'd tell her. 'There's too much uncertainty . . . too much that can go wrong. I mean, what if you decide you don't want to commit to me? What if you decide you'd rather be with Brad instead?'

'Danny how many times do I have to tell you? There's nothing going on between me and Brad! We're just friends! I want to be with *you*, OK. I just need you to wait for me until I'm ready.'

'I hate this waiting . . . you know I hate it.'

'Yeah, I know. But if you love me, you'll do it.'

And so I did. And so throughout October, I grew more and more anxious, I grew more and more melancholy, and this sorrow poisoned the rest of my life. It made it so difficult to study. It made it so difficult to write. I started falling behind all over again, and I was fucking livid with myself for it.

Do you want all the other scholarship holders to kick your ass again? I'd ask myself. *Do you want to feel inadequate again? Do you want to feel like a failure again? No? Then fucking pull yourself together and knuckle down and focus!*

But no matter how hard I tried I just couldn't manage to do it. Chanel was tearing me apart – so much so that at times I thought I should just forget about her and call it quits for good.

If I was single, I rationalised, *then I'd be able to focus and achieve my goals, and then I wouldn't feel so disappointed and frustrated and angry with myself all the time.*

But I couldn't leave her. For whatever reason, I thought she was "the one". At times I really, genuinely, thought she was the one. I clung to the belief that we were just going through a rough patch – that we'd soon get through it and it would all be worth it.

She knows how much I care about her, I convinced myself. *She'd never do anything to hurt me. We're going to get married and spend the rest of our lives together.*

November, 2007

But after the end of year exams were finished, Chanel told me that she'd changed her mind – that she liked being single and that she no longer had any intention to resume dating me again. I asked her why, I asked her what had changed, but she just kept reiterating that she wanted to remain unattached.

'Is this because of Brad?' I asked.

'No! For the last time, Brad and I are just *friends*! It's not because of him or any other guy! I just don't want to be in a relationship right now.'

I was crushed. It was like breaking up with her all over again. That night, I went to a rat-hole of a club and got piss-blind drunk, just having one drink after another after another after another, desperately trying to drown out the anguish, to suppress the agonising grief that was all I could feel. Eventually I took a cab to my best friend Casey's house, where he consoled me for the rest of the night.

'This hurts so much, mate,' I murmured, holding back tears. 'I waited weeks for her . . . and now all of a sudden she just says it's over.'

'I'm sorry, bro,' he said.

'I love her so much, man . . . all I want is just to be with her.'

'I know you do cuz, I know you do,' he said, clapping me on the back.

We kept talking into the early hours of the morning.

'At least you can move on now,' he said once I'd calmed down a bit. 'You can start to forget about her and get on with your life.'

I sighed deeply.

'Yeah. You're right.'

'This is it, mate,' he continued. 'No more Chanel. Just cut off all contact from her – just leave her in the past. It's all about the future now.'

I nodded.

'Yeah, man. This is it. I'm done with her for good.'

~~~

I was only studying three subjects that semester – one less than usual so I could have more time to write. Given that I was doing less than a full course load, I didn't think there was any excuse for not getting a High Distinction average. So when I only got 82%, I was furious with myself.

What the fuck is wrong with me? I yelled in my head. *I was only doing three fucking subjects, and I* still *couldn't achieve my goal! That's fucking hopeless. That's fucking pathetic. And I can't even say that the reason I messed up was because I was writing so much, because I didn't get that much of my book written at all. It still isn't even finished yet! The reason I screwed up was because I spent the whole fucking semester fighting with and fretting over and worrying about Chanel. I was so fucking lovesick that I let her get in the way of achieving my goals. That's fucking disgraceful. I should be ashamed of myself that's so fucking pitiful. I fucked up. I failed. Again. Just like I have in everything I've tried to do this year.*

~~~

The following week, a mutual friend of Chanel and I organised an event at a club, and we both ended up going. At some point in the night, I got talking to a girl I knew from high school. Under the influence, we started flirting. Then Chanel got upset and another fight ensued.

'I can't believe you've moved on already! It's only been a week!'

'Look, I haven't exactly moved on,' I said honestly. 'I still love you, OK, and I still want to be with you. But you don't feel the same way. So it's over. And given that it is, you have no right to get pissed off with me for talking to other chicks.'

'I'm not pissed off. I just got so jealous seeing you talk to another girl.'

'Why did you get jealous?'

'Because I still have feelings for you.'

'Then why aren't we dating then?'

'I told you! I don't want to date anyone right now.'

'Even though you have feelings for me?'

'Yes.'

I sighed.

'Does this have anything to do with Brad?'

'Shut the fuck up about Brad!' she screamed. 'How many times do I have to tell you it's got nothing to do with him?'

For a while, no-one spoke. Immeasurable frustration hung in the air as we both brooded in silence.

'So we like each other, but we're not going to date,' I eventually summed up. 'So where does that leave us?'

'I don't know,' she shrugged.

December, 2007

So there I found myself again, trapped between a rock and a hard place – that insufferable no man's land I'd so hated before.

'I'm so confused,' Chanel would always say. 'I know I have feelings for you, but I just don't want to be in a relationship right now. This is crazy, Danny . . . I have no idea what to do. Nothing makes sense to me anymore.'

I had it in my mind that the reason she didn't want to be with me was because she was scared – of commitment, of intimacy, of who knows what. So I stuck it out hoping that she'd come around, miserable day after miserable day. The pain of not being with her, of knowing she was single and could be hooking up with any given guy at any given time was so tormenting that over the course of the month, I gradually lost my ability to function. I could hardly write. I could barely eat. I'd lie up night after night unable to fall asleep.

This isn't worth it, my head would tell me. *Just make a clean break for it and forget Chanel ever existed.* But my heart was telling me that she was beautiful, that she was special, that she was my one true love, and that it was worth doing whatever it took to make it work with her.

By the end of the month, however, I couldn't take it anymore. I'd devolved into an exhausted shell of myself, a nauseous wreck of a person who was rapidly withering away. Something had to give. Something had to change.

'I can't do this anymore,' I finally told her. 'It's just too much uncertainty, too much worrying, too much pain. I need to know where I stand with you – once and for all this time.'

I sighed.

'So I'm going to give you until New Year's Eve to work out what you want. If you decide you want to be with me, then that's great. But if you don't, then I'm done for good. I'm moving on. For real this time.'

New Year's Eve, 2007

From the moment I woke up I was stricken with nerves, so I went to a friend's place to drown them in alcohol. I spent the day getting pissed playing beer pong with my school mates, doing my best to enjoy myself instead of tensely counting down the hours until night when I was due to meet Chanel at a party. By five o'clock I'd had half a dozen beers and a bottle of bourbon, and was able to escape by passing out on the couch. But when I woke up it was seven and time to go, and once again I was consumed with apprehension.

The boys and I arrived and joined the other guests on the balcony. We sat in a circle and talked for a while, drinking beers and passing joints as my anxiety heightened.

This is it, I kept telling myself. *She's going to be here any minute. I'm only moments away from knowing whether she'll be my girlfriend or an ex I'll never speak to again. Soon I'm going to be either deliriously happy or miserably devastated.*

A touch after eight she arrived with some friends, looking beautiful as ever wearing a white strapless dress and red high heels. I walked up to her and gave her a peck on the cheek, and said hello to the rest of her friends. A couple of my mates then went to greet her, and one of them ended up talking to her in a corner of the room for 20 minutes. He came to speak to me straight afterwards.

'You're in, mate,' he said. 'It's gonna be fine.'

I mixed up another big bottle of bourbon and cola and finally got talking to her myself. She was shooting me flirtatious looks, teasing me playfully, rubbing my arm whenever she spoke. The vibe was good. The signs were all there. At some point we got drawn into a drunken group hug, and as we pulled away, our eyes locked. Our heads moved closer together. And then for the first time in two months, we kissed.

It was slow. Ardent. Breathtaking. Her arms were wrapped around me, clutching me tightly as I zestfully ran my fingers through her thin brown hair. Our hearts were pounding. Our bodies were one as we rediscovered each other's lips, wrestled each other's tongues, leapt into each other's mouths. When we finally pulled away, we gazed into each other's eyes with giddy smiles on our faces, and in that moment, I remember thinking that everything was right with the world. I remember thinking that it had all been worth it: all the fighting, all the angst, all the despair – even the disruption to my degree and my novel – because it had all turned out so wonderfully in the end. It was New Year's Eve and I was on a balcony overlooking stunning Sydney Harbour, kissing the girl who I was now sure I'd be spending the rest of my life with. I felt spectacular. *Thank-you, God,* I whispered in my head.

But then Brad got furious.

'If you're just going to hook up with Danny all night, then I'm going to leave!'

He stormed away. Chanel went after him.

'Hold on a second, Danny,' she said over her shoulder.

I could see them at the foot of the steps that led to the street. They were talking to one another, and I was making small-talk with someone else, just passing the time until Chanel and I could get back to making out on the balcony. I was fantasising about kissing her on the dot of midnight, seeing in the new year with her wrapped in my arms, and then taking her back to my place so we could celebrate it properly. I thought it was going to be one of those magical nights that we'd never forget, one of those nights we'd one day be telling our kids about: *the time when Mummy and Daddy got back together again . . .*

Those were the thoughts that were dancing through my mind when I saw her kiss Brad.

My jaw dropped. I stared at them, bewildered. Aghast. But on some level I think I always knew.

She saw me gaping at them and quickly jumped up and pulled me inside. Of course I was furious. I accused her of lying to me the whole time.

'No! No!' she protested. 'That was just a drunken mistake! He means nothing to me! *You're* the one I want!'

She hooked up with me and then Brad got pissed off, so he pulled her away to talk to her. I sat stewing by myself as all the anguish and the stress and the misery of the last five months came roaring right back before Casey put the nail in the coffin:

'I'm sorry bro, but I just overhead her telling him the same thing that she just told you – that kissing you was a mistake, that you mean nothing to her, and that he's the one she's always wanted.'

The rest of the night was a disaster. As the fireworks brought in 2008, the three of us yelled and screamed at each other in the middle of the street while a bunch of our friends watched on around us.

'You always said that Danny was just your friend!' Brad yelled at her. 'You always said that he was obsessed with you but that you never liked him! You always said that no matter how many times you told him it was over he never got the message!'

'What the fuck!' I yelled. 'Chanel, the whole time you were telling *me* – '

'No! No!' she screamed. 'Both of you – just settle down! Brad, let me talk to you for a moment. Danny, don't go anywhere – I want to talk to you afterwards.'

By then it was obvious she'd been leading a double life, particularly since she kept trying to separate Brad and me like so to avoid us comparing stories. On one such occasion I remembered that I had her six day old $1,200 iPhone that had been imported from overseas for Christmas. Chanel had clearly been lying through her teeth, so I decided to read through the messages she'd been sending Brad to try and get closer to the bottom of what'd been going on. Within a minute, I found a text she'd sent him three days earlier.

'You're my soul mate,' it said.

I was infuriated. I'd never been so angry before.

'I feel like smashing this fucking phone,' I told Casey.

'Do it,' he said.

'Do it,' the rest of my school mates said.

I'd been drinking for the past 12 hours – nearly half a case of beer, the first bottle of bourbon, and a good portion of the second bottle of bourbon – not to mention that I'd also smoked one or two joints. I was overwhelmingly pissed off and my judgement was not what it usually was.

So I smashed it to pieces.

Eventually, Chanel and Brad went their separate ways, and that was the end of it. I stayed at the party, furious and heartbroken. My worst fears had come true: *Chanel and Brad were never "just friends". She was playing me the whole time. I loved her with all my heart but she never gave a damn.*

My mates did their best to comfort me, but there really wasn't a whole lot they could do. Eventually, I decided to take a cab home. As I waited on the side of the street, I found myself feeling so overwhelmed, so horrifically distraught that I collapsed by the gutter. I started coughing up bile, began trembling uncontrollably, and in that moment, I couldn't see how I'd ever recover from such a devastating experience.

January, 2008

I was racked with grief. There was just so much emotion bottled up inside me. I was irate at the fact that I was always being lied to, and by the way that I'd been so ruthlessly betrayed. I was embarrassed by the way she'd played me in front of everyone. And above all, I was heartbroken that I was all alone after I thought I'd found "the one". I'd never been so shattered before. Never been so devastated. It was the worst time of my life.

On the other hand, I knew I needed to move on. I was at a crossroads – I could either collapse and fall apart or pull myself together and get on with my life – and I knew I needed to do the latter.

I can't change what happened in the past, I told myself, *but I can control what I do from this point forward. And what I need to do now is forget about everything that happened last year and channel all my energy into achieving my goals. I need to work my ass off to get* Chrysalis *finished, and once uni starts I need to study really hard so that I can keep on top of things this time and get a High Distinction average. Last New Year's Eve was a mess, but if I work hard this year then I can spend the next one celebrating getting great marks at uni and publishing my novel. That's the right way to respond to this – by achieving my goals. If I achieve my goals then I'll be happy again, just like I was when I started uni.*

February, 2008

There was still a lot of anger festering inside me, but I tried my best to forget about Chanel and get on with my life. It was hard to write with a clear head, but I managed to do OK. I edited *Chrysalis* to the point where I thought it was ready to be published, and then decided to get it professionally critiqued just to make sure. I caught a break and was lucky enough to be put in touch with Nick Bleszynski through the New South Wales Writers' Centre, an author who's written three bestsellers and mentored two writers who ended up signing major publishing deals.

Once he's read my manuscript, I'll make the changes he suggests and then submit it for publication, I thought.

I figured that after that I'd then be able to switch my attention to my degree, and I was confident that without my novel to worry about I'd be able to study as much as I needed to in order to get a High Distinction average.

~~~

In February, I also decided to spend my savings going to South America at the end of the year to volunteer at an underprivileged school in Cusco, Peru. I found out about the opportunity from a friend, but it was Mr Williams' words at the scholarship dinner the previous year that made me want to do it:

'You've been blessed with so much,' he'd said. 'You've been brought up in a wonderful neighbourhood; you're surrounded by a loving, supportive family; and you've got the opportunity and the ability to do anything you want to in life. I hope you always use your blessings for good. I hope you always do charity work, and I hope you always try to help people. Remember, Danny: to whom much is given, much is expected.'

He's right, I thought. *Even though I'm going through a rough patch right now, I am a very lucky person. I do have a terrific life. And it's my responsibility to start giving back, and lend a helping hand to those less fortunate than myself.*

March, 2008

I did *not* rape her.

But that's what I started hearing when I got back to uni.

'To justify her intimacy with you to Brad, she said that you'd force yourself on her. She said that she wouldn't want you to but that you wouldn't take no for an answer.'

I couldn't believe it. I seriously couldn't believe it. I cherished that girl every day we were together. I treated her like a queen. I would've turned the world upside down to make her happy. So to have her accuse me of something as vile and despicable as rape made me sick to my stomach. It made me so fucking angry.

It made me so fucking angry that I wanted to kill her.

I'm not just saying this – I literally wanted to kill her.

I never, ever actually would've done it. I strongly believe the best revenge in those cases is simply living well. I knew that the right way of responding to everything she'd put me through was to channel my fury into achieving my goals and then go on to live a happy life. I did know that, and that's what I was focused on doing. But after I heard those allegations . . . I'd be lying to you if I said I never got the urge to pick up a baseball bat and smash in her face. I was that enraged.

I mean, lying to me throughout our whole relationship was bad enough.

Two-timing with one of my best friends was even worse.

But saying that I raped her to explain our intimacy?

I don't even know what you call betrayal that extreme.

And being a self-confessed mamma's boy and someone who's always held women in the highest esteem and regard, there's not a more repulsive, heinous act anyone could have possibly accused me of.

April, 2008

I was still finding it so hard to deal with – the heartbreak, the hatred, and most recently my complete and utter disgust at the rape accusations. But what had begun to really tear me up the most was the impact it was all having on my ability to achieve my goals. Half the time I'd be too distraught to study or write properly, so I'd end up barely absorbing anything in lectures or writing crap that I'd later have to toss in the garbage. And as a result, it started happening all over again: I wasn't getting much quality writing done and I'd fallen way behind at uni. So I didn't do well – I didn't get High Distinctions – and the other scholarship holders did, and then I felt so hopeless, felt so inadequate, felt like such a failure again. And I hated that feeling so fucking much. Like I've said, I wanted to be the best. I wanted to be the guy that everyone looked up to. So the fact that I wasn't at the top of the cohort made me overwhelmingly upset with myself.

I need to stop being such a fucking pussy! I'd yell in my head. *I need to pull myself together. Everything with Chanel ended four months ago! There's no way it should still be bothering me now!*

But it did. And the more it bothered me, the more I failed. And the more I failed, the worse I felt.

~~~

Dear Danny,

*Below is my assessment of your work. On the plus side, I think your story has potential – it has a clear plot and the power to be inspirational. However, you have **a lot** of work to do in order to bring your manuscript up to a publishable standard.*

Nick then went on to detail the problems with the draft: *"the writing style is terrible – way too many clichéd similes, unnecessary big words, awkwardly worded sentences, melodramatic scenes and too much repetition"*. It was *"very poorly researched – the kryptonite for any work of historical fiction"*. I had the Caucasian male protagonist fall in love with a coloured girl, a development which had to be *"deeply rethought"*, since *"the racial aspect of the novel isn't dealt with well at all, nor is her love with the protagonist believable – they don't share nearly enough experiences for them to fall in love"*. The motifs I'd employed were *"amateurish"*. The poetry I'd written and inserted here and there was *"awful"*. My use of punctuation was *"neither proper nor effective"*. The ending was *"contrived"*. Nick then offered suggestions for improvement and noted that it takes a long time to write a book of publishable quality, but that I could get there in the end if I worked really hard.

I read through it several times until words like *"terrible"*, *"poor"*, *"amateurish"*, *"contrived"* and *"awful"* began to sink in and I grew furious with myself.

For fuck's sake! I thought. *How did I think this was going to be so easy – waking up one day and deciding to write a novel? No training, no practice, nothing – just waking up one day and deciding to write a novel and thinking I can have it done and dusted in a year writing it part-time. That's ridiculous. That's insane. What the fuck is wrong with me? How the fuck could I be so stupid? How the fuck could I be so naïve? I've failed again. Again. Again and again and again.*

June, 2008

Adolescents need to be educated about depression.

In my humble opinion, they need to be educated about depression in school, and they also need to be educated about depression at home – in the same way they're educated about safe sex and drink driving.

Adolescents need to be educated about depression so that if they find themselves experiencing the symptoms, they can realise that they're suffering from an illness, and can then go about seeking treatment from there.

But if they don't know what depression is?

Then they won't seek help, and will thus prolong their suffering.

Just like my main character Jimmy does in *I Will Not Kill Myself, Olivia,* they might self-medicate with drugs and alcohol and develop an addiction – which, it should be noted, significantly exacerbates depression, since alcohol and some drugs are, of course, depressants.

They might self-medicate with sex, and thereby vastly increase the risk of unwanted pregnancies and STDs.

Like Jimmy also does, they might self-harm.

And worst of all, they might kill themselves.

Some parents think that depression is taboo – something that shouldn't be talked about; something that's too dark for their teenager to be exposed to. If you do think like that, then let me give you some stats:

At the time of writing, in the US, the UK and Australia, as many as 20% of teens will experience depression before they reach adulthood.

Measuring rates of self-harm has proved difficult for a variety of reasons, but there have been studies that estimate that 6-7% of 15-24 year olds intentionally hurt themselves, and other studies that suggest the figures are as high as 12-20%.

For youths aged 15-24, suicide is the third leading cause of death in America.

For the same age group, it is the second leading cause of death in the UK.

And for the same age group in Australia, it is *the* leading cause.

Depression is persecuting youths all over the globe. It's a worldwide epidemic that's everywhere you turn – even if you don't know it, even if the sufferer themself doesn't know it. Regardless of age, gender, sexuality, religion, colour or creed, teens are at risk for a myriad of reasons. Isn't it best that they're educated to spot the warning signs if they do fall victim?

In my opinion, not educating an adolescent about depression because it's too "dark" for their "innocent" mind is nearly as dangerous as not teaching them safe sex because it encourages fornication. I once met a girl who'd been raised like that. After a few drinks at a bar we went back to her place, and she wanted to do it without protection. That shit isn't safe.

The reason I bring all this up is because when I was 19, I couldn't have known any less about depression. I knew what I was feeling – I knew I was in pain – but I had no idea I was starting to develop an illness. If I did I would've gotten the help I needed, and this story would probably end right here.

Alas, it continues . . .

After that semester's exams were finished, I found myself in a seedy motel room in Kings Cross, 25 standard drinks in. My friends were across the room talking amongst themselves, but I was slouched against the wall completely zoned out and still drinking, drinking. Despair tugged at my soul. I felt so overwhelmed. *How am I ever going to work my way out of this mess?* I thought desperately. *I try so hard, but it's never enough. Whenever I study hard enough to get the marks that I want to get, I hardly get any writing done. Whenever I write more, I fall behind at uni. I feel so inadequate. All the other scholarship holders are doing such amazing things with their lives – travelling the world, founding charities, interning at the United Nations, or representing the country in sport or debating or who knows what else. And then there's me: getting marks way below my potential and writing books that are so bad they practically need to be rewritten. I feel like such a loser. No matter what I do I can't achieve my goals. It's so frustrating, so disappointing. I feel so unhappy. And I didn't rape her! I did not rape her!*

And this is where it's all led me: to a seedy motel room where I'm still drinking, drinking. And I can't stop. I can't stop. I just can't stop.

July, 2008

I kept fucking up at uni – my average was only 76% that semester – and *Chrysalis* was nowhere near finished. I always felt like such a failure, and that made me always feel miserable. And because I was always miserable, I was always drunk. It had gone way beyond the point of what's socially acceptable. Every time I went out I'd plough through 20 or 30 standard drinks and end up losing control of myself. It got to the stage where my friends were pissed off with me, and the ones that weren't were worried. I just couldn't stay sober. If I had one drink then I'd end up having another and then another and then another and then before I knew it I'd had 25 and was a complete and utter mess.

One of my mates told me that he'd started to drink a lot less so that he could be in a better position to look after me when I inevitably needed him to. That was a wake-up call that something had to change. Craving booze in the middle of the day, that was another wake-up call. Standing still while some punk kept punching me in the face outside Star City and being too drunk to feel it – that was another wake-up call that I really needed to stop drinking.

After I admitted I had a problem to myself, I then admitted it to my parents. They were really understanding, as I knew they would be.

'We're not here to pass judgment on you, Danny. We're your parents. We love you, and we just want to do whatever it takes to help you get better.'

We talked for a long time, and I agreed to see a psychologist who specialised in treating people with an addiction.

~~~

For the third time that week I found myself on the edge of my bed, sweating, clutching my hair, panting through gritted teeth. I wanted booze so badly. My whole body was begging for it. Like I say in *I Will Not Kill Myself, Olivia,* craving a substance is like being really, really hungry, and fighting it is like not eating. It's wholly consuming. There's nothing else you can think about, nothing else you can do until it has mercy on you and passes. But seeing the psychologist had been helpful, and I tried to use some of the techniques she'd taught me as I kept panting, kept sweating, kept ripping strands of hair out of my head:

Just hold off drinking for the next hour, I told myself. It's what I'd told myself an hour beforehand, and it's what I'd have to keep telling myself to get through the night. The idea was to break down a seemingly insurmountable task into a number of surmountable ones. Simple I know, but it worked.

Just hold off drinking for the next hour . . . I'd murmur. *It's only an hour . . . it's only an hour . . . you did it last hour so you can do it this hour, too. Just stay strong . . . keep fighting . . . don't give in. No matter how much you want to you cannot give in . . .*

August, 2008

By the end of the mid-year holidays I felt so much better. It'd been five weeks since I'd touched alcohol and the cravings were gone, and with the passing of time, my anger towards Chanel had begun to fade. For the first time in months my mind felt clear – I was able to wake up and just write, write, write. It was so enjoyable, and over the previous couple of weeks I'd gotten so much done. It was just great to be able to live freely again, instead of always floundering.

Finally, I thought, *all of the drama is behind me – all the shit with Chanel, and the alcoholism, and the misery. And now that it is, I'm ready to throw myself into clocking up a High Distinction average and getting my novel published by the end of the year. I'm going to smash it! I can't wait for the next semester to start!*

PART II

OR

IT'S REALLY HARD TO GET BETTER IF YOU DON'T GET HELP

September, 2008

In *I Will Not Kill Myself, Olivia*, Jimmy's girlfriend is called, as the title suggests, Olivia. They were high school sweethearts and on their way to the altar, but then for reasons that don't need to be dealt with here, Jimmy falls victim to a crippling depression. From that point on in the novel I start exploring what can happen to a couple when they become a threesome: i.e. the man, the woman, and the serious mental illness.

What sort of chaos can it lead to?

How does it change the relationship? Does it bring both of them closer together or does it rip them apart?

Is the healthy partner's love and support enough to get the depressed partner through it, or does he/she still need to receive professional treatment?

And, even if the depressed partner does get better, will their relationship ever be the same?

I never had a girlfriend throughout my war with depression like Jimmy did, but I did have a close friend called Sylvia, who if truth be told, was the inspiration for Olivia herself. The two situations were hardly the same – Jimmy and Olivia were ardent lovers who wanted to spend their lives together, whereas Sylvia and I were friends living on opposite sides of the globe. Nevertheless, we often used to reach out to each other for advice and support, and some of the relationship-related questions I explore in my novel were based on real life events that happened between Sylvia and myself.

And so, she enters this story with a Facebook message:

> *Hey Sylvia,*
>
> *I thought I was better. I honestly thought I'd beaten it. But somehow I've fallen right back into that state of almost permanent despair. Striking the right balance between studying and writing has trumped me again. It's only been six weeks and I've already fallen behind at uni and progress on my novel is slow. I feel like such a fucking idiot. How did I think this semester would be any different from the last ones? Every semester I've had at uni has*

been a failure, and I'm well on my way to failing this one too. I hate this. And I hate myself for making it like this.

As usual, my solution is to work harder. I think if I could study and write for a total of 60 hours a week, then I should be able to achieve my goals. I think working 60 hours a week would allow me to get a lot of work done and still give me plenty of time to tutor high school kids, coach basketball, play basketball, go to the gym, and go out with my friends. Then again, maybe 60 hours a week isn't enough either. Maybe I need to be pushing myself harder. Maybe I should be working 70 hours a week. Maybe 80. Maybe more. I'm going to feel miserable until my novel's published and I've achieved a High Distinction average, so maybe I shouldn't be doing anything else apart from studying and writing. Fucking hell . . . I don't know. I just feel so overwhelmed. Everything seems so hopeless. I've lost so much confidence. So much of my self-belief has disappeared. I never thought I'd say this, but I don't know if I can achieve my goals anymore.

I hope you can say something to help, Sylvia. I'm really struggling at the moment and could use your support.

Love,

Danny.

She replied a few days later:

Hey Danny,

I'm so sorry to hear that you're hurting again. I know it must be hard being so unhappy and feeling like you can't achieve your goals, but whatever you do, just keep hanging in there. You've faced some really hard challenges before and you've always overcome them, and I know you're going to do the same here too. Remember back in high school, when you never used to study and all you cared about was basketball? You were so devastated when you injured your knee and you had no shot at going pro anymore – and because you were in the bottom 20 out of 160 students everyone said you were dumb and would amount to nothing – but you turned your life around and finished school in the top 0.4% of the state. I've always found your ability to overcome setbacks really inspiring, and I know you're going to overcome this too. You're one of the strongest people I know, Danny. Seriously – I've never met anyone with the kind of will power and determination you have. So remember that, and know that it will let you achieve what you want. It always has.

But at the same time, it might be a good idea to try and not be so hard on yourself all the time. Seriously, Danny – you always put so much pressure on yourself to achieve such difficult goals, and that's really what seems to be making you so unhappy. I mean, if you get an average of 75- or 80% instead of 85%, is it really the end of the world? Those marks are still really good by almost anyone's standards! And what about your book? Does it really matter if you finish it and get it published this year or the next? Either way you'll have written and published a book, right? That's incredible! How many other 19 year olds can say that?

But aside from that, Danny, just keep at it. Keep believing in yourself, keep having faith in God, and know that I believe in you too. You can do this – I know you can. So just keep working hard and soon you'll get your High Distinction average and be a published author.

Love always,
Sylvia.

In the same way Olivia does for Jimmy, Sylvia had a way of filling me with hope. Having her say that she believed in me meant the world, because as I've intimated, I wasn't someone who was used to being believed in. My family were great and had faith in me no matter what, but aside from them I was always being doubted. There was everything that happened after I busted my knee, but even after I did do well in school, when I told the same people I was going to write a novel, they laughed at me again.

'You've got to be joking!' they all said. 'You're only good at "maths" subjects. English was your worst by far. You can't write. You struggled with *essays,* for crying out loud! How do you, of all people, think you can possibly get a novel published?'

I'm going to do it because I have the right attitude to succeed, I'd think. *I have a tireless work ethic and relentless determination, and I never, ever, ever give up. That's how I managed to overcome my knee injury and succeed in school, and it's also how I'm going to get my novel published. With the attitude I have, anything is possible, and even though I may struggle and fall, I'll get up every time and get what I'm going for in the end.*

But aside from my family, Sylvia was the only one who saw that, which is why I cherished her belief in me so much. In fact, I treasured it even more than my family's faith in me, for the same reason that it means more to a teenage girl when the football captain says she's beautiful than when she hears it from her father. Having Sylvia say that she had confidence in me and that I had what it took to achieve my goals always gave me hope that everything would turn out well in the end. It gave me strength. It inspired me. And when I felt hopeful, strong and inspired, I stopped feeling depressed.

I didn't agree with what Sylvia said at the end of her message, though – that it didn't really matter if I only got 80% instead of 85% or if *Chrysalis* got published later than I hoped.

I need to be at the top of the cohort, I thought. *I need to be the best. And 80% is not the best. A few of the other scholarship holders get High Distinction averages, so that means that I have to get a High Distinction average. Anything less is unacceptable. Anything less is a failure. And I need to finish* Chrysalis *this year and get it published as soon as possible because as much as I enjoy writing it, it is a huge disruption to my degree, and getting a High Distinction average would be a whole lot easier if I wasn't writing a novel at the same time.*

So I was convinced that Sylvia wasn't right on that front. Instead, I thought the solution was to just work harder: *if I can work for a total of 60 hours a week, then I should be able to achieve my goals and then everything will be fine.*

October, 2008

Life is such a fight. Such an all-out slog. I work so hard. I drive myself to exhaustion. But no matter how much I try I keep on sinking. Every week I fall further behind at uni, and progress on Chrysalis *is far from good. It's just too much. It's all just too much. Every week I feel under more and more pressure, I feel more and more suffocated, so much so that the fun's been sucked out of everything. I get no pleasure out of life anymore. Nothing exists for me except despair. And the worst part is that at times, I can't see myself ever waking up from this nightmare. At times there's nothing to indicate I'm ever going to get better. And when I feel that hopeless, I start craving booze. I just want to lock myself in my room with that litre bottle of Beam and sit on the floor and drink and drink and drink until I eventually pass out. And when I feel like that, I can't study properly, I can't write properly . . . and then I feel even more miserable, and then I want to drink even more, and then I'm even more useless, and then I get even more unhappy, I get even more overwhelmed. I mean what the fuck am I supposed to do? I'm already trying my best. I'm already running myself into the ground. And it's never enough. It's never enough. So what the fuck am I supposed to do?*

~~~

I'm fucking hopeless. I'm fucking pathetic. I'm such a lazy fucking piece of shit. Who the fuck can't work 60 hours a week to achieve their goals? It doesn't matter how exhausted I am. It doesn't matter how dreadful I feel. Only working 54 hours this week is a fucking disgrace. That's fucking pathetic. I'm such a fucking slacker. I should be ashamed of myself I'm so fucking lazy.

~~~

Sylvia,
    I'm cracking, I'm breaking at the seams. I work so hard to try and keep it together but no matter what I do it's never enough. I just keep getting more and more miserable. I know I'm going to

hang in there, I know I'm going to keep on fighting, because that's who I am, that's all I know how to do – but right now it all seems to be in vain. I just can't see how I'm going to achieve my goals, and so I can't see how I'm ever going to be happy. And somehow even after all these months, I still have so much fucking anger pent up towards Chanel.

Put it all together and I'm desperate to drink. The cravings are insatiable. I try to fight through them but they won't go away. They just keep growing, more and more intense. So I thought I'd Facebook you. It was either that or drowning myself in booze.

Please say something, anything to help.

Love,

Danny.

~~~

For the third night that week I found myself on the edge of the bed dripping with sweat, gripping my hair, gasping through gritted teeth in desperation for the bottle. I was so miserable. So overwhelmed. I just wanted to forget everything, just wanted to escape but I knew it wasn't right. So once again I retrieved Sylvia's Facebook message from my pocket – the one she'd sent me in response to my previous one when I was feeling that way and begging her for help. I read it through, one, two, three times, and then I kept rereading the part where she said that I was strong and that she believed in me and that everything would turn out well in the end. I was clutching it so tightly that it was crumpling, that it was getting tattered and frayed in my frenzied grasp, but as I kept reading it, hope gradually breathed back into me, and the clenching, the sweating, the panting finally came to a halt.

As it always did, hearing Sylvia say that she had faith in me strengthened my resolve. It gave me confidence when I needed it most.

She's right, I eventually concluded. *I am strong, and I can achieve my goals if I keep working hard. I'm behind the 8-ball at the moment, but the mid-semester break's coming up next week and I can catch up then. So I'm going to be OK. I'll work really hard and then everything's going to turn out well.*

And now that I was feeling refortified, I didn't feel the need to drink. I folded up Sylvia's message, put it back in my pocket, and stood at the foot of my bed to do my prayers:

Dear God,
Thank-you for blessing me with food, shelter, my family, and the opportunity and the ability to pursue my dreams.
I pray for everybody who is suffering right now, and I pray that you take care of them – just as well as you take care of me.

I paused for a moment, recalling all the loving, kind, inspiring things Sylvia had said in her message as I became flushed with gratitude.

And I thank you for blessing me with Sylvia's compassion. I thank you for bestowing me with such a caring friend.
I love You, God.
Amen.

I then turned out the light and crawled into bed to try and catch a couple of hours sleep before class the next day.

~~~

What the fuck is wrong with me? I tell myself I'm a hard worker, I tell myself I have the discipline to achieve my goals, but then this week I only manage to work 53 hours? There are no excuses – that's fucking atrocious. That's a fucking disgrace. I'm such a fucking slacker. Such a worthless fucking piece of shit.
Enough. This cannot happen anymore. This is fucking ridiculous, and it can never happen ever again. Never, ever, ever again.
So I came up with a plan to make me work harder:
I'm going to start cutting myself.
Starting just above the wrist, I'm going to cut myself with a steak knife every time I don't work 60 hours a week. It makes sense. When I do something wrong, it's my fault. And if it's my fault, then I deserve to be punished. So whenever I don't work hard enough so that I fall behind at uni or don't get as much of my novel written as I need to, I'm going to

cut myself. Maybe if I do this I won't be so lazy. Maybe if I do this I won't fail so much.

I never actually ended up harming myself, but it's a testament to my rapidly deteriorating mental health that doing so seemed completely normal to me. That's what depression does – it bends straight lines, complicates simple equations. But because I'd never been educated about it, I still didn't know I was depressed. I thought I was just going through a rough patch – I had no idea I was suffering from an illness. So instead of getting the help I needed, I just continued spiralling further and further downwards.

~~~

The following week, I snapped. I broke my three month sober stretch. Drank a bottle of bourbon alone in my room. Even Sylvia's message couldn't save me then. The anxiousness, the misery, the pressure, how overwhelmed I felt . . . it became unbearable. I was desperate for an escape and I didn't care how I got it.

~~~

I remember my first fantasy about death like it was yesterday. It was four in the morning, and I was cramming for a stats exam I was way behind on.

'You're gonna fail, you're gonna fail,' whispered a voice in my head.

'You're gonna fail, you're gonna fail.'

I tried to push it to the side, I tried to forget about it, but no matter what I did it was always there, heckling me, taunting me.

'You're so far behind. You'll never catch up. You're going to fail. Again. Just like you always do.'

It fed my fear, heightened it, made me want to scream.

'You're gonna fail, you're gonna fail.'

I need an escape, I thought. *Relief from the ceaseless dread.*

'You're gonna fail, you're gonna fail.'

Need booze. Fucking gagging for it.

'You're gonna fail, you're gonna fail.'

Shut up! Shut the fuck up!

'You're gonna fail, you're gonna fail.'

I want to die! I just want to die!

I hate my life so much that I just want to die!

At that point, the "low battery" notification flashed across the screen of my laptop:

Only 10% remaining. Connect to a power source immediately.

I retrieved the charger from my bag, and as I was about to plug it in to the power point, I remember hoping that something would go wrong – that there'd be some sort of technical malfunction – so that when I plugged in the chord I'd be electrocuted to death.

And I remember feeling dejected that I wasn't. I remember feeling disappointed that I was still breathing in a world I no longer wanted to be a part of.

November, 2008

I hardly slept during the exam week that semester. I had to study round the clock to try and catch up, and even then I was still badly prepared, having to resort to learning coursework on the day of the exam. I felt so burnt out, so horribly drained, like a horse that'd been flogged to the point of death. And on the night of my last exam, as I tried to fight off the fear of failure that had been progressively engulfing me; as I tried to swallow down the sick feeling lodged deep in my throat; as I ran to the bathroom thinking I was going to puke; as I coughed and spluttered up bile in the sink; and as I stared into the mirror at my black-rimmed eyes that were puffing out from my exhausted, unshaven, sorrowful face, I knew that something had to change. Studying Commerce/Law full-time, writing a novel, tutoring high school students, coaching basketball, playing basketball, going to the gym – it was too much. I realised I was going to self-destruct if I kept going like that.

~~~

My average was 74% that semester, and my novel was still nowhere near finished. I talked over what I could do with my parents, and after we'd analysed each option to death, we all agreed that the best thing for me to do would be to ease my workload the following year by only doing one subject a semester instead of four. I figured having effectively a year off uni would give me time to finish my novel and get it published, after which I could come back refreshed, and with my writing done and dusted, I'd have enough time to keep on top of my subjects and get a High Distinction average. I hated the fact that it had come to this. I hated the fact that I was delaying my corporate career a year. I hated the fact that I was falling behind the rest of the scholarship students. But I knew it was just something I had to do. It was, as they say, the lesser of two evils.

December, 2008

The days were better after uni was finished, because I didn't have to worry about studying – but I was still far from happy. Two years beforehand, happiness and I were bundled together, but since then it'd been kind of like the Big Bang, myself and happiness stretching further and further apart until it seemed like nothing more than a dim pinprick in the great blackness of space. It felt like I had no sun. In my world it was always winter. I tried to write but my mind was too hazy. I had the focus of a bored child.

A vivid memory I have of that time is being on my flight to Chile. Before I left, everyone was saying that I'd have the time of my life. But whenever I thought about it, I just couldn't see how. I just couldn't fathom the concept of enjoying myself. In my dismal state, the idea of pleasure seemed too foreign. Too farfetched. And in those silent, pensive hours, when the lights were switched off and the whole plane was asleep except for me, my thoughts kept returning to the same lone question:

Will I ever be happy, again?

And also to the same answer:

I don't know.

I really, genuinely, truthfully don't know.

Santiago, Chile – New Year's Eve, 2008

I was plastered for the second time in three days. I knew I shouldn't have been drinking, given my history with alcoholism, but I didn't care. I was finally enjoying myself, and I didn't care. I was sick of being unhappy and I was prepared to do anything to feel good again.

'Hey Danny, do you want to snort some coke?' a bloke at the hostel asked.

'Never had it before, bro. What's it like?'

'Oh it's so good, man. It makes you feel so alive. It makes you feel on top of the world. Two snorts and you'll be flying, man.'

I just wanted to be happy. I'd been miserable all year and I just wanted to feel happy again.

'Yeah, let's do it, dude.'

So we went to a club and got blazed. We stayed there all night long, dancing, drinking, coking and having the best time I'd had in months before the club closed at five and I had to go back to the hostel and pack so that I could take my 9am flight to Cusco, Peru.

Cusco, Peru – January, 2009

Particularly since Mr Williams had emphasised it, I'd been very mindful of the fact that I'd been tremendously blessed. I was very grateful to have been brought up in a wonderful neighbourhood; to be surrounded by a loving, supportive family; and to have been gifted with the opportunity and the ability to do anything I wanted to in life. I knew that I was a lucky man – but I never knew how lucky until I went to Cusco.

Before I went there, I'd never been to a place where 56% of the population lived on less than US$1 a day, where 85% of children never attended high school, where the school drop-out rate was 40%, where the unemployment rate was 42%, where the underemployment rate was 74%, where the literacy rate was 18%, where the infant mortality rate was 5%, and where the average life expectancy was 41 years.

I'd never met any children who wore the same World Vision clothes to school every day.

I'd never been to a school where not a single kid was fat, nor had I ever been called fat by anyone else, which is what some of the children thought the volunteers were because we weren't bone-skinny.

I'd never had 10 year olds try to sell me cigarettes on the street at two in the morning on a school night to help support their family.

I'd never been too embarrassed to tell someone I had a swimming pool in my backyard, like I was when my host family – who lived in a flat barely larger than my living room – had asked me to describe my home to them.

I'd never lived in a place where only ice-cold water came out of the taps, meaning that I had to heat it with a kettle and use a bucket and cup to shower.

I'd never seen villages of houses that didn't have any windows and were made out of mud bricks, much less had I helped build chimneys out of bamboo for said houses so that smoke wouldn't suffocate the air when the families cooked over a fire.

I'd never been to a place where all the adults looked 20 years older than their actual age, and where people as young as 30 had dry and wrinkled skin.

I'd never met a kid who grabbed other peoples' crotches and stuck his fingers up their bums during a school yard game of dodge ball.

'Why does he do that?' one of the volunteers asked.

'Because . . . he gets sexually abused at home.'

'By who?'

The volunteer manager released a painful sigh.

'By his father.'

We were all flabbergasted.

'How come . . . how come no-one's reported it?'

'We have.'

'And?'

He sighed again.

'The police . . . it's not like in your country. There's so much corruption . . . it's not like in your country.'

'But surely something can be done about it?'

'I'm afraid not.'

Seeing this poverty, this exploitation, this corruption, this perversion; waking up every morning and staring it in the face . . . it can change you. And it certainly changed me. Like I said I was aware of it before, but working in that community made me realise just how immensely privileged I really was. And when I looked into the eyes of those skinny kids wearing World Vision clothes, I knew that it was up to me as one of the extremely fortunate people in this world to step up and give them a helping hand. So I did whatever I could there, whether that was helping to build a chicken coup or a vegetable patch so the children could have eggs and vegies as a constant source of food, helping to build chimneys for the houses in the villages, or working on a new classroom for the school. And as I hammered away, I knew that that wouldn't be the end for me. I knew I wouldn't just go back to Sydney and forget about that place. I knew it was the start of something big. In time, I knew that I was going to be making a much bigger contribution to that community than just pounding nails.

~~~

I was feeling great while I was in Cusco, because I was loving all the volunteer work I'd been doing. But the other reason I'd been enjoying myself so much was because of all the partying. Five nights a week I was hitting the town, drinking until midnight before getting on the marching powder and flying until four. I thought being high on coke was the best feeling in the world. Whenever I took it I felt like I could run forever, fly, conquer the world. I just felt so confident, vivacious and energetic. I felt the exact opposite of depressed. And when I was dancing on top of the bar at three in the morning, fucked out of my mind and fist-pumping like hell to the music, I felt so incredible that it was hard to imagine I ever was.

February, 2009

After six weeks in South America, I went to Auckland, New Zealand for a week-long stopover on the way home and dived back into writing my novel. I'd missed it so, so much, and it was great to return to it after all those weeks. Every morning I'd stroll down to Esquires, order myself a milkshake and a ham and cheese croissant and just write, write, write. Now that I was no longer so stressed out with uni, working on my novel was back to filling me with indescribable joy. I was on a high all week, just from being able to do what I loved. And when I wasn't writing, I was thinking about writing: my characters, plot twists, how it all tied together. And when I wasn't thinking about writing, I was fantasising about getting published. I'd imagine how incredible it would feel, receiving that phone call where I'm offered a contract and falling to the floor with overwhelming happiness, crying deliriously into the palms of my hands. I wanted it more than I'd ever wanted anything before. I didn't think there was a single thing on earth I wouldn't do – aside from hurting someone else or violating my ethics – to achieve my dream. It was an obsession that dominated my thoughts. There were nights I'd just lie awake, thinking about it, longing for it, aching for it. Even then, I knew that if it happened it would be the best moment of my life.

~~~

I nearly missed my flight because I was passed out drunk and slept through my alarm, but somehow I managed to make it and there I was, flying back home seven weeks later a brand new man. I had an amazing time, and I was so excited to get back to Sydney and start my year of writing. *I can't believe how lucky I am!* I thought. *I mean, I actually get to spend the whole year working on my dream! How amazing is that?* I just felt so happy again. *Gone are the days when I feel worthless, when I feel so overwhelmed that I want to lock myself in my room and drink until I'm numb, when I feel so miserable that I wish I was dead.* My self-esteem, my self-confidence, my exuberance for life was back, and for the first time in a long time, I felt free, like an eagle, wings mended and ready to soar through the sky, chase my dreams, catch them, and live happily ever after.

~~~

On my first weekend back in Sydney, I'd organised to catch up with some of my friends in Darling Harbour. About an hour and a half before my mate Cal was coming to pick me up, I mixed myself a stiff bourbon and cola and continued working on *Chrysalis*. After South America I didn't have much money to spend at the clubs, so I wanted to get as smashed as possible before I went out so I didn't end up sober and have a shocker of a night.

Cal came when he said he would, by which time the litre bottle of Beam was close to finished and I was shitfaced. I went to greet him at the door, stumbling already.

'Sup man?' I yelled.

'Danny . . . are you trashed already?'

'Yeah, bro! Let's go hit the clubs!'

He didn't even look shocked. I was in the same condition when he saw me the previous night too.

We met the other boys at Darling Harbour and decided to go to Cargo Bar. The guys got let in, but when I went to give the bouncer my ID he shook his head.

'You can't come in tonight,' he said.

'Aww, why not man?' I slurred.

'You've had too much to drink.'

'Naahhh, bro. You've gotta let me in!'

He shook his head and told me to leave. My mates tried to talk him into letting me inside but he stood his ground.

'That guy was a fucking cock!' I said loudly as we were walking away. 'Why the fuck didn't he let me in?'

My mates shook their heads.

'Anyway fuck Cargo!' I kept ranting. 'Let's go to Bungers!'

We lined up at Bungalow8 but it was the same story there too. I lined up again and again, hoping that a different bouncer would card me and let me in, but I was refused entry every time. We gave up when they threatened to blacklist me from the club and call the police if I didn't leave.

'Why are all the bouncers being such fucking assholes tonight?' I yelled.

'They're not being fucking assholes,' one of my mates finally said. 'You're wasted as fuck. You shouldn't even be out.'

'Naahhh, man! They're all just being fucking assholes tonight!'

Eventually we got let in to Strike Bar down the road. I headed straight for the bar and started smashing back cocktails.

'Stop drinking, stop drinking,' everyone was telling me.

But I couldn't stop. When some guys go out their entire night's about trying to get laid, but with me it was all about trying to get as much booze into me as possible. Once that switch got flicked I craved it and it became all I could think about.

I was being loud and obnoxious. My friends got more and more pissed off and at some point left without saying goodbye. Cal said he'd take me home, so I stumbled into his car and passed out in the front seat.

He woke me up when we reached my house. I got out of the car and staggered away in the opposite direction. He tried to guide me inside but I broke free and kept lurching away, stumbling and falling in the neighbour's garden. Eventually he gave up and went to get my mum. It was late at night. She answered the doorbell, shocked to see him.

'Cal? What's wrong?' she panicked.

He sighed.

'Hi Mrs Baker. Danny's drunk too much again. Could you please help me get him inside?'

My parents were livid the next day.

'This is disgraceful! What the hell were you thinking! You know you're not supposed to be drinking! You know that if you do you're going to ruin your life!'

I thought about how pissed off my friends were with me. I remembered how completely out of control I'd been. There was no escaping the conclusion: *my parents are right. I can't keep drinking. I have to stop.*

After my parents stopped berating me, I started berating myself.

What the fuck is wrong with me? How the fuck could I let it get to this stage? How the fuck do I not know by now that I can't control myself when I drink? I'm such a fucking idiot. Such a fucking loser. Such a stupid fucking piece of shit.

I was so disgusted with myself for fucking up again. I felt so worthless. I felt like such a failure. And as a result, it was back.

Depression.

Surrounding me, swarming me, throttling me ruthlessly as ever. It was the depression that always came with feeling like a failure, but this time, it was greatly exacerbated by the fact that I'd previously tricked myself into thinking I was healthy again. I thought I'd beaten it, but nothing could've been further from the truth and it scared the shit out of me.

How the hell could I feel so good, feel so certain that I'd conquered my demons, only to feel like this seven days later? It's been a whole year now – how can I still feel so miserable after all these months?

And then came the most terrifying thought that a person with depression can possibly have: *will I always feel this way? Is this just the way I am? Will I forever be condemned to a life of insufferable pain and despair?*

If at the end of the day, all people want is to be happy, then is this feeling – *will I forever be condemned to a life of insufferable pain and despair?* – not the most terrifying feeling we can possibly experience?

As I state in *I Will Not Kill Myself, Olivia*, the fact that it haunts everyone in the throes of a prolonged depression – not to mention that by definition, patients are, to say the least, unhappy – is what makes clinical depression such a horrific illness.

March, 2009

There were days when I felt myself – when I was cheerful, when I was excited to be pursuing my dream, when the future seemed bright and full of promise. But it was like I was walking on a tightrope, where the slightest hit would knock me off and send me spiralling into despair. I was so wildly unstable, smiling one moment but then so angry with myself, so overwhelmed with self-hatred, so distraught the next – and always over the simplest of mishaps: missing the bus, forgetting my wallet at home, being five minutes late to class. It was scary as hell, how volatile I was. And I didn't even have booze to weather the storm. I was sober as a nun, for fuck's sake. I was fighting unarmoured. I'd been trying to read to relax but when you're craving bourbon, reading to relax is like hugging when you're horny. I didn't know how to balance without a bottle. Hell, I didn't know how to balance, period. I was a fucking train wreck, a ticking time bomb, set to explode at the slightest provocation.

~~~

And then one morning, I did.

I had a writing course – "how to develop romantic relationships between characters" – at the NSW Writers' Centre in Rozelle at 10am. I took the 7:46 bus to Queen Victoria Building in the city from the top of my street; it was meant to get there before 9 o'clock, but the peak hour traffic was worse than usual and it didn't arrive until 9:11. I checked the bus time to Rozelle at the stop opposite Town Hall.

Fucking hell, I swore.

The next one left at 9:25.

That's pushing it, I stressed. *That's really fucking pushing it. What if I'm late? What if I miss something really important? What the fuck am I going to do then?*

Wait . . . I finally said to myself. *Just try to relax. Nine twenty-five – I should still be OK. Just calm down. Try not to get so anxious over everything all the time.*

I boarded the bus, reached Rozelle at 9:45. I saw the sign that read "NSW Writers' Centre", so I pressed the button to stop the bus. When I got off I was standing in front of it, but all I could see was a big grassy area and a large complex of buildings.

Where the fuck is this place? I fretted.

I nervously walked through the field, studying all the buildings, but nothing indicated that any of them were the Writers' Centre. With mounting panic I circled them, once, twice, three times, but I still couldn't find where the damn place was.

Then came the self-abuse:

What the fuck have I done? Why the fuck didn't I look up exactly where this place is on a fucking map? Why the fuck didn't I ask for directions? Why the fuck am I so stupid? Why the fuck am I such a fucking moron?

I checked the time on my phone. Three minutes to ten.

Fucking hell! I'm going to be late! I'm going to be late! What the fuck will I do if I'm late?

I let out a loud, desperate groan and ran back to the main road. I looked around hopelessly, but I was lost. I had no idea where I was. Eventually I ran down the street before I saw one perpendicular to the road I was on: Alberto Street. It meant nothing to me. I doubled back through the field and the buildings and hysterically searched for the Writers' Centre but to no avail. I checked the time again: 10:10.

I'm such a cunt! I screamed in my head. *Who the fuck can't get to a fucking course on time! What the fuck is wrong with me? Why the fuck am I so fucking pathetic? Fucking hell! I'm such a cunt, I'm such a cunt, I'm such a cunt!*

I was so angry with myself that I collapsed in a heap beneath a tree and burst into tears. I completely broke down, so overwhelming was my vehement self-loathing, my nauseous distress, my ghastly misery that all I could do was cry and cry and cry. I sat there for what felt like hours just balling my eyes out, and all I could think was, *my life is so fucked up, my life is so fucked up. My life is so fucked up that I wish I was dead.*

Eventually I staggered up, drifted through the streets, tears still streaming down my cheeks. I couldn't think of anything else but death. It's not that I – like most people suffering from severe depression – particularly wanted to die – rather that I was just desperate to escape my harrowing anguish, and death seemed to be the only conceivable way. I imagined how soothing it would be. The answer to all my problems. Just blackness. Gentle, calm, soothing blackness. I fantasised about all the different ways I could do it: slitting my wrists, overdosing, electrocuting myself, poisoning myself, hanging myself, drowning myself, gassing myself . . . and then I saw a bridge, only 50 metres away. I felt a surge of energy and ran towards it.

I felt less overwhelmed the closer I got. To me, the bridge was a salvation, perhaps like what land is to those lost at sea. I felt like I controlled my own destiny again. In a strange way I felt empowered.

I found myself standing at the top of the bridge. I looked down. Instantly I felt a rush of disappointment.

The bridge isn't high enough.

Instead of dying I'll get screwed by luck and just break all my bones.

Racked with grief, I pulled myself away, lurched down the street. I saw a pub and headed straight in.

'What can I get you?' the bartender asked.

I thought about how blissful it would be to taste the bourbon on my lips, to have it pumping through my veins before I melted into numbness. So good. So. Fucking. Good.

'What can I get you?' the bartender repeated.

'Ah . . .'

He raised his eyebrows.

'Um . . . Coke.'

'Just Coke?'

'Yes.'

I can't do it, I finally realised in a moment of strength.

It's not right.

Now's not the time to get drunk. Neither is it time to kill myself. It's the time to sort this mess out. It's the time to face my demons and man up and beat them.

That's the right way to overcome this.

Not by drinking – which will get me into even more trouble.

And definitely not by committing suicide – which is a permanent solution to a temporary problem.

So I sat down at a table with my glass of Coke and called my mum.

'Danny? Why aren't you at the writing course? Is everything all right?'

'No.'

'Why? What happened?'

'Can you . . . can you just come and get me? Please?'

She came. By then I just felt drained. I mumbled what happened on the way home. When we got there, we sat on the dining room couch and talked for a while.

'I can't . . . I can't believe what happened today,' I murmured. 'That whole thing with the bridge . . . I mean that's just . . . that's just *so* screwed up.'

I paused.

'Why am I like this?' I asked. 'What's wrong with me?'

Mum was holding my hand, squeezing it tightly.

'It's going to be OK,' she said. 'Dad, Mathew[3] and I are all here to support you, and tomorrow, we'll go to the doctor and make sure you get the help you need.'

She squeezed my hand even tighter.

'Just keep having faith, Danny. Whatever you do, you can't ever lose hope.'

~~~

The next day, I saw my general practitioner Dr Kramenin and told him everything. He responded by saying that I was showing classic signs of clinical depression.

I remember being confused. I remember not really getting it.

'Clinical depression?' I asked. 'What do you mean?'

'Clinical depression,' he repeated. 'It's an illness, Danny.'

I still didn't get it.

'What is it, exactly?'

'In lay man's terms, it's basically an intense state of unhappiness, experienced over a prolonged period of time.'

'But . . . but doesn't everyone feel unhappy from time to time?'

'From time to time, yes. But not for prolonged periods. People with depression feel constantly miserable, almost without relief. And the intensity of their despair is usually far greater than that experienced by a non-depressed person. Some people with clinical depression hate

---

[3] My brother, who's three years younger than me.

themselves. Some self-harm. Some kill themselves. Clinical depression is an illness, Danny, and it can be very serious.'

I nodded. The description fitted like a glove.

'So you think I've got clinical depression, then?'

Dr Kramenin filed through his drawer before handing me a checklist called SPHERE, a scale he said was developed to increase the identification rate of mental illnesses like depression. I started reading it:

For more than TWO WEEKS have you:

Felt sad, down or miserable most of the time?
OR
Lost interest or pleasure in most of your usual activities?

If you answered "YES" to either of these questions, complete the symptom checklist below by circling the symptoms that are applicable to you:

Behaviours

Stopped going out;

Not getting things done at work;

Withdrawn from close family and friends;

Relying on alcohol and sedatives;

Stopped doing things you enjoy;

Unable to concentrate.

Thoughts

"I'm a failure";

"It's my fault";

"Nothing good ever happens to me";

—

"I'm worthless";

"Life is not worth living".

Feelings

Overwhelmed;

Unhappy, depressed;

Irritable;

Frustrated;

No confidence;

Guilty;

Indecisive;

Disappointed;

Miserable;

Sad.

Physical

Tired all the time;

Sick and run down;

Headaches and muscle pains;

Churning gut;

Can't sleep;

Poor appetite/weight loss.

I answered "yes" to "in the last two weeks have you felt sad, down or miserable most of the time" and then circled "relying on alcohol and sedatives", "unable to concentrate", "I'm a failure", "I'm worthless", "it's my fault", "overwhelmed", "unhappy, depressed", "guilty", "disappointed", "frustrated", "miserable", "sad", "irritable" and "life is not worth living". After I was finished, I handed the test back to Dr Kramenin.

'You circled 14 symptoms,' he said. 'According to the authors of the test, you are likely to have a depressive illness if you circled at least three.'

Dr Kramenin then asked me a few additional questions, like whether I was also experiencing periods of mania or whether I'd had any hallucinations, for the purpose of ruling out whether I was exhibiting symptoms of other mental illnesses like bipolar disorder or schizophrenia. After being satisfied that I wasn't, he concluded that I was in fact suffering from depression.

'What . . . what do I do?' I asked concernedly.

'I'm going to place you on an antidepressant medication,' he said.

Once again I was confused.

'Medication? For depression? How can that be?'

'If you have depression, then it means you have a chemical imbalance in your brain – a deficiency of either serotonin, dopamine, adrenalin or noradrenalin. We use medication to treat depression in the same way we use medication to treat physical illnesses. There's no difference, really.'

I was shocked. I'd never heard of such a thing before. Then again like I've said, I hadn't heard of clinical depression before, either.

'I'm going to place you on a selective serotonin reuptake inhibitor,' he continued. 'This SSRI will increase the amount of serotonin in your brain, and thereby work to correct this chemical imbalance. You should feel better after that.'

He gave me a sample packet of pills and a prescription for more when the sample ran out.

April, 2009

I feel so much better! Ever since I started taking antidepressants a couple of weeks ago my brain has felt a hundred times clearer! My suicidal thoughts have vanished, and every day is so much easier without that voice in my head telling me that I'm a loser and a fuck up and a failure. I actually feel healthy again – probably as healthy as I've felt since back in 2007 before my symptoms began making their way to the fore. I'm so stoked! I know I've said this a hundred times before, but I really think I'm cured! I think I'm finally cured this time! All I needed was antidepressants! Now all my problems are solved and I can get on with writing my novel and trying to get it published by the end of the year!

The fact that I thought I'd beaten it once again just goes to show how little I knew about depression. While medication can be very helpful, unfortunately recovery isn't as simple as just popping a pill.

May, 2009

Hey Sylvia,

I'm so depressed again. I have no idea how. I've been taking my meds, but I think they've stopped working or something. So what am I supposed to do? How am I supposed to beat this illness? I keep thinking I've beaten it but I never have. I feel like I have no control over my brain. I feel crazy.

I'm becoming such a recluse. I don't want to talk to my friends anymore, because I don't think I'll have anything non-depressing to say. So don't worry about replying to this message or my last one. You must hate having to keep hearing about my problems all the time, so I'm going to stop dumping them on you and just leave you alone. You're better off without me, anyway.

Danny.

She replied that same day:

Oh my God Danny please don't think that you're dumping all your problems on me or that I'd be better off without you! Seriously, nothing could be further from the truth! I want to be here for you whenever I can because you're my friend, Danny – I care about you so much and I want you to keep telling me about what you're going through so that I can try to help if I can. So please don't ever forget that. Seriously – thinking that you're dumping all your problems on me or that I'm better off without you is absolutely ridiculous! You're my friend and I'm here to support you and that's all there is to it.

That being said, Danny, I'm not a psychologist, and I really think you need to start seeing one. I am only about to finish my second year of Psychology at uni, but one thing my professors have really hammered into me is that just taking the drugs won't necessarily fix everything . . . or anything. The aim of medication is to treat the symptoms you're feeling, whereas therapy aims to deal with the underlying causes as well as the symptoms. Sometimes the reason people are depressed is because of the way they think about one or more aspects of their life, but with Cognitive Behavioural Therapy, you can actually learn to rewire the way you think and thus make yourself look at things in a way that doesn't make you feel so depressed. I know your mum has been telling you to see a psychologist too, so I think you should definitely do it. Maybe then you can conquer your depression for good and stop having so many relapses.

Apart from that, Danny, just keep hanging in there. You're so strong, you can get through this. Just keep fighting and you'll beat it in the end. I know you will.

Love always,
Sylvia.

~~~

In light of everything my mum and Sylvia were telling me, I scheduled another appointment to see Dr Kramenin.

'Do you think I need to see a psychologist?' I asked. 'I've heard they can be really helpful – that sometimes the reason you're depressed is because of the way you think about certain aspects of your life, and that therapy can, among other things, rewire the way you think so that you can look at things in a way that doesn't make you feel depressed. What do you think? Would it be a good idea for me to see one?'

Dr Kramenin shrugged his shoulders.

'Danny, the reason that *you're* depressed is because of your situation – struggling at uni and battling to get your book finished. If you change your situation, then you won't feel depressed anymore. And for you, that means getting *Chrysalis* finished and doing well at uni. That's the key to you beating your depression.'

It's what I'd been thinking all along: *I've been depressed because I haven't been achieving my goals, so if I achieve my goals then I won't be depressed anymore.* To me, that line of thinking made sense. *So what's the need to see a psychologist?* I thought. *I don't need therapy to "change the way I think", and in any sense, I've got Sylvia to talk through my problems with. Like she said in her last message, she'll always be there for me, so seeing a psychologist would be redundant. It would only waste time that could better be spent working towards achieving my goals, so it would actually do* harm *rather than good. So it's out of the question. No way am I going to see a psychologist.*

This was the first time – and unfortunately not the last – where I put my faith in Dr Kramenin's hands and he fucked me over.

July, 2009

There were still days when I was horribly depressed, when I would've rather be anyone else than me, when I wanted to lock myself in my room and drink myself to death. But on the whole, I was feeling much better than I did when I got back from South America. The bad days were becoming fewer and farther between, and I was starting to return, ever so slowly, back into my usual confident, exuberant self. It was coming at the right time, too – Sylvia was an instructor at a holiday camp until September and barely had access to the internet, so she wouldn't have been able to support me if I crashed and burned again.

Without a doubt, the antidepressants were one reason why I'd been feeling a lot better. I'd definitely been more stable and level-headed since I'd been on them, instead of getting suicidal over the slightest thing all the time like I was before. But what'd also been great was having been able to settle into a routine where I got to spend the majority of the day doing what I loved: writing. As usual it filled me with enormous pleasure, and what's more, around that time I started discovering how cathartic writing could be, which enabled me to enjoy it on a whole new level. It was interesting – over the course of the year, I found myself putting so much of my soul into my novel. For example, when my protagonist was living in a shanty town and struggling to make ends meet, I made him turn to alcohol to escape. When he failed to reach the target amount of money that he wanted to make in a day, I had him falling into depression. At one point, I had him on the edge of a bridge about to jump. Hell, even the relationship between the protagonist and his lover started to mirror mine and Sylvia's, in the sense that it played a big role in helping him through his despair.

It was no accident that this happened – nearly all artists explore their struggles through their work. It helps us deal with it in a way. When I was writing about how my protagonist overcame his alcoholism, it reminded me that I needed to keep it together and not relapse. When I was writing about how he didn't jump off the bridge because he decided that he'd rather face his demons and beat them instead of running away, it reinforced the idea that I needed to stay strong and do the same. When I was writing about him achieving his dream at the end of the novel, it helped me remember that if I just kept working hard and never gave up, then I too could achieve mine. In this way, my protagonist became the man that I wanted to be. He helped give me strength, helped give me hope, helped me keep believing that my best days were ahead. He helped inspire me to keep on going.

By July, the next draft was almost finished. I planned to send it to Nick by the end of the month.

I really hope he says it's ready to be published this time, I remember thinking.

August, 2009

Dear Danny,

First off, I'd like to say that this draft is much, much better than your last one. You really brought the time period to life, and a lot of the silly schoolboy symbolism you used beforehand was eliminated. The ending was far less contrived. Good job.

However, I still feel you have a significant amount of work to do before you submit your novel for publication.

Just like last time, Nick then went on to detail the problems with the draft. Firstly, he said that although my writing style had improved immensely, that the novel still wasn't as well written as it needed to be. Secondly, the hardships that befell the protagonist occurred too close together, making large chunks of the novel too dark to be enjoyable. With regards to the main character falling in love with a black girl, Nick said that I still hadn't portrayed the "racial" issue anywhere near well enough. He also said that the poetry still wasn't up to scratch.

Part of me was encouraged: *Nick says it's much better than my last draft, so that's obviously a positive sign. It's good that I've been improving, and because I'll continue working hard and never give up, I have no doubt that one day, I'll have produced a novel that's worthy of being published.* I really did believe that. What I was worried about, however, was my dwindling amount of time. *What if I can't make all these changes before uni starts?* I stressed. *Then I won't get a High Distinction average. Then I'm going to be depressed. Then I'm going to want to kill myself again.*

I can't put myself through that again, I thought. *I just can't. So come hell or high water, I need to get this book finished by the end of the year.*

September, 2009

I started getting involved in quite a bit of volunteer work in the second half of the year. In August I did the 40 Hour Famine to raise money for World Vision, and in September I signed up to participate in Movember to fundraise for prostate cancer research and the mental health charity Beyond Blue. I guess I felt like I was doing my bit, but I really wanted to be doing more.

I kept thinking back to the poverty I saw in Peru: the skinny kids wearing World Vision clothes every day; the 10 year olds selling cigarettes on the streets at two o'clock in the morning on a school night; and the tiny homes made out of mud bricks. When I was there, I promised myself that I was going to make a difference once I got back to Sydney, so while I was raising money for Movember, I started looking into the feasibility of founding my own charity to help the people I worked with in Peru and others like them around the world.

'But is now really the best time for you to be starting up a charity?' Mum questioned. 'It's a nice idea, but right now, you're suffering from depression – you're hardly in the best state of mind yourself. Don't you think you should just focus on you for the time being and then worry about helping others once you're 100% healthy?'

I shook my head.

'I am going through a hard time right now, but eventually I'm going to work my way out of it. I'm going to beat my depression. I'm going to be OK. But those kids . . . they need people to help them. They're not in a position to be able to save themselves.'

I paused.

'I am in such a position to help them though, and I don't want to put off doing so any longer. I want to help them now.'

I paused again.

'Every day those kids are suffering – when you look at it like that, I've already waited long enough.'

October, 2009

I had my good days and my bad days, just like anyone else – but on my bad days I felt suicidal, and wanted nothing more than to put a gun to my head and blow my brains out. That was more or less the state of my depression in October, and I figured it to remain that way until I achieved my goals, because it was when I struggled to achieve them that I was sent spiralling into despair. With only one subject at uni at that point in time, my mood was basically pinned to my writing. If I felt like *Chrysalis* was on track to being well and truly finished by the start of the first semester of 2010, then I felt good. If I felt like it was still going to be at the draft stage, then I wanted to die. It was that simple, really.

November, 2009

Towards the end of the year, I found myself developing feelings for Sylvia. I knew we lived on opposite sides of the world, I knew we'd been friends for years and it was a dangerous line to cross, but the heart wants what the heart wants. I just kept thinking about how she'd always been there for me, about how she'd always helped me in my hours of need. No matter what I'd told her she'd always stuck by me, lifting me up again, giving me hope, inspiring me to keep on fighting. Just like Olivia is for Jimmy, Sylvia was the most compassionate, genuine, caring girl I'd ever met, and I found myself wanting her, despite all the warning signs.

She was coming back to Sydney for two weeks after Christmas. My plan was to wait until then and then tell her how I felt.

December, 2009

When I sent the next draft of *Chrysalis* to Nick, I felt really good about it. I was confident that it was ready and that it wouldn't leak into the upcoming semester. But all I could do was nervously wait and see.

In the meantime, I founded my charity – I partnered with a friend and we made it happen. We called it the Open Skies Foundation, and once it was fully set up, we planned on funding projects that created sustainable change in Third World Countries. Our first one was going to be to build greenhouses in the villages I visited while I was in Peru; this would allow vegetables and flowers to be grown year-round instead of only 3-4 months a year using open air fields, and thus provide the community members with a sustainable source of food and income. But unfortunately we were still a while off from being able to fundraise, as there were a lot of burdensome and time-consuming legal and administrative hoops to jump through before we obtained the requisite license to do so. *I really wish there didn't have to be such a delay,* I remember thinking. *I really wish we could start right now.* The urge to make a difference burned so strongly inside me, particularly whenever I saw an old photo of one of those kids wearing World Vision clothes in Peru. But as with everything else in my life, I knew that I had to be patient, and trust that everything would work out well in the end. Frank and I had a clear vision, and we were dedicated to growing Open Skies so that one day it would be operating in Third World Countries all over the world. That was our goal: to change hundreds of lives across the globe. It was not a commitment for the next month, or the next year, or even for the next decade, but rather a lifelong pledge to help those less fortunate than ourselves. Once again, it was those words that inspired me:

'Remember, Danny: to whom much is given, much is expected.'

January, 2010

We held each other in bed, gazing into one another's eyes. It was the end of a two week fling – she was heading back to the States the next day.

'What am I going to do without you?' I asked seriously.

She laughed.

'What are you talking about?'

I was thinking about how warm, how tender, how loving, how supportive she'd been through thick and thin. She was my rock, my saviour, and I couldn't bear to see her go.

'I'm going to miss you so much,' I said. 'Sydney won't be the same without you.'

'I'll miss you too. But we'll always have Facebook.'

It didn't seem like enough anymore. Our two weeks together had been amazing, and I'd fallen head over heels for her. *How can we go back to talking only once or twice a week over the net?* I thought.

'Maybe I could come and visit you sometime?' I asked.

I expected her to be excited at the prospect, but instead she looked shocked.

'Huh?' she gaped.

'Well, I've never been to mainland America before. You could show me around. It would be so nice to see you again.'

She looked away.

'Uh . . . well . . . I don't know. Let's not think about it right now, OK?'

I looked into her eyes and smiled, still not sure what I'd done to deserve someone as caring as her.

February, 2010

This is great! I thought. *I just got my review back from Nick, and he says* Chrysalis *is more or less finished! All I have to do is make a few changes, tinker with a few scenes here and there, tidy up the writing style in various places and I'll have a completed product! That's incredible! Particularly after everything I've been through! It's been such a long, slow, arduous process that's really tested my resolve, but I got there in the end and here I am, soon to be submitting my manuscript to agents and publishers. I can't wait!*

Uni's also starting in a couple of weeks. I'm taking all third-year economics subjects, including all the honours stream ones. I'm not quite sure exactly what line of work I want to pursue in the corporate world, but I know it's definitely not law. In fact, that's why I'm taking the honours stream subjects – once I've finished this year and gotten my Bachelor of Commerce, I'm almost certain that I'm going to quit my law degree and do an honours year in economics, followed by a Masters of Applied Finance at hopefully Oxford or Cambridge or one of the Ivy League schools in the States. Honours in economics and then an MAF will have me very well placed to get a job at one of the top management consulting firms in the world, which is the industry I'm leaning towards entering. It all starts with this year though, and I want to smash a High Distinction average and finish my bachelors on a high. And now that I've more or less finished my novel I'm primed and ready for it. Bring it on!

I feel as if I'm in a really good place right now. For the first time since uni started, I'm really pleased with the direction my corporate career, my writing and my charity work is heading in, and that's something to really feel good about. Now that my goals are on track to being achieved, I feel like I'm back to my old self again. Once again I'm full of hope and confidence, brimming with energy, coursing with desire. And my depression? That's long gone. Done, finished, kaput. Goodbye, you bitch. I've beaten you. You tried to break me but you couldn't.

With the benefit of hindsight, it is easy to see that ignorance is bliss.

PART III

OR

'THANK-YOU, DR GREGOR'

OR

'FUCK YOU, DR KRAMENIN'

March, 2010

On the first day of my Advanced Microeconomics Honours class, the professor ran us through the course outline and the assessment regime before delving straight into game theory in extensive form. Within a few minutes I was horribly lost. I had no idea what was going on. I tried my best to catch up while the lecture continued:

'It is imperative to note the critical distinction between actions and strategies. Suppose player "I" in an extensive form game has "L" information sets: "I.1", "I.2" . . . "I.L" etcetera, and that she has a choice of M_K actions at her "K-th" information set. Then, player "I" has "M_{1}" x "M_2" x . . . x "M_K" strategies. If an agent has only one information set, strategies and actions are synonymous for that player. In particular, for a simultaneous-move game, the notions of strategies and actions coincide for each player.'

I was so confused. *What the fuck is he talking about?* My notes were a mess – he was speaking far too quickly for me to get everything down. I scanned the room in panic, hoping to see everyone just as lost as I was, but they were all listening intently and calmly taking notes. Some students were even asking perceptive questions that pleased the lecturer. But I still had no idea what was going on. I started berating myself.

What the fuck is wrong with me? How the fuck is it that everyone understands what's going on except for me? Everyone here must be smarter than me. Hell, of course they're smarter than me. I'm dumb. I'm an idiot. I'm a fuckwit. I'm a complete and utter failure.

And the more I abused myself the less I could concentrate, and the less I could concentrate the more I fell behind. In two hours I hardly absorbed anything, and all my old demons – anxious dread, self-loathing and a lust for death – stormed back into my life and butchered my psyche.

I left class feeling suicidal. Despair throttled me, as did that torturous uncertainty of not knowing whether or not I'd ever be able to douse depression's roaring fires that once again were burning me alive.

For fuck's sake! I thought I was cured! I felt cured. But I'm not. I'm as depressed as ever.

I fought back tears.

Will I ever get better? I fretted. *Is this just the way I am? Am I forever destined to a life of excruciating misery?*

I went home and tried to work through the lecture material but I was too depressed to function. I took a break and tried again, but it was the same story all night long. Eventually I gave up and tried to get some sleep, although I should've known there was no chance of me being able to just shut my eyes and drift away. I was far too disturbed. I was far too terrified. I was in full-blown panic mode.

I just couldn't believe it.

How the fuck can it be back?

How the fuck can my depression possibly be back?

~~~

Sylvia, where've you been? I'm going fucking mad here. My depression's back and I don't know what to do. What am I supposed to do? My doctor's put me on a stronger antidepressant but it's not making any difference. Nothing is. Fuck. Just please say something to help me. I'm going to pieces and I really need your support.

Love,

Danny.

~~~

I was more depressed than ever. It started on my first day back at uni when I left class feeling like a failure, and was multiplied by the horrifying reality that I'd never in fact conquered my depression and maybe never would. Feeling that depressed made it difficult to study, so I fell behind at uni, which made me even more depressed, which made it even more difficult to study, which made me even more depressed . . . and so the cycle went. The pain lasted for days at a time. To use Jimmy's analogy in *I Will Not Kill Myself, Olivia,* I felt like a starving journeyman lost deep in a forest, blindly wandering in the hope of making it out alive. The journeyman has no food. He goes for three or four days, sometimes even a week, without eating. Eventually he'll catch something, wolf it down, but it's only a quick fix. Not long after he'll be famished again.

Replace hunger with depression and that was me. Food was my equivalent to all forms of escape: T.V., reading and masturbation. They were temporary as fuck. Depression always prevailed.

I would think of suicide as much as the starving journeyman would think of food. We had the same goal, too: get through the day. Live til tomorrow. Sometimes that seemed too overwhelming, so I'd use the trick my addictions psychologist taught me and break it down into smaller sub-goals: *just survive the next twelve hours. The next ten hours. Hold off killing yourself until then.* It was so hard but I knew that I had to keep on fighting, I knew I couldn't lose faith that one day I'd get better. Every day I prayed to the Lord: *God . . . I am suffering . . . I am drained . . . please give me strength . . . please give me the fortitude to beat this illness.* My life was such a disaster but I had not abandoned hope. That's the one thing I had going for me. To steal another line from *I Will Not Kill Myself, Olivia*, hope and depression are bitter rivals until one inevitably defeats the other. As long as I had hope I was in with a shot.

~~~

Sylvia, what's going on? I've tried texting you but you won't reply to my messages. Everything's so fucked up. I don't know how to beat this illness and I'm just getting worse and worse and worse. I'm so lost. So confused. Help me. Please.

~~~

I kept floundering, kept sinking. One night in particular stands out in my mind. It was three in the morning. I lay on a couch paralysed with anguish. I was in so much mental agony that it was affecting me physically. I felt so heavy, so lethargic. I could hardly move. Hardly speak. Mum was beside me, clutching my hand. Tears were rolling down her cheeks.

'D-Danny . . .' she sobbed. 'Danny pr-promise . . . promise me you'll never . . . end your life . . .'

She clenched my hand even tighter.

'Do you promise?'

I managed to move my head, nod ever so slightly.

'Because if you do . . .' she cried, 'you might as well take me with you.'

I knew I'd never do it. *No matter how much I want to I can't commit suicide,* I thought. *Suicide's quitting. Suicide's selfish. I am not a quitter, and I'm not going to leave my family without a brother and a son.*

'Don't worry,' I murmured. 'I won't.'

~~~

Sylvia, what's with you lately? You never reply to texts, take ages to reply to Facebook messages, and don't want to talk on the phone. Something about you seems so . . . distant. Seems so foreign. It's like I . . . don't even know you anymore. Seriously, Sylvia . . . what's going on?

~~~

Look, Danny – maybe I have been distancing myself from you lately, but I have my reasons. You're depending on me more and more and . . . I care about you, OK, and I want to be there for you – but you've got to understand that it's putting a hell of a lot of pressure on me. I'm only human, Danny, and I'm not a qualified psychologist either. I'm your friend, OK? I've been supporting you as your friend and I want to keep doing so, but you have got to realise that it can be very hard for me, particularly when all you seem to feel is depressed these days. You're not even seeing a psychologist, so you're depending solely on me. Not to mention that your feelings for me are growing and growing and you're contacting me at rapidly increasing rates and . . . look, it's all just a lot of pressure, OK? It's scary. It's too much for me right now and I don't know how to deal with it.

Just like Olivia eventually does, Sylvia was beginning to reach the end of her tether.

~~~

We talked back and forth for the next few days, but everything basically came to a boil. Sylvia was feeling uncomfortable about the extent to which I was coming to her with my problems and about how attached I was getting to her, and once she aired those sentiments, I felt too self-conscious and uncomfortable to talk to her at all. So that was pretty much the end of it.

The timing couldn't have been worse. As if I wasn't depressed enough already, I'd now messed things up with Sylvia, a very important person in my life and my main support system. It was depression on top of depression. A whole new low.

In a moment of reflection, I found myself thinking back over every attempt I'd made in the last two years to try and beat my illness: trying to drink my way out of it; working myself to exhaustion at uni and on my novel; snorting coke in South America; working my ass off again on my novel and at uni; depending on Sylvia for help and support. *And where has it gotten me?* I thought. *I'm an alcoholic, suicidal on a daily basis, and I just lost Sylvia because I smothered her too much.*

There was no escaping the cold hard reality:

Nothing I have tried to beat my depression has worked. Every one of my attempts has failed.

I released an exhausted sigh before reality landed me another kick in the balls:

I don't know how to fix my depression.

Admit it: I've got no idea how to fix my depression.

'Danny, will you *please* see a psychologist,' my mother begged.

I knew Dr Kramenin said I didn't need to see one, but I felt like I was out of options. I was the most depressed I'd ever been, and I didn't know where else to turn.

'OK, Mum,' I said. 'I'll see a psychologist.'

April, 2010

It took all of my energy to heave myself out of bed and make it to my first appointment. I arrived at Dr Gregor's office feeling dreadful, and sat slouched in the waiting room with my head lulled lethargically back against the wall until he called me in. He was a tall, middle-aged man with brown hair, an unassuming posture and soft, gentle features. His handshake was prolonged, full of the warm familiarity of a mate, and his smile was broad and friendly, inducing me to reciprocate even though I felt like shit. When he introduced himself he spoke in a calm, soothing voice and looked me earnestly in the eye. My immediate impression of him was that he was an amiable, down to earth bloke who wouldn't judge me no matter what I told him.

He led me from the waiting room into his office, where we sat down in comfortable arm chairs that faced each other. Then without further ado, I described to him everything I'd been through. I'd always thought it would be difficult – opening up my soul and sharing my darkest, innermost thoughts to a stranger – but Dr Gregor was warm and non-judgmental, and even if he wasn't, I felt far too depressed to give a shit what he thought of me anyway.

'And the worst part is,' I finally summed up, 'that I don't know what more I can do to beat my depression. I've worked so hard on my book and at uni but it's never enough. I always fall back into it. I keep thinking I've beaten it but it always comes back. I've tried everything to beat it but it always comes back.

Dr Gregor frowned gently.

'I don't think that's true, Danny,' he said.

'You don't think what's true?'

'That you've tried everything you can to beat your depression.'

'But I have,' I insisted. 'For two years I busted my ass but no combination of writing and studying worked to achieve my goals. Then I took a year off purely to write – I delayed my corporate career an entire year! – and that didn't work either. And now I'm back at uni and trying my best but it's still not enough. Nothing's changed. I've worked as hard as I can but I'm still so depressed.'

'That's not what I mean,' he said calmly.

'What do you mean, then?'

'In all the time you've been depressed – two years, now – have you ever once seen a psychologist?'

'Yes.'

'For depression?'

'No, for alcoholism.'

'What about for depression?'

'No.'

'Never?'

I shook my head.

'This is my first ever session.'

'Why didn't you see a psychologist earlier?' he asked.

'Because I didn't think I needed to. I thought that all I needed to do to beat my depression was to get a High Distinction average and get my novel published. I thought that after I achieved my goals I'd be happy again. That's what my GP's been telling me – fix your situation and you'll stop feeling depressed.'

Dr Gregor's eyebrows jumped.

'Your GP told you that?'

'That's what he always tells me.'

Dr Gregor shook his head.

'I don't think that's very good advice,' he said.

I was surprised.

'How do you mean?'

He sighed.

'Let me put it this way: what's going to happen if you don't achieve your goals? Are you going to be depressed forever?'

I flinched. It was such a brazen, confronting question.

'I . . . I mean . . . I think I will achieve them. But if I don't . . . if I don't I'll . . .'

'Even if you do achieve them this time round, what about your goals after that? What if you struggle to achieve those, just like you've struggled with uni and your novel? Does that mean you'll go through another huge bout of depression? And what about your goals after that, and the ones after that? Are you going to get depressed every time they don't go 100% according to plan?'

I was speechless. My whole world was crashing down around me. I was so sure that all I needed to do to beat my depression forever was to get a High Distinction average and get my novel published. That's what Dr Kramenin had always told me, and to me, it had always made sense. But the questions Dr Gregor was asking me . . . I'd never thought of them before. And now that I was, my life seemed destined to be bereft of happiness. It seemed that my depression would keep coming back, again and again and again, until the day I died Consternation engulfed me. I was so scared that I literally wanted to puke.

'Yes,' I managed to croak.

Dr Gregor nodded.

'This is why the advice Dr Kramenin gave you wasn't very good. All he told you to do to fix your depression was to change your situation, and as you can see, in your case at least, this would have set you up for a lifetime of relapses. Now, sometimes overcoming depression *is* as simple as changing your situation – but often the reason people suffer from depression is not actually because of their situation itself, but rather because of the way they *think about* their situation. And this is what I think your problem is – one of perception, as opposed to one of circumstance. You feel suicidal every time you struggle or "fail", as you put it, to achieve your goals – and it doesn't have to be this way. My role as your psychologist will be to help you get to the bottom of why "failing" to achieve your goals depresses you so much, and then help you to perceive this "failure" in a way that doesn't make you feel depressed.'

At the time, it seemed unimaginable. But I tried to be hopeful.

'Do you really think I can get to that place?' I asked.

He nodded.

'If you commit yourself to therapy, then I'm confident you can.'

Our session eventually finished. I agreed to see Dr Gregor again at the end of the week, and we shook hands and parted. What he'd said sounded promising, but I just couldn't for the life of me ever envision a world where not getting a High Distinction average or my novel published didn't plunge me into a life-threatening bout of depression. Hell, in the state I was in then, anything but depression seemed impossible to fathom.

~~~

The new medication Dr Kramenin prescribed was giving me splitting headaches, so he placed me on a different one yet again – this time a relatively new drug that was part of the serotonin-norepinephrine reuptake inhibitor class of antidepressants. Mum was hysterical over it.

'Danny, you should *not* be taking that medication! In Beyond Blue's *Clinical Practise Guidelines for Depression in Adolescents and Young Adults*, it specifically states that for the type of drug you've been placed on, further research is required before any conclusions can be drawn about its effectiveness and harms. For this reason, its use is *not* recommended for adolescents or young adults under the age of 24.'

'But Dr Kramenin prescribed it, so it must be OK.'

'That does *not* mean it's OK! All that proves is that he hasn't read the guidelines!'

'He's the GP, Mum! I'm not going to go against what he says!'

'I don't care if he's the GP! You need to tell him to change medications again! You can't keep taking this one! You're only twenty-*one*!'

We argued about it for hours, and eventually I was able to get Mum off my back. She was still distraught about the antidepressant I was taking, but the matter of my medication was just one too many things for me to deal with at that point.

I'm just trying to get through the days without necking myself, I remember thinking. *What medication I'm on is up to Dr Kramenin. It's his job to make sure I'm taking the right one.*

~~~

The days dragged along. This was the worst I'd ever felt. Period. There was no relief from the ceaseless dread. I could barely function. Paying attention in class was almost impossible. Studying was too overwhelming. I'd fallen absurdly behind. I hadn't touched my book in days. I'd quit my job at the law firm, too – needed all my free time to try and catch up on uni. But there was never enough time. I was constantly exhausted. Drained of life. Depression sucked at my soul. My spirit withered. My goal for the day got broken down even further: *just survive the next six hours. The next four hours. Hold off killing yourself until then.*

I'd previously thought I'd get better. I'd always thought it true that hope and depression were bitter rivals until one inevitably defeated the other, and I'd always thought that hope would win out in the end. But for the first time in my life, I was void of hope. I honestly believed that being depressed was just the way I was, and that being depressed was just the way I'd be, for the rest of my life. And because I was so convinced that I'd never get better, there seemed no point in fighting my illness. Instead of willing myself to "hang in there" because I believed that my suffering was temporary and that everything would be better one day, I comforted myself with the knowledge that human beings are not immortal. That I would die, one day. One special, glorious day. Then I could spend the rest of eternity mouldering in a grave, free from pain. You might be wondering why I didn't just kill myself if I wholeheartedly believed that my future consisted of nothing more than excruciating misery. Well, first of all, I still was not a quitter. But more importantly, I didn't want to hurt the people that loved me.

It's not fair to commit suicide and ruin their lives, I thought. *So I have to hold on. No matter how much it hurts me I have to hold on.*

Hence why I drew comfort from the thought that one day I'd die and finally be free.

When you're that depressed, that insanely and utterly depressed that you genuinely believe you'll suffer that acutely for the rest of your days, life seems to lack all purpose. *After all,* I remember thinking, *what's the point in working, fighting, striving for a better life if I'm sentenced to one of chronic anguish and despair? There is no better life. There is no life outside of pain. So what's the point in doing anything but waiting until death finally arrives on my doorstep and whisks me away to the Promised Land?* I was still studying, and I still planned on finishing my novel and trying to get it published, but it was more out of force of habit than anything else. My passion had been drained. My zest for life asphyxiated. I was like a ghost, just drifting through the ghastly days.

'Shit! What's wrong, mate?' an old friend once said when I ran into him at uni. 'Perk up, brother!'

I was shocked. One of the most well-known attributes of depression is that it is entirely possible – and very common – to suffer horrifically without anybody knowing. But somehow without realising it, I'd crossed the line from a place where I was able to put on a front and fool people into thinking I wasn't depressed to a place where I was so sick that it was obvious to people I hadn't even seen for a year. When I got home I looked in the bathroom mirror, and realised that I was staring back at a man whose eyes were exhausted slits, whose whole face shrieked of agonising misery. I was staring back at a man whose spirit had been broken, whose soul had been destroyed. I was staring back at a man who, for all intents and purposes, was already dead.

Three days later

I'd always taken a lot of pride in being a fighter, which in my books, meant having a tremendous work ethic, relentless determination, and most importantly, a never-say-die attitude. And because I was a fighter, I'd always believed I could handle anything life threw at me, and that even though I may struggle and fall, I'd get up every time and succeed in the end. That'd been my MO, and that's what I hung my confidence on.

But drifting through life a spiritless, broken shell of a man?

Giving up on happiness and resigning to a life of misery?

Letting depression destroy the next 60 years of my life?

That's not fighting, I finally realised. *That's quitting. And that's not me. I'm not going to let depression break me. Not now, not ever. I don't know when, I don't know how, but somehow I'm going to beat this illness and live a happy, healthy, fulfilling life.*

May, 2010

It took five intense weeks to understand the issue forming the crux of my depression – the "underlying issue", as Dr Gregor chose to call it. Over that time we were able to dig deep into my psyche, and after analysing my behaviour and the way I thought, Dr Gregor concluded that the primary culprit of my depression was a very unhealthy level of perfectionism.

'You relentlessly seek excellence, Danny, and you always set extremely challenging goals and then throw yourself into achieving them. Being perfectionistically goal-driven like this is fine in and of itself, but the problem with you is that you measure your self-worth entirely in terms of whether or not you achieve these goals. If you don't achieve a goal that you set out to achieve – like getting a High Distinction average or getting your novel published by a particular point in time – you hate yourself. You feel worthless and inadequate. You feel like a failure. And you feel this pain so intensely that you'd rather be dead.

'You're human, Danny, and humans, by our very composition, are not perfect. Humans make mistakes. Humans don't always achieve their goals. You need to accept this, and not be so hard on yourself. You need to accept this, and be able to love yourself regardless. You need to be able to love yourself regardless of how you go in your uni exams and no matter what happens with your novel. Even if you fail every exam for the rest of your degree and your novel never gets published, you should still be able to love yourself. You should be able to find elements of yourself that you love that will be there no matter what. That will let you love yourself no matter what.'

He paused for a moment.

'If you can do this, then I think you'll go a long way towards conquering your depression.'

~~~

Over the next several days, I managed to find things about myself that I liked. The fact that it took me an entire week to do so may seem downright absurd to you – maybe you can list a dozen things you like about yourself right off the top of your head. But me? I sure as hell couldn't do it. It wasn't something I'd ever considered before. All that mattered to me was whether or not I was achieving my goals. If I was, or was on track to, then I loved myself. If I hadn't, or was not on track to, then I hated myself. The concept of loving myself regardless of whether or not I succeeded was completely foreign to me.

But after a long time pondering, I finally had a list written:

> *I like it that I'm a kind person – someone who always treats other people with respect.*
>
> *I like it that I'm an honest person who acts with integrity.*
>
> *I like it that I'm compassionate and that I do volunteer work to try and help other people less fortunate than myself.*
>
> *I like it that I have the determination and the work ethic to pursue my dreams through to completion.*
>
> *I like the fact that I'm a positive person. I like the fact that even after everything I've been though, I still feel tremendously blessed, still feel immensely fortunate to have everything the Lord has bestowed upon me. I like the fact that instead of thinking of myself as unlucky for having suffered such a severe depression, I think of myself as lucky for having all the support I'm getting to help me beat it.*
>
> *I like it that I'm religious – that I have God in my life to guide me and to keep me safe. I like it that I trust Him so deeply that I'm faithful no matter what.*
>
> *I like it that I'm a fighter. I like it that I can handle everything life throws at me, and that even though I may struggle and fall, I have the strength to get up every time and beat it in the end.*

And when I focused on those things, I could actually see that there really was a lot to love about me.

I actually am a good person, I thought. *And this really is true, regardless of what my marks are at uni or whether or not my novel ever gets published. These are the reasons why I can love myself, and whether I succeed or fail has nothing to do with it.*

~~~

For the next few days it was all I could think about – this idea of thinking of myself as an inherently good person and loving myself regardless of whether I succeeded or failed. And its strength, its conviction, only grew with time. For the first time in a very long time I was really able to see the good in me, and now that I could, I didn't feel worthless anymore. I didn't hate myself. I didn't feel inadequate. Instead, I felt confident, and proud of myself. And I didn't feel depressed at all.

~~~

I shared my psychological epiphany with Dr Gregor the next time I saw him.

'This is excellent, Danny,' he said. 'Measuring your self-worth entirely in terms of productivity and accomplishment is not healthy – but this – what you've just told me – *is*. And combined with you taking your new medication which now seems to be working, I think it's the key to you overcoming your depression.'

Hearing that made me feel so empowered, so unburdened. But it also made me feel a pang of unease.

'But Dr Gregor . . . I like being a perfectionist. I like setting challenging goals for myself and then working hard to achieve them. Are you saying that it's not healthy to do that?'

He shook his head.

'Of course not, Danny. It's perfectly healthy to have goals and to pursue them passionately. It's good, even, and you should continue to do it. But it's critical that you love yourself, regardless of whether or not you achieve those goals.'

He paused.

'There are many good aspects of perfectionism, Danny. Like we've said, it obviously pushes one to strive for excellence and to reach their true potential. And in your case, I suspect it was the underlying reason why you never killed yourself. To you, suicide would've been quitting – the ultimate failure. And there is nothing, *nothing* a perfectionist hates more than failing.'

He paused again.

'It's a double-edged sword, perfectionism. The challenge for you, Danny, is going to be to retain the positives of it while banishing the negatives. And if you can remember and apply what we've talked about today, then I think you'll be able to do it. I *know* you'll be able to do it.'

~~~

Two weeks later, I was waiting at my computer to get the results of my Mathematical Economics mid-semester exam mark back. Due to my work with Dr Gregor I'd been feeling much better over the last few weeks, and with a few all-nighters and help from my friends, I was able to catch up on most of the uni work I'd missed out on. I'd done well in my mid-semester exams so far, getting 80% for Monetary Economics, 88% for Advanced Microeconomics Honours, and 90% for Regression Modelling. I'd run out of time to properly catch up on Math Econ, so I knew I wouldn't go as well in that – but I was hopeful I could scrape together a 75 and, due to the other exams being worth more, have my marks balance out to a High Distinction average.

Five PM came. I logged in and went to the "Exam Results" section.

Nine out of 20.

Nine.

Forty-five per cent.

A fail.

I couldn't believe it. I'd never failed an exam at uni before. Never even come close. I was absolutely gutted. *Fucking hell,* I thought. *A mark like this is really going to drag my average down. It's really going to make it difficult to get a High Distinction average this semester. This is bad. This is fucked. Fuck fuck fuck fuck fuck.*

I stewed in disappointment for the next half an hour before deciding to get laced up and head to the gym. I popped into the bathroom before I went, and then it hit me while I was taking a piss.

Wow! I actually exclaimed out loud. *I just got a shocking exam mark and I didn't go to pieces! I didn't abuse myself! I don't feel inadequate. I don't feel suicidal. I only feel disappointed. Not depressed – just disappointed!*

I could hardly believe it. Before I saw Dr Gregor, an exam mark like that would've destroyed me. It would've made me feel horribly inadequate and plunged me into an almost suicidal depression. But now, all I felt was disappointment – a perfectly healthy emotion. *I've had a setback, yes,* I thought, *but that doesn't mean I'm worthless. It doesn't mean I'm a failure. I'll learn where I went wrong, I'll do better next time, and I'll go on to live a happy, fulfilling life. That's all there is to it.*

Wow, I thought to myself. *I never thought I'd say this on a day I failed an exam, but I actually feel great right now. I think I've finally conquered my demons. God sent me a huge test, and I passed with flying colours! Regardless of how I went in my exam today, I truly have succeeded.*

I never thought I'd say that, either.

~~~

I told Dr Gregor what happened with my exam mark at our appointment a few days later.

'That's great, Danny!' he beamed. 'That's really, really great.'

I was beaming too. The high hadn't worn off yet.

'I feel really good,' I said. 'I think I've actually conquered my depression. Once and for all, this time.'

Dr Gregor nodded.

'You've done exceptionally well in these last couple of months, Danny. You came to me an emotional wreck, and you've transformed yourself into a brand new man. You ought to be congratulated. I know it hasn't been easy but you've done a great job.'

I smiled at him gratefully.

'Thank-you so much for all your help, Dr Gregor. Like you said I was such a mess when I first came to see you, but now I really do feel well again.'

I paused for a moment, looking him earnestly, emotionally in the eye.

'You've saved my life,' I said.

He smiled at me and we shared a warm moment together.

July, 2010

Halfway through the year, I finally finished *Chrysalis*. It took me the rest of the semester plus all of the holiday break, but I eventually managed to work in all of Nick's comments and do enough final read-throughs for me to be entirely happy with it and feel that at last it was ready to submit to literary agents. The way it usually worked was that you had to submit a one page "query letter" describing your novel; based on that, the agent might ask to read your manuscript, and if they liked it, they might offer to represent you. Once you've been signed, your agent would then present your work to publishing houses to try and get you a deal. It would be a long process, and it all began with the query letter, so I started reading everything I could find on the internet about how best to write them, after which I planned to write, rewrite and profusely edit my own. It was kind of like writing a second novel in the sense that it had to be as close to perfect as possible before you submitted it to an agent. You could write a great book but if the query letter wasn't up to par then you wouldn't get anywhere, so it was well worth taking the time to get it right.

~~~

Uni was due to start at the end of July, and once again I was aiming to get that so far elusive High Distinction average. I got almost 80% in the first semester, which, while disappointing, Dr Gregor had taught me to view as actually pretty good, considering the circumstances. That was something we were constantly working on – trying to get me to not be so hard on myself, to offer myself compassion, to learn to think of things in shades of grey rather than so black and white. No more *80% < 85% = fail*. Rather, *it's good, considering that for half the semester I was really sick, and now that I'm well again I'll work hard to achieve my goal this time.* That sort of stuff.

I felt good at the time. I could feel myself getting healthier and healthier, due to all the therapy I'd been continuing to do, and I was excited to embark upon my publication journey and jump right back into uni. I felt it was time to start a new chapter in my life, one where I was depression-free and ready to achieve my goals.

August, 2010

Mum was still stressing out about the medication I was on.

'You shouldn't be taking this antidepressant, Danny! You're too young! Like I keep trying to tell you, it's not recommended for young adults under the age of 24!'

'Mum I'm sick of talking about this! I'm doing well now – I don't want to change medications. And Dr Kramenin doesn't want me to, either.'

'Dr Kramenin hasn't read the research! He's got no idea what he's doing! Don't you get it? Not enough research has been done on this drug to know its effects on young adults under 24! You're like a guinea pig! Who knows what's going to happen down the line?'

'Dr Kramenin said it's fine.'

'Dr Kramenin doesn't know what he's doing!'

'Mum can you just drop it?'

'But Danny – '

'I said drop it, Mum! I told you – I'm sick of talking about this!'

~~~

Throughout the year, my co-founder and I had been working hard to get Open Skies off the ground. We were making progress, but unfortunately everything was moving at a snail's pace. We were still waiting on receiving the government's approval for our License to Fundraise, and until then were forced to play the waiting game with great frustration. In the meantime though, I'd started doing volunteer work at 180 Degrees Consulting, which is a non-profit organisation that does pro-bono work for other NGOs. The first project I was assigned to do was to work closely with a charity that combatted violence against women. Broadly speaking, my team's role was to advise them how to achieve their objectives more efficiently, so we started breaking down the organisation into its various components and analysing where improvements could be made. Just like the previous charity work I'd done, it was a very eye-opening experience – as the project progressed, I gained a much deeper appreciation of the hardship that battered women endure, and also of some of the reasons why many victims can't just simply "pack their bags and leave" – often they have nowhere to go, are financially dependent on their abuser, think their abuser will kill them if they do, or can't bear to leave their children behind. In the same way witnessing Peru's confronting poverty did, learning about the suffering of these poor women shed even more light on just how lucky I really was, and further strengthened my belief that as someone who'd been tremendously blessed, it was my obligation to help those less fortunate than myself. Open Skies was my baby, my pet project, and as soon as we got our License to Fundraise I hoped to do incredible things with it – but in the meantime, I still wanted to do whatever I could to help others in need.

September, 2010

Things were still a mess with Sylvia. We tried to work through it but couldn't make any headway, and by September we weren't speaking at all. It'd been bothering me, so I started talking to Dr Gregor about it.

'I think the problem you guys had is that you had a very uneven relationship – and what I mean by that is that Sylvia was more your de facto therapist than your friend. You came to her with all your problems and she helped you through them, and the more this happened, the more you came to depend on her, the more emotionally attached you became to her, the higher a pedestal you placed her on and the more you thought of her as some sort of angel of healing, and the more, I suspect, she thought of you as something along the lines of a mentally ill patient in need of help. It got to the stage where you became needy and started asking too much of her, and that made her feel pressured and scared and she started putting up barriers, and when that started happening, it bothered you to such an extent that you felt too uncomfortable to ever open up to her again. And the end result is that you're no longer talking to each other.'

I was confused – not about Dr Gregor's analysis of mine and Sylvia's relationship specifically, but about the general conclusion that it seemed to be implying.

'But then . . . but then are you saying that it's not healthy to turn to a friend or a partner or whoever for support? Are you saying that it's healthier to just keep to yourself?'

He shook his head.

'Of course not, Danny. You never want to keep things bottled up inside you. It's good to talk to your friends, your partner and your family and to have their support, but when you have a mental illness, it's never good to rely on someone to such an extent that they become a *substitute* for a psychologist – which is exactly what was happening with you and Sylvia. It's not good for the relationship, as you've seen, and it's also detrimental to you on a broader level. When you have a mental illness and you rely on someone as a substitute for a psychologist, then you're not getting the help you need. Love and support from the people closest to you is invaluable, but it can't take the place of professional help. It needs to be in addition to it, not as a replacement for it. Think about it, Danny: if you had a physical illness or injury – a broken leg, diabetes or cancer for example – you'd never refuse professional help and rely solely on the support of your loved ones to get through it. And it's exactly the same with a mental illness – nothing should take the place of professional help.'

I nodded. It made sense, and I wished it was something I'd known earlier. It reminded me of that old adage "experience is the comb life gives you once you're already bald".

We kept talking.

'So do you think I'll ever be able to be friends with Sylvia again?' I asked.

Dr Gregor nodded.

'If you're both able to put the past behind you and start fresh, then I think you'll be fine. But don't rush it. Give it time. You're doing well now, Danny – the best advice I can give you is to just keep doing what you're doing. Keep focusing on getting better, keep honing your coping mechanisms so you don't have any relapses. Then you can see how things stand with Sylvia when the right time comes.'

To bring this sub-story to a close, it was a couple of years before we reconciled, but in 2013 Sylvia and I were able to start fresh and are now friends again. Just like Dr Gregor said, all we needed was time.

October, 2010

So after a lot of thinking, I finally settled on what I wanted to do in the corporate world: become a management consultant. According to my classmates and all the recruiters from the big firms who were always visiting the campus, you basically got paid a ton of money to travel all over the world and consult on a multitude of fascinating projects for a diverse range of organisations. It sounded great, particularly the part about getting paid a heap of money. *I could live the life I've always envisioned!* I thought excitedly. *I could own a big house on the harbour, have a couple of sports cars parked in the garage, and take my family on overseas holidays every year! How cool would that be?*

There was no one path to take to become a management consultant, but I planned on doing Economics Honours in 2011 followed by a Masters of Applied Finance at Oxford or Cambridge or one of the Ivy League schools in America. By then I would've had more than enough education under my belt to get a job at one of the top tier firms.

I decided not to finish my law degree. I found it dry and unenjoyable and it wasn't where my strengths lay. So I applied for honours and planned on quitting law as soon as I'd been officially accepted. But until then I had to focus on my bachelors. My exams were only a couple of weeks away, and I wanted to smash them and end my degree on a high.

November, 2010

How the fuck can this still be happening? After all I've been through . . . after all I've done to get better . . . how, for fuck's sake, how?

I was suicidal again.

For the first five days of November I was horribly depressed, and what was most bewildering was that I didn't know why. Unlike before, my depression didn't seem in the slightest bit related to my perfectionism. Whenever I'd been depressed in the past, it was because I thought I'd failed at something. I could always point to a "cause" – like a bad book review or an exam mark below 85%. But this time there was no such cause. I'd just wake up and want to die – that's it. And for that reason, I couldn't use any of the techniques Dr Gregor had taught me to work through my despair. Being reminded of all the reasons why I ought to love myself wasn't working this time.

I was so shocked. So mind-numbingly terrified. *For fuck's sake!* I stressed. *How could I feel so well again, feel so certain that I'd overcome my depression, only to have the urge to kill myself again? It's been three years now! I'm working with my psychologist, I'm taking my medication – what more can I possibly do?* Back came all the petrifying questions, the ones that would nosedive me even deeper into depression and chill me to the bone:

Will I ever beat this illness?

Is this just the way I am?

Am I destined to live a life that's forever riddled with suffering and despair?

Who knows? Who the fuck knows?

I wish I could kill myself, I remember thinking. *I wish I didn't have any family so that I could just blow my brains out and nobody would care.*

~~~

Then all of a sudden, life was sublimely rapturous.

The days are so beautiful! I remember thinking. *I'm so lucky to be alive! God, thank-you for the gift of life! For giving me the senses to be able to see, smell, hear, taste and touch this beautiful planet that you've graced us with! Thank-you for blessing me with everything anyone could possibly want! And please help everybody who's less fortunate than me . . . please help everybody who didn't wake up this morning feeling that today is a glorious gift from above!*

Wow! The world is just perfect! It's such a splendiferous oasis! Such a magnificent confluence of beauty! Like Victoria Park next to uni! I love just strolling around and marvelling at the gorgeous green grass, smiling at the ducks in the pond, picking flowers off the jacaranda trees and twirling them hypnotically between my fingers, which is seriously like, the most beautiful thing in the world. And how about technology these days! I mean talk about incredible! The fact that we can speak to people on the other side of the planet is absolutely amazing! I was chatting to an old flame the other day and I was just thinking, "how are we not together?" Like seriously, we would be so good for each other! It's like that letter I sent her last year with the flowers, when I was talking about picking them all and laying them at her proverbial feet, and it just made so much sense, and it still makes so much sense, because I'll treat her so well, and she gets me, like we really click! I don't know what my brother's talking about, saying that it doesn't make any sense. He doesn't make any sense! He doesn't understand how beautiful the world is! He doesn't understand how deliriously happy I am! Like, wow! This is the best I've ever felt in my entire life! I feel so invincible! So strong! So powerful! So indestructible! When I look up into the sky and sense the Lord's presence, it's like we're the same. I feel like God! I feel like God! I am so insurmountable that I feel like God!

~~~

And then I was depressed again.

I was depressed two days before my first final year exam.

I was depressed two days after the most blissfully happy week of my life.

And I still had no idea how.

What the fuck is going on? I remember thinking. *What the fuck is wrong with me?*

I was back in wanting-to-die mode, more so than ever before. I tried to escape through life's momentary pleasures: masturbating; over-eating; sleeping, if I could manage to get it. But it never lasted beyond the moment. Depression always prevailed.

I wish I didn't have any family, I kept thinking. *Then I could just end it.*

At the time, I remember feeling that love was a terrible burden.

~~~

A week later, I was back to being high as a kite. I felt so energetic, so vivacious, so almighty again. Dr Gregor said I was exhibiting classic symptoms of bipolar disorder – a condition where, when untreated, the sufferer oscillates between the nodes of extreme depression and extreme mania. I seemed to fit the description, but psychologists provide therapy as opposed to diagnose mental illnesses, so Dr Gregor advised me to see a psychiatrist. I really hoped someone could figure out what was wrong with me. I felt so wildly unstable, so horrifically disturbed. And the "mania", if that's in fact what my highs were, was really starting to freak the shit out of me. I liked it at first, I think because I was so relieved not to be depressed anymore. But after a while it was just plain fucking scary.

Feeling that I'm a superhero?

That I'm the greatest human being on earth?

That I'm as powerful as God?

Like what the fuck! That's so ridiculous! I mean seriously, what the fuck is wrong with me? I'm crazy! I'm actually crazy!

And the worst part was that I was actually aware of it. I *knew* that I'd lost my mind. I *knew* that I'd gone completely mad.

It was the most confronting, horrifying experience I'd ever had in my life. I'd rather have been suicidal any day.

~~~

Got my wish – six days later I wanted to kill myself again.

I remember trying to study in a group for my exam the following day . . . made progress, but I knew my depression was right there, ready to swarm.

I had dinner with my parents afterwards. I could no longer run from it. The beast throttled me, reduced me to a blob of agony. Mum and Dad spoke to me but I couldn't talk back. I just didn't have it in me. I was too drained. Too exhausted. There was nothing left but pain.

The next day

Woke up feeling ghastly. Dad drove me to uni for my exam. Silence all the way.

He dropped me off. I dragged myself to the exam room in a soulless, debilitated shuffle. When I got there I fell to the floor, sat slumped against the wall. My classmates talked to me, asked me questions, but still . . . nothing.

We got called in.

'Ten minutes reading time, starting now,' the announcer said.

I tried to read. I understood the words on their own, but put together they made no sense. I flicked through the exam. Not much of it did.

The exam itself began. I reread questions I knew I'd studied for, but in the moment the answers were a blur. I felt like I was in a trance. The world seemed a black hole. A vacuum of agony. I couldn't see any escape. The only possible salvation seemed death.

I scribbled down a few answers before the end of the exam.

'How did you go?' one of my friends asked. But I just shook my head and shuffled spiritlessly away.

I pulled myself into the streets. It was pouring down with rain. I had no idea what to do next. *Should I go home? Go back to uni and study? Go to a coffee shop? Call a friend? Get smashed at a bar?* Every possibility seemed brutally unbearable. The only one that didn't was killing myself. As you know, I'd always thought suicide was selfish, because even though it might've given me peace, I knew it would've left my family in ruins. But right then, on what was, unquestionably, the worst day of my life to date, I started to think that maybe I was wrong. I started to think that perhaps I'd been too narrow-minded.

Because I swear, I vividly remember thinking, *if my family knew how depressed I am right now . . . if they could comprehend the gut-wrenching severity of the pain I'm in . . . I swear they'd want me to put myself out of my misery. I swear they'd want me to end it all and finally be free.*

It was a dangerous revelation.

Does this mean I can die now? I thought. *Guilt-free and with my family's blessing?*

I stopped walking, let the rain pound down on top of me.

Can I do it? Can I really kill myself? Jump in front of a speeding car and join the rest of the road toll casualties?

I stood at a right angle to the road, watched the cars zooming by.

Is this really it? Can I really end it all right here?

My mind was a warzone. So much conflict. But eventually there emerged a definite answer.

No.

I can't do it.

It's the answer I'd always reached, but this time, the reason was different.

It wasn't for me.

It wasn't even for my family.

It was for those less fortunate than me.

Regardless of how depressed I feel right now, I thought, *I know that I've been tremendously blessed: with a loving, supportive family; with First World privileges; and with the opportunity and the ability to do whatever I want to in life. Regardless of how I feel right now, I have had a lot bestowed upon me, and I have to use my good fortune to help others who aren't as immensely privileged as I am. If I kill myself, Open Skies will disband. All the charity work I'd planned on doing will never get done. I'd be abandoning all the people I have the capacity to help. And no matter how much pain I'm in I just can't do that. To whom much is given, much is expected. I can't kill myself. Not now, not ever.*

I felt it so strongly, with such paramount force that it couldn't be doubted. It was as if it was a calling, a message from God in my hour of need:

> *I put you on this earth for a reason, Danny. You can't leave it. There's so much work that you need to do . . .*

So I stepped away from the road. I called my mum.

'Hello?'

'Ma . . .' I croaked.

'Danny? Are you alright?'

I murmured something inaudible.

'Danny?' she panicked. 'Is everything OK?'

'Come and get me . . . please. Wynyard.'

I met her there, crawled into the car, muttered in broken sentences what happened.

'Danny, we would *never* want you to kill yourself!' she stressed. 'Never, ever, ever, ever! Suicide is a permanent solution to a temporary problem! You know that, don't you?'

I eventually managed to nod my head. From the corner of my barely opened eye, I saw Mum fighting back tears as she tried to drive through the rain. At some point she pulled over to call my dad. She talked to him while I sat motionless in the front seat.

After a long time, she finally hung up.

'Danny . . .' she murmured. 'Danny we think . . . we think it's time you be admitted to hospital.'

She paused solemnly.

'What do you think?'

I just wanted to get better. I was so tired of feeling sick and I just wanted to get better.

'OK,' I managed to say. 'I'll go to hospital.'

~~~

Arrangements were made and I was placed on the waiting list for a psych ward recommended by Dr Gregor, in all likelihood to be admitted in the next couple of days. Just knowing that I was about to go to a place where I could get better was enough to lift my spirits, so much so that I could crack a smile here and there and even joke around a bit with my brother. The way I saw it, going to hospital was a reason to be positive. In hospital, I'd have daily access to a psychiatrist, I'd be doing group therapy two or three times a day, and I'd have nothing to focus on except getting well again.

With all the support I'm going to get, hopefully I can get healthy again and return to life a healthy, stable human being, I thought.

~~~

Mum drove me to the hospital. I filled out some forms at reception and was then shown to my four person dorm. I sat pensively on the bed, waiting for my appointment with one of the in-house psychiatrists. It may sound a little strange, but I actually found myself hoping that she'd diagnose me with bipolar disorder. Of course it wasn't an illness that I wanted to have, but at least it would explain why the previous month had been so consummately fucked up, and hopefully with the right treatment I'd be able to get better. Being in that limbo where I didn't know what was wrong with me, where I oscillated from being horrifically depressed to being mad as a hatter . . . I couldn't take it anymore. I was desperate for answers. Sometimes anything's better than not knowing.

~~~

An hour later, I saw the psychiatrist and told her everything, and she concluded that I had "medicine-induced bipolar disorder". The bipolar part didn't come as a surprise, but the "medicine-induced" part was a hell of a shock.

'What . . . what do you mean, exactly?' I asked.

'The medication you were taking had a bad reaction with your brain, and it's caused you to develop bipolar disorder,' she said.

So it turned out that Mum was right – I should never have been taking that medication. My doctor was a quack. A bad apple. A person who I trusted who then completely fucked me over. You'd think I would've been furious at him, but anger was really the furthest emotion from my mind. Hell, I'd just been told that I had a life-threatening illness – did it really matter how I got it? I just wanted to do whatever it took to get it under control. I wasn't going to dwell on how it happened or feel pissed off or bitter or sorry for myself. I knew that wouldn't get me anywhere. Instead, I was going to focus on getting myself healthy. Anything that was taking away from that was just wasted energy.

The psychiatrist and I kept talking.

'Is bipolar disorder a permanent illness?' I asked. 'I know depression is generally more of a temporary affliction – something one often suffers from for a period of time before they at some point overcome it. But how long does bipolar disorder usually last for?'

I swallowed apprehensively.

'Is it something I'll have to battle for the rest of my life?'

'It's hard to say, Danny,' the psychiatrist said. 'Most people who have it do need treatment for the rest of their lives. But in saying that, bipolar disorder is very manageable. Through a combination of medication, therapy and maintaining an active, healthy lifestyle, many patients become stable enough that they can live a happy life that isn't impeded by their illness.'

~~~

After five days at the psych ward, I began to feel immensely better. When I switched from the antidepressant to a mood stabilising medication I stopped feeling suffocated by depression, and also ceased to experience the madness of mania. For the first time in weeks I was on a fairly even keel, and felt like I could think clearly again. Things were definitely looking up.

But in saying that, I found myself living in constant trepidation. Every day I'd go to group therapy and see 30, 40, 50, 60 and 70 year olds tell the same old stories:

'I've been depressed for the better part of my adulthood.'

'My bipolar disorder has had me in and out of hospital ever since I was 25.'

'Mental illness is just a part of who I am. I've learned to live with it, but I know I'll never beat it. It will be with me until the day I die.'

Being in the psych ward made me realise that this was my biggest fear: being forever shackled by my illness. Not being able to live a normal life. Hell, just not being happy. I would never give up on happiness – after everything I'd been through, I knew that about myself. *But what if the balance of chemicals in my brain prevents happiness from ever being possible?* I thought. *What if my life is genetically predetermined to be a ghastly rollercoaster where I oscillate between insufferable depression and delusional madness? What if my destiny is this: a psych ward. I feel much better now, but how long will it last? Is a relapse through hell inevitable?*

~~~

But after ten days in hospital, I had my answer.

No.

My brain chemicals do not control my destiny.

I – Danny Baker – control my destiny.

Through group therapy, I learned a lot more about the 30, 40, 50, 60 and 70 year olds who had been persecuted by their illness for decades of their life.

A lot of them drank.

Many of them were overweight, continued to eat unhealthily, and admitted to not exercising.

They had only tried a handful of medications.

They had only read one or two self-help books.

They didn't actively see a psychologist and never had for an extended period of time.

I was so surprised when I heard this. All I could think was, *how can they have such a serious illness and not do any of the right things to combat it?* At some point I delicately asked as much.

'I saw a psychologist for a couple of sessions, but I didn't like it much so I stopped going,' one said.

'Self-help books are a drag.'

'I like eating junk food.'

'Exercise is hard work!'

'I've tried a few different medications. None of them worked.'

And the most universal conclusion:

'Depression is just a part of me. I've accepted it. I know I'll probably be back in this psych ward next year sometime, but that's just who I am. Why fight it?'

I was flabbergasted. I couldn't believe it. I felt like saying:

'Mate! It doesn't have to be who you are! There are dozens of different medications on the market – how do you know that one of the ones you haven't tried won't work?

'You live in Sydney – there are hundreds of different psychologists here. You've tried a couple, but how do you know that another one won't be able to help you?

'What about all those self-help books? There are dozens of them written by some of the best psychologists in the world. Thousands of people have claimed that they've changed their life. Isn't it possible that you might get something out of them?

'And eating healthily, sleeping well, exercising frequently and not drinking are the most basic principles of managing a mental illness. Don't you think you'd feel better if you abided by them?

'How can you just surrender yourself to your illness before you've thrown everything but the kitchen sink at it? There's so much you haven't tried. You've barely scratched the surface. You can fight it! You can beat it! Depression does not have to be destiny!'

But I couldn't be so blunt. The most I could do was gently ask if one of these options may be of help to them. So I did. They shrugged. Someone changed the subject and that was the end of it.

And that's when I reached the conclusion that I controlled my own destiny. *Depression and mania and psych wards do not have to be a permanent feature of my life,* I realised, *because the means exist for me to conquer this illness. The means exist for me to live a happy, healthy life like any other bipolar-free person, and if I do the right things, I will. So for the rest of my life I will eat healthily, exercise frequently, and lay off the grog and other substances. I will never stop honing the techniques I've learned to prevent me from getting manic or depressed. I currently feel stable on the medication I'm on, but if at some point down the line I find myself struggling again, I will work with my psychiatrist to up the dosage or change medications.*

I'm not going to let this illness beat me. I'm going to fight it and fight it and fight it until I get better. I'm going to fight it and fight it and fight it until I'm happy again.

December, 2010

After two weeks I left hospital feeling infinitely better than when I arrived, ready to return to life a healthy, re-energised man. I was looking forward to starting work on my honours thesis for 2011, and I couldn't wait to get back to submitting my novel to literary agents and working to get Open Skies' License to Fundraise as soon as possible. I felt good. Hospital was great for me – exactly what I needed. But I never wanted to go back there again. And I planned on doing everything in my power to make sure I didn't.

PART IV

OR

LEARNING HOW TO BE

HAPPY

January, 2011

At the start of the new year, everything went haywire at uni. My Economics Honours application was rejected because it turned out that I hadn't done one of the pre-requisite subjects. It was never clear that that subject was a pre-req – it was a zero credit point *law* subject – so I spent days sending emails all over the faculty trying to talk them into letting me do honours regardless, or at the very least, letting me do the pre-req concurrently with honours. But they weren't having a bar of it.

'Rules are rules,' they said. 'You'll just have to wait to do honours in 2012.'

Wait until 2012? Are you fucking kidding me? I thought. *All for a zero credit point law subject that couldn't be any less related to economics?*

It was exasperating. Uni-wise I'd had everything planned out, but this technicality had completely fucked everything up. I was so pissed off about it, but there was nothing I could do. Studying honours that year was no longer an option.

I spent the next few weeks trying to work out what to do instead, and finally decided to just complete my law degree. It definitely wasn't ideal – I'd wanted to quit law, remember? For months my plan had been to do honours and then a Masters of Applied Finance. But I knew a law degree would open the same doors for me, since many of the skills you learn studying law are also useful for management consulting. And if it meant not delaying my corporate career another year, then I preferred to just suck it up and finish it over the next two years, even though I didn't like it very much. The way I saw it, anything was better than stalling my career another year. *I've already pushed it back by writing in 2009*, I figured. *I'm behind the 8-ball enough already – all the scholarship holders I started uni with are about to finish and enter the workforce – so I can't fall behind anymore. I have to study law. I don't have a choice. I wish I didn't have to but I don't have a choice.*

February, 2011

By this point in time I'd wanted to have been signed by a literary agency, but unfortunately I was still at the start of the long, rocky, winding road that would hopefully lead to publication; the agents who I'd submitted my query letter to in September and October had rejected me, and due to having been so sick, then going to hospital, then studying for and resitting the exams I'd missed, and then having to sort out all the drama at uni, I hadn't resumed since. On the bright side, however, one agent in particular gave me some valuable feedback on the start of my manuscript – she said that she didn't like my use of a prologue to open the novel, and recommended a few other ideas. I didn't agree with her, and I knew my mentor Nick was a big fan of the prologue, but I was always open to constructive criticism, so I was experimenting with her suggestions before I got back to querying other agents. To date, the process hadn't gone as smoothly as I would've liked, but I was still optimistic. There were literally dozens and dozens of agents I hadn't queried yet, and I was praying every day that one of them would pick me up and then go on to make my dream come true.

March, 2011

I'd been working hard to get Open Skies off the ground, but we were still stuck trying to get our License to Fundraise. The relevant government department was stretched so thin that it was taking forever. They'd receive our application, take three months to review it, ask for additional information, take another three months to review that, then ask for even more information, etcetera, etcetera. It was a frustrating process, but I was hopeful we'd get our license soon so that we could get straight to work.

In the meantime, I was volunteering with a few other charities. I was doing a second stint with 180 Degrees, this time doing pro bono consulting for an organisation that was combatting sex trafficking in South East Asia. The second NGO I was working for was the Australian League of Immigration Volunteers (ALIV), who worked with refugees in community detention. In January I volunteered at a holiday camp where we spent a week taking disadvantaged children to the beach, theme parks and other fun places to brighten up their day, and since then I'd been involved in ALIV's monthly weekend program where we did the same thing. Thirdly, I'd been visiting an online mental health forum to lend an ear to sufferers who needed someone to talk to, and to try and offer them the support of a person who'd been there. It was all so eye-opening, and as charity work had always done to me in the past, it hammered home just how lucky, just how immensely and richly blessed, I really was.

How else can I feel, I remember thinking, *when I hear stories of thousands of girls as young as five or six being sold into prostitution by their very own families? How else can I feel when I hear about them being tortured, beaten unconscious or having a bucket of live snakes or maggots dumped on them as "punishment" for fighting back when a violent client tries to rape them? How else can I feel when I hear about how their vagina often rips during sex so they get infected with AIDS and die before they're 20?*

Then there were the refugees. *How can I not feel tremendously grateful for the education I've received when I do reading practice with a 15 year old from Sierra Leone who can't pronounce the word "football"? How can I not feel even more grateful for being raised in a nurturing, peaceful country like Australia when every afternoon at camp an eight year old boy from Iran begs me to sit with him by the Parramatta River and silently gaze at the soothing, tranquil water because it "relaxes" him? Or when I meet a child who's fresh off the boat from some other war-ravaged country but whose family didn't make it to the Promised Land with him?*

And then of course there was everyone I'd speak to who had a mental illness, and it was those people, more so than anyone else, who made me realise just how good I really had it. *I mean how else can I, of all people, not feel inexpressibly thankful for all the treatment I've received when I talk to teenagers who are suicidal, manic or psychotic yet whose parents "don't believe in mental illnesses" and thus refuse to get them help? I mean fuck, these kids were* me *last year! Particularly the ones who have bipolar disorder – they're as unstable, suicidal and deluded as I was. But my parents had been supportive. They were kind, and loving, and got me the help I so desperately needed.*

And it got me to thinking:

Where would I be right now if I hadn't had anyone to help me? If my parents were like these kids' parents and said the whole thing was a farce and that if I didn't snap out of it they'd kick me out of home?

I certainly wouldn't have recovered, so they inevitably would've thrown me out.

There's no way I could've held down a job being that sick, so where would that have left me?

Homeless?

Probably.

And what does life hold in store for a homeless man who's gone completely mad?

Nothing.

Except death.

April, 2011

You may have been wondering when I started writing *I Will Not Kill Myself, Olivia.*

The idea first came to me when I re-read my favourite novel *Candy* by Luke Davies for the fourth or fifth time:

In the same way that Candy *is a gritty story that explores the lives of two lovers who are both trapped in the throes of a heroin addiction, I could write about something similar that's centred around mental illness instead of addiction. If there's one thing I know it's depression, and I think I could draw on everything I've been through to write a really engaging fictional story.*

These same musings were also holding me back from submitting *Chrysalis* to more literary agents, because I knew *I Will Not Kill Myself, Olivia* would overlap with it to some extent. Like I've said, while I was suffering from depression I started inserting a lot of my own experiences into it, and I wasn't sure how it would work having some of the same stuff in another novel. And there was no doubt in my mind that *I Will Not Kill Myself, Olivia* had far more potential than *Chrysalis* ever did. While I thought *Chrysalis* was a good story, I could admit that there was probably nothing special about it – nothing that made it stand out from all the other books on the market. But I was confident that *I Will Not Kill Myself, Olivia* could be exceptional. *At this point in my life it's the best book I have in me, so don't I owe it to myself to write it and see what happens? But then what about* Chrysalis? *What's the best thing to do with that?*

I kept thinking.

~~~

Apart from trying to work out what to do with my novel, I was also studying law full-time – and I wasn't enjoying it at all. Every day I'd sit through hours of lectures that I couldn't care less about.

'The identification of the ground of judicial review is contingent upon which remedial model is applicable. Under the "common law remedial model", the overarching question is whether an error which gives rise to a particular ground of review can be classified as a jurisdictional error, because some remedies (specifically, prohibition and mandamus) only issue for such errors. If it cannot, the error may still attract a remedy (i.e. certiorari) if it is an "error of law apparent on the face of the record".'

Who gives a fuck? I remember thinking. *This shit is boring as hell.*

I wish I didn't have to study law. I hate it that I'm trapped in this life. But it is what it is. This degree's just something I have to suck up and finish, regardless of whether I like it or not.

May, 2011

I kept going back and forth on what to do with my writing. Sometimes I thought I should just submit *Chrysalis* because I'd spent three and a half years writing it and it would be a waste not to. But most of the time I thought I should go with *I Will Not Kill Myself, Olivia* because it was a much better concept, and if it was a choice between the two, then I owed it to myself to produce the best manuscript I could.

I met up with Nick to talk it over.

'*Chrysalis* is a good book, but it's not a great book,' he said.

'But this new idea . . . it could be.'

He was confirming what deep down I already knew. Decision made.

On the drive home, I felt exhilarated. I felt so amped up, so full of life. Just giddy for it. I was about to start writing the story of my soul, and I couldn't wait to jump right into it.

~~~

So I began writing *I Will Not Kill Myself, Olivia*, and it was going great. Whenever I'd start I'd get so absorbed in the plot, so enveloped in the characters' lives, so lost in my imaginary world that I'd never want to stop. I knew I had to be careful, though – this was the same sort of thing that had gotten me into trouble during my first degree – too much writing and not enough studying. So I made a rule: *I can only write after I've finished all my law readings for the day.* I thought that would prevent me from getting the balance out of whack.

Another thing I thought it would do was give me some extra (and much needed) motivation to get my law work done. I'd been falling behind in class, purely because I disliked it so much. Whenever I'd study I'd get so bored and frustrated and miserable that before long I'd get fed up and stop. It was awful. There wasn't a single thing in any one of my subjects that interested me in the slightest.

I wish it didn't have to be this way, I remember thinking. *I wish I wasn't forced to do something I hate. I wish I could just forget about law and write all day. What a wonderful, invigorating life that would be. What a beautiful, ethereal existence.*

What a fantasy.

June, 2011

In the past, it had taken me by surprise. It had shocked the shit out of me. It had seemingly come so out of the blue that I hadn't known what had hit me. But this time, it was almost expected.

It was back.

That harrowing despair. That anxious dread. That feeling that life is so overwhelming, so insufferable that I wished I was dead.

Depression.

This time, my relapse was the consequence of being forced to do something I hated, hour after hour after hour, day after day after day. My exams were in a week, but I couldn't study for 20 minutes before depression would paralyse my mind and coerce me to stop. I just loathed it so much that I wouldn't be able to go on. So I was up Shit Creek. I was completely fucked. And the more I fell behind, the more depression strangled me. Every day it squeezed tighter and tighter, so tight that I was gasping for air, I was spluttering like mad and I wanted to kill myself again.

'I fucking hate law,' I told Mum one night. 'It's making me so miserable . . . so suicidal. I'm a wreck again. I need to go back to the psych ward – get some help so that I can put myself back together.'

Mum nodded solemnly.

'That sounds like a good idea, Danny. If you think you need to go back to the psych ward, then you should go.'

She paused.

'I also think it would be a good idea for you to drop out of law.'

I flinched.

'W-what . . . ?' I stuttered.

'If it's making you so miserable then I think you should quit.'

I was speechless.

'I c-can't . . . I can't do that,' I finally stammered.

'Why not?'

'Because . . . because I . . . because I need a law degree to get into a good management consulting firm. A bachelor's degree isn't enough.'

'What about an honours degree?'

'What do you mean "what about an honours degree"? I couldn't do honours this year. I hadn't done the pre-req, remember?'

'But you've done it now. So why don't you just quit law and do honours next year, which is the course you wanted to do all along anyway.'

'But I can't do that. I can't delay my corporate career any longer. Don't you get it? I *have* to finish law. I don't have a choice!'

'Of course you do, Danny. You always have a choice.'

'No I don't – '

'Yes you do, Danny. You always have a choice.'

July, 2011

Over the next few weeks I spent a lot of time talking to my parents, with the aftermath being that I decided to quit law and do honours in 2012 instead. Mum and Dad helped me realise that I do in fact have choices in life, and that it's a mistake to travel a path that isn't right for me – which law sure as hell wasn't. It may've been good for my corporate career, but all it was doing was rushing me straight back to the psych ward. So I decided that that was the end of it. And when I quit, I stopped feeling depressed. I felt well again. Of course I did – I was no longer spending my days doing something I hated.

I also came to be at peace with the fact that I was delaying my career another year. Something my parents and Dr Gregor helped me understand was that I had to go through life at my own pace. I couldn't be comparing myself to others and thinking that I'd "fallen behind". There was no such thing as "falling behind". What everyone else was doing was irrelevant. I had to do what was right for me. And if that meant that I entered the workforce a little later than everybody else, then that's what it meant.

It was a period of realisations for me. As anyone who knows me will tell you, I'm a diehard NBA basketball fan, and around that time I started thinking a lot about something that Oklahoma City Thunder coach Scott Brooks had said:

'Even though we finished third last in the league in 2009, the whole year I was telling my guys, "we're not losing games . . . we're learning how to win them".'

Over the next two years, the young Thunder continued to get more experienced, and after a while began to reach their potential. In 2011, instead of finishing 28th in the league, they finished in the top four, losing to the eventual champion Dallas Mavericks in the Western Conference Finals.

'We're not losing . . . we're learning how to win.'

I loved the inherent positivity behind it, loved the implication that as long as the Thunder were learning as they lost, they would inevitably start winning. The notion struck a chord with me, and it got me thinking about my mental health.

I could say a similar thing about my illness: I could say that I'm not suffering from depression, but that instead, I'm learning how to be happy. I'm learning how to be happy because I'm learning to understand myself better. I'm learning what triggers those plummets into despair. I'm learning, through therapy, how to pick myself back up again whenever I do take a plunge. And, I'm learning valuable life lessons from my parents and my psychologist that I'll carry with me for the rest of my life. It's as if there's a fortress surrounding my brain that's there to protect me from getting depressed, and every time I learn a bit more about how to be happy, another armed guard gets posted outside it. Sure depression's army still gets through from time to time, but that just means there aren't enough guards defending it yet. But if I keep learning how to be happy like I have been over the last few weeks, then – combined with diligently taking my medication, eating well, sleeping well and exercising frequently – I'll eventually have so many guards protecting me that depression's army will be shut out for good. It'll have no way of getting through.

If they stay together, then I think it's only a matter of time until the Thunder win the championship.

Just like I believe it's inevitable that I'm going to beat my illness.

~~~

Since I'd quit law, I was back to writing full-time again. This was more like it!

It's hard to describe the pleasure writing gave me. I tried on numerous occasions to articulate it, but I was never able to come up with a perfect explanation. The best I could do was say that, when I was writing, and when I really lost myself in it, I felt as if I was transported to a different place. All my pain just melted away, and I felt at peace with the world. I felt blessed to be alive. I felt more blessed than ever to be me. I felt a pulsing rush . . . of excitement, of joy, of inspiration, all at the same time. I felt invigorated. I felt alive. I felt free. And above all else, I felt happy. Purely and utterly happy.

October, 2011

Towards the end of the year, 180 Degrees announced its first ever international consulting project, in partnership with a grassroots organisation in Cambodia that ran a range of programs supporting underprivileged children who'd been the victim of physical and/or sexual abuse, parental neglect, human trafficking, or had been orphaned. I was fortunate enough to have been selected as part of the team, and in December we were set to start looking at ways in which the organisation could achieve their long term objectives before flying to Cambodia in February for two weeks to work closer with them and help out on the ground. I was really looking forward to meeting the team and starting the project, and also to volunteering in another Third World Country. Open Skies was still in the process of getting its license, and until I could really get going with that, I relished the opportunity to support other charities.

November, 2011

At the start of the month I sent the first draft of *I Will Not Kill Myself, Olivia* to Nick, and while I was waiting for him to read it, I started doing some preparatory work for honours the following year – revising a lot of the bachelor's degree material I'd need to know and doing some early research for my thesis. I wanted to get a head start, because my goal for honours was to get the university medal.

It would do wonders for my corporate career, I thought. *If I was able to get it, I'd be almost guaranteed to be accepted into my choice of Ivy League school to study a Masters of Applied Finance, and then I'd be in a prime position to get a job at one of the top management consulting firms in the world. The upside is so big that I have to go for it. I have to do whatever it takes to try and get the medal.*

Economics was my forte – I knew I could do it. But I also knew that I'd have to be more dedicated than I'd ever been. To average 90%, I'd need to have a near-perfect mastery of the subjects, and I'd also need to write a killer thesis. It was doable, but there was no margin for error. I knew I'd need to study really, really hard. I'd have to put absolutely everything I had into it. I'd have to go for it to the exclusion of almost everything else.

But then it got me thinking, *what about my writing? When am I going to get a chance to work on my novel if I'm pulling 12 hour days busting a gut to get the medal? These last six months have been incredible, being able to dedicate myself solely to the thing I'm passionate about. I've always known it wouldn't last, that I'd have to scale it back once uni started – but the way honours is shaping up now, I don't see how I'm going to have time for it at all. And if I can't write, if I have to shun the thing I love, then how will it be possible for me to be happy?*

~~~

The tension continued to mount in my troubled mind.

I really want the medal for all the doors it will open, but how can I not write for a year? I'll be miserable if I don't write for a year, but given my corporate world goals, I won't be able to live with myself if I don't go for the medal, either. So what am I supposed to do?

Balancing life's competing priorities like work, family, friends, hobbies, exercise, relaxation, travel, volunteer work and spiritual devotion is something a lot of us struggle with, and I strongly believe that finding the right harmony is one of the biggest keys to good mental health. At its core, it requires you to have the self-awareness to be able to answer one very important question:

What makes me happy?

And at that point in my life, I still wasn't able to answer it. I wanted to do what was best for my corporate career, and I wanted to do what was best for my writing, but both options were mutually exclusive. My "balance" seemed destined to get completely out of whack the following year, and there seemed to be no way to keep it at a stable equilibrium. I felt like I was imprisoned in a Catch22, where the only possible outcome was depression. And in anticipation of being depressed all through 2012, I once again fell into a horrific depression then. All the excitement, the inspiration, the vivacity, the liberation of the past five months vanished, and I was back to feeling suicidal every day. Every day was once again choked with excruciating misery, and was once again a ghastly war I won if I didn't kill myself. And as was so often the case, my suffering triggered the urge to drink. I started having those nights again where I'd be clutching my hair on the edge of my bed, sweating through my clothes, panting through gritted teeth, desperately trying to fight off the cravings. Usually I wouldn't give in, but on one occasion the pain was so overwhelming that I thought *who gives a fuck if I have a drink,* so I went out and had 20 or 30. I stumbled home and wanted to keep drinking, so I opened the liquor cabinet and got another bottle to take to bed with me.

'Please put it back,' my mother pleaded. 'Please, please put it back.'

'I need it, I need it! Don't you get how much I need it?'

'Danny I'm begging you!' she cried. 'Please put the bottle back . . . please . . . *please* . . .'

It was such an ugly scene that I eventually did so out of guilt, but that didn't stop the cravings, it didn't stop the pain, and that's why I started experiencing the insatiable impulse to cut myself. At times I just wanted to get a steak knife from the kitchen and rip it through my flesh. I wanted to slash up my arms and watch the blood spurting out, just so I could feel something different, just so I could escape my psychological agony, just so I could release some of my built-up fucking tension and try to settle down a bit.

The urges were so strong – to drink, to cut myself, to kill myself. But I knew that drinking was a mistake, I knew that cutting myself was an even bigger mistake, and I damn well knew that killing myself was the ultimate mistake. No matter how overwhelming the desire, I knew I couldn't give in. I knew I had to keep on fighting.

Hang in there . . . don't give up . . . trust the Lord, he knows what's best, I'd tell myself. I knew I could get better, but I also knew that it would take work to do so. I knew that what I needed to do was take a time-out from everything and resolve the conflict that I needed to resolve.

So I organised to go back to the psych ward.

~~~

A few days later, I was admitted. Mum and Dad drove me there. We talked a bit on the way. Well, they talked – I mumbled what I could. Mostly there was silence. Hell, we were on the way to a psych ward. It wasn't exactly a joy ride.

After I got settled into my room I saw my psychiatrist. She decided to give me an additional medication to take on top of the sodium valproate I was already taking. It was sure to help stabilise my mood, but I knew I couldn't just rely on the drugs. I knew I needed to put in the hard yards myself and sort out my problems from within. Only then was I going to get lastingly better.

~~~

For the first few days after I started taking my new medication I was too drowsy to do much, but on my fourth day I was feeling much more with it. I took Dr Gregor's advice and started reading a self-help book by the world-renowned psychologist Dr Martin Seligman called *Authentic Happiness.*

By page 14, I'd learned the lesson that I'd needed to learn to work my way out of my despair.

~~~

On page 13 going on 14, Dr Seligman speaks of doing activities that leave us feeling invigorated, and of doing activities that leave us feeling drained. If my interpretation of the text is correct, what he's basically saying is that you will have greater happiness in your life if you do more of what leaves you feeling invigorated and less of what leaves you feeling drained.

The idea resonated very strongly with me, because the dichotomy Dr Seligman speaks of so perfectly characterised how I felt after writing and studying economics. Writing left me feeling inspired, and exhilarated, and completely alive. But studying economics – even though I found it somewhat interesting – would leave me feeling mentally exhausted. It would leave me feeling like a flogged horse. Afterwards I'd just want to watch TV, or go to the gym, or play basketball, or go out with my friends – anything to clear my head and get away from it. So what Dr Seligman said got me to thinking, *what would the rest of my life be like if it was full of pursuits that left me feeling invigorated – i.e. writing – instead of pursuits that left me feeling drained – like studying economics and presumably the corporate work that would follow?*

And that's when I had my epiphany:

I would be happier if I spent my days writing instead of studying economics or working at a management consulting firm.

It was an extraordinarily powerful realisation, because I'd never contemplated the idea of writing for a living before. I'd only ever planned to publish just the one book. What actually got me writing in the first place back in 2007 was sucking at English all through Year 12 and having it mess up my perfect UAI score – getting 99.6 instead of 100. I'd wanted to prove to myself and everybody else that I could in fact be good at the written word, so I decided to write a novel, thinking I'd be vindicated if I could get it published (I know, I know, it's perfectionism gone mad – there's a reason I was getting therapy for it). Over time however that stopped being my motivation, and I wrote purely because I loved it – but even then it was always supposed to be a one-and-done thing – achieve my dream of getting published and then dedicate myself to a lucrative career in the corporate world. The idea of being a full-time author had been the furthest thing from my mind. But this revelation had unlocked that door, and now that it was open I wanted to run right through it.

~~~

By the time dinner was served at six, my entire outlook on my future had changed. I was no longer an Economics Honours student/budding management consultant who was writing a book on the side. Instead I was an aspiring author, who studied Economics Honours so that I could become a management consultant if I couldn't make it as a writer. I still wanted to have that back-up plan in place, because I didn't want to end up a "starving artist" – I still did want to be rich. *But if I can make it as an author then I'm definitely going to hop ship,* I thought. *From now on, that's going to be my focus, which means that next year, I'm not going to put off my writing and go for the university medal – instead, I'm going to keep working on my novel, and study just enough to get the minimum marks required to get into one of the schools that I want to get in to* (75-80% instead of 90%).

With that issue resolved, the balance in my life was back, and since it was, I didn't feel depressed anymore. On the contrary, I felt excited, and inspired, and elated over my newfound epiphany, and at the prospect of trying to make it as an author. I couldn't wait to get the hell out of hospital and dive headfirst into it.

December, 2011

I stayed in hospital for another seven days, but it was really just to keep an eye on things, just to play it safe more than anything else. I stopped feeling depressed as soon as I'd had my revelation, and a week later I was discharged feeling great.

Will I ever have to come back here? I recall thinking on my way out.

I hoped not. The lesson leading to my epiphany was one more very important one that I knew I'd take with me forever, and I hoped that, combined with everything else I'd learned over the years I'd been suffering from depression and bipolar disorder, that it would be enough to prevent another relapse in the future. To use my war metaphor again, I hoped I now had enough soldiers surrounding my fortress to prevent depression's army from ever attacking my brain again. But only time would tell whether my defence was strong enough. Until then, I was focused on Nick's review of the first draft of *I Will Not Kill Myself, Olivia*. He was bound to send it to me any day then, so first order of business was to get straight back to work on the manuscript.

~~~

Dear Danny,

In summary, I think this draft is a great start – the best writing I've seen from you so far. This novel is bold, raw and confronting – nothing is left at home – and the writing style suits it well – it's fast and edgy like the protagonist. The whole notion of depression/suicide is also very topical, as it is an area of life that has not been understood. A number of prominent people have recently taken their lives and brought the issue to the forefront of public consciousness. It's also a recurring theme as we look at the psyche of the post-modern world: why are so many people unhappy when we're better off, materially, then at any time in history?

But as with all first drafts, there are things that need fixing in the second. The opening chapters of the book for one are not up to par, because you don't do a good job of setting the scene. Manly in Sydney is one of the most beautiful places in the world, but you wouldn't know it from the way it's currently portrayed in your novel. You need to paint the picture properly – make the reader feel it. See my notes on the attached manuscript for ways to do this.

Aside from the opening, I thought there was much to admire in the first half of the book. It was easy to read, had good character development, some great insights, and most importantly, it felt real and authentic. Until about halfway I was rooting for Jimmy fighting against all the odds and caught up in his story. But I found the second half of the book too dark and introspective. The personal stories, day-to-day events and the characters that have leavened the story up to this point have run out, and then it's just Jimmy's depression. I think people will be interested, then fascinated, but will then feel that it's too harrowing. You want to take them out of their comfort zone, yes – and you do a very good job of doing so – but not hold them hostage.

You have created an excellent basis for a great fictional story, but to make it really exceptional you are going to have to weigh it right. This is the tricky thing about such a dark journey – particularly one that is rooted in reality. You need to get the right balance between light and dark, between informing and entertaining. Again, see my notes on the manuscript for how to do this – particularly in the second half of the novel.

Great work, keep it up.
Nick.

~~~

After almost two years, Open Skies finally got its License to Fundraise! I was so happy, and I couldn't wait to start helping the communities we'd chosen to work in. In Peru our first project was to build the greenhouses, and at the end of the year we also set up a project in Siem Reap, Cambodia, where we planned on paying instructors to teach disadvantaged women how to weave products from natural resources, which they'd then be able to sell in hotels and other markets. Like I said,

I couldn't wait to start fundraising and giving back to a world that's given so much to me.

At the end of 2011, I felt like I was in a really good place. My writing was going great and Open Skies was finally ready to go. I was doing what I loved, and not surprisingly, I felt the best I'd felt in years.

PART V

OR

EAT, PRAY, LOVE: THE YOUNG ADULT'S VERSION

OR

STILL LEARNING HOW TO BE HAPPY

January, 2012

I'd delayed it as long as it was wise to, but when the new year started I began feeling the pressure to come up with a topic for my honours thesis.

'You need to make sure you pick something you're passionate about,' the course co-ordinator and all the ex-students said. 'You'll have to spend the majority of the year working on it, so you'd better make sure it's something you like.'

I had a look through all the recommended topics: twenty-first century fiscal policy. Post-GFC government regulation. Labour laws and the European Union. All the shit that was happening in Greece.

Then I started researching more obscure topics: happiness economics; the economics of time; something about speed limits and accidents and politics. Whatever. Each topic seemed as boring as the next.

I felt exhausted just thinking about it, so I pushed it to the side and returned to hustling up donations for Open Skies and moving forwards with *I Will Not Kill Myself, Olivia*. The money was coming in and the paradisiacal setting of my novel was starting to come to life as I worked at painting Manly's idyllic picture: the sun, the cool ocean breeze, the clear blue sky, the salt on your lips washed away by an ice cold beer, the serenity of the beach and the great Australian outdoors. It was all going so well, but after another week I knew I had to stop for a while and get back to my thesis.

I did some more research to try and come up with a topic, but I just couldn't find anything I was passionate about. After I'd looked into practically every branch of economics there was, my mentality turned from *I need to find a topic that I'm passionate about* to *I just need to do whatever will get me a good mark*. So I spoke to one of my friends who'd gotten the university medal the previous year.

'I did my thesis on microfinance. My supervisor was amazing – if I was you I'd just pick a topic in that area and let him guide you. You'll kill it if you do.'

So that's what I ended up doing.

'What in the area of microfinance interests you?' the supervisor asked when I met up with him.

I shrugged.

'Is there any chance you can just choose a topic for me? Maybe something that *you* find interesting?'

He considered this for a moment.

I'm currently focusing a lot of my research around competition and microfinance,' he said. 'How about something to do with that?'

I shrugged again.

'Yeah. Why not.'

'OK. Well how about I give you some journal articles to read? You could have a look at them and come up with a more specific topic yourself, and then I could guide you from there.'

So that's what I started doing, plodding through journal article after journal article: *Competition and Microfinance; Competition and the Performance of Microfinance Institutions; How Rising Competition Among Microfinance Institutions Affects Incumbent Lenders; Microfinance in Times of Crisis: The Effects of Competition, Rising Indebtedness, and Economic Crisis on Repayment Behaviour; Microfinance Trade-offs: Regulation, Competition and Financing; Competition and the Wide Outreach of Microfinance Institutions;* etcetera, etcetera, etcetera.

Within the week, depression's army had blown past my soldiers and charged straight through my fortress. Only two months after I'd left the psych ward, my brain was under siege again.

February, 2012

To my grave dismay, I realised that I was about to begin an honours year I no longer cared about. I'd started my thesis and looked over the course work, and all it did was bore me senseless.

I didn't know how this had happened. I thought I wanted to do honours. I thought I'd enjoy it. But it was all just so dry and uninspiring compared to writing my novel.

'I think you'll just have to suck it up for a year,' my parents said. 'You need to do honours if you want to be able to become a management consultant.'

So I really started thinking about what it was going to be like to be a management consultant, and that's what had ignited depression's attack. For the first time I wasn't focusing on the big fat dollar signs; on the harbour-side mansion, the sports cars and the overseas holidays; and I was actually looking at it for what it really was.

Management consultants help organisations improve their performance.

And just like honours, it didn't inspire me like writing did. If I ever needed a reminder, on my second day of being in Cambodia for the 180 Degrees project, I met a man called Tok Vanna who'd been forced to fight in the Khmer Rouge against his will. When he went to get some food during a break from training, a landmine went off in front of him. He was unconscious. When he came to, he realised his arms were gone.

He said he wanted to kill himself.

'There was no future for me. What could I do? How could I get a job, get married and support a family without any arms?'

There was a grenade in a bag attached to his waist. He arched his body around and tried to reach it. He wanted to pull out the pin and end his life, but his friend saw him just in time and took the grenade away.

Tok was then taken to hospital, where he stayed for the next nine months. When he eventually left, he was too embarrassed to go back to his family and rely on them for help, so he started begging on the streets.

Months later, Tok's mother found him and took him home, but he soon had to go back to the capital city for more treatment. Tok used up all his money on hospital bills, and ended up back on the streets again.

Luckily, an aid worker soon found him, and he was given a job selling local crafts and gifts to tourists that were visiting Angkor Watt. He then fell in love, got married, and had two children. Now Tok runs his own business, selling books at a stall in Siem Reap.

'I'm very happy now,' he told me.

I took his contact details – it was such an incredible story that I had the thought of writing his biography once I'd finished *I Will Not Kill Myself, Olivia*. It was a story that the world should hear, and I thought I could use some of the proceeds to pay for his ongoing medical bills and to put his children through school.

That was the kind of thing that excited me: meeting incredible people, writing incredible stories, and giving back to the world. That's what got my juices going. But helping billion dollar organisations improve their performance? Nothing.

'But you can do all that other stuff in your free time,' my classmates said.

That was what I used to think too, before I took off the money goggles and really thought things through. Then I was asking myself, *when will I have the time to write, to really try and make it as an author, if I'm working 60, 70 hour weeks?*

'But you only get pumped that hard in your first five or ten years,' my classmates rebutted. 'It all eases up after that.'

I wasn't convinced that was always true in practice, *but even if it is,* I thought, *how am I going to have time to write when I'm over 30 and married with kids, even if the hours have reduced to around 50 a week?*

I'd worked so hard for one of those jobs without really thinking about it, because I thought all the money would make me happy. At a top tier management consulting firm, you make close to six figures in your first year out of uni, half a million after 5-7 years, and in the vicinity of a million after 10-15. You've got it made. You're as secure as can be. But now I was finally thinking realistically, and the idea of working 60 hours a week helping organisations improve their performance made me want to shoot myself.

So I was self-destructing, I was exploding at the seams.

For fuck's sake, my back-up plan's a disaster! Another one-way ticket to the psych ward and a life of relentless, agonising despair. So where the fuck does that leave me?

I felt so insecure, so vulnerable, so terrified, and more so than anything else, so horrifically suicidal. The urge to run away, to quit, to buy that automatic and put a bullet through my head was stronger than ever before.

But I knew that I wasn't going to do that. I knew exactly what my problem was, and what's more, I knew exactly how to fix it. The only question was whether or not I had the balls to do it.

I mean fuck . . . can I really abandon my back-up plan – the guaranteed, lifelong financial security for myself and my future family; the most sure-fire way of getting rich that I'm ever going to get – and instead chase some crazy artist's dream?

~~~

The questions kept coming as I tried to fight off depression's onslaught. *Can I really ditch my back-up plan? Can I really bail on management consulting after all these years to put all my eggs in one basket and try to make it as an author? What about the financial security? What about my mental health?* I was locked in turmoil. For days I kept going back and forth and back and forth, racking my brains trying to work out what to do. It helped to have someone to talk it over with, so like I'd been doing most nights, I Skyped my mum on the other side of the world.

'If I work a corporate job, I know I'm going to be depressed. I know that it's sensible to have a back-up plan, and I know that management consulting is a "great job" from the standpoint that I'll make a lot of money. But what's the point if it's just going to make me suicidal and send me straight back to the psych ward? The reason I've always fought like hell to pull myself out of the abyss in the first place has been so that I could get another crack at life. It's been so that I could get another chance to be happy. And working 60 hours a week in a job I'll hate, just to make a lot of money, just so that I have a back-up if I can't make it as an author, is hardly giving myself a chance to be happy. But going all out with my writing, throwing myself into the thing I love and doing everything in my power to make a life out of it . . . *that's* giving myself a chance. *That's* listening to my heart. *That's* living the dream.'

I'd never articulated such a sentiment before. Just hearing myself say it . . . it was so obvious what decision I needed to make.

'So that's what I'm going to do,' I said. 'I'm going to forget about management consulting and just give it my all to try and make it as an author.'

'I think that's really wise, Danny,' Mum agreed. 'You have to do whatever you think is going to make you happy. Dad thinks exactly the same thing.'

I knew my parents would be supportive. A lot of parents might object to their son throwing away a safe corporate career to chase a wildly unpredictable artistic one, but my parents have never been the kind to pressure me into living the life that they want for me instead of the life that I want for myself. While they've always given me advice, they've at the same time left those decisions up to me, and given me the freedom to follow my own path. They never had any fixed ideas about what job they wanted me to have – they just wanted me to be happy and healthy. So if that meant bailing on management consulting and pursuing creative writing, then that's what it meant.

I kept talking to Mum.

'So,' she said. 'Do you think you'll be able to make it as an author?'

I'd thought that question over a thousand times that month, and I knew exactly what my answer was.

'Yes,' I said confidently. 'I really believe I can make it, because I know I have the right attitude to make my dreams come true: I have a tireless work ethic, relentless determination, and I never, ever, ever give up. I really believe in the novel I'm writing, and even though it's not ready to be published yet, I know that in time, it will be. It's inevitable that it will be, because I'll keep at it and at it and at it until it is.'

'I believe in you, Danny, and because you have a good attitude, I have no doubt that you'll eventually have a manuscript that's worthy of being published. But you still need a bit of luck. What if the agent reading your query letter is having a bad day and they just gloss it over, assume your book won't be worth publishing like the other hundreds of books being pitched to them, and then pass on it? What if the only agents that would be interested in representing you don't have the time to take on new projects? What about that interview you told me about when an agent actually admitted to at times requesting to see manuscripts based on the author's *initials*? Like you've often said, there's just *so* much luck involved. What if it doesn't fall your way?'

I'd thought a lot about that over the last month, too.

'That part's up to God,' I said. 'I trust Him.'

~~~

So I quit honours, and as soon as I did, depression's army retreated. The war was over. It had taken a lot of hard work – a lot of self-analysis to understand myself better and work out what I really wanted out of life – but like I've said, that's all part of learning how to be happy. In that respect I'd taken a huge leap forward, and as a result, I felt so liberated. So inspired. Instead of dreading my future, I was now looking at it with unbridled excitement.

This is incredible! I mean, I actually have the freedom to chase my dream! How amazing is that?

I felt so elated. So overjoyed. I couldn't wait to fly back to Sydney and start my new life.

March, 2012

When I got back home, I started telling my friends that I'd scrapped my back up plan and was going full tilt to try and make it as an author. To be honest, I didn't expect them to understand. I thought everyone would think I was crazy, abandoning what many consider to be the Holy Grail of careers to chase one that's so risky and uncertain. I thought I'd get heaps of 'what the fuck were you thinking's and a myriad of starving artist jokes. And of course I got some. But to my surprise, a lot of people thought what I was doing was really cool. And to my even greater surprise, some people even seemed . . . envious.

'I wish I could do what I'm really interested in,' one of my mates said. 'I'd really like to be a journalist, but instead I'm working 80 hour weeks at a law firm.'

'I'd love to go to the Caribbean for a year and be a scuba diving instructor,' another friend said. 'But now I'm working six days a week as a management consultant.'

'I've always dreamed of going to a little village in Africa and doing hands-on work for an NGO. Instead I'm working as an investment banker. I don't even like it. I really wish I could just do what I enjoy.'

'But you *can* do what you enjoy,' I said. 'You guys are only 23 – you're still so young! If you want to be a journalist, then be a journalist. If you want to be a scuba diving instructor, then be a scuba diving instructor. If you want to work for an NGO in Africa, then work for an NGO in Africa. Now's your chance. Go for it!'

They all just stared at me, shocked, unable to say anything.

April, 2012

For the first month after I quit honours, I'd wake up every day and just write, write, write, completely smitten with my brand new life. By then the next draft was finished so I sent it to Nick, confident that I'd successfully taken on his feedback and produced what would be close to a finished product. I knew it would take him 4-8 weeks to review it, so I then got a job at a call centre to make some quick cash in the meantime. Accordingly, I spent the first two weeks of April sitting at a desk with nothing but a phone and a thick stack of paper, dialling up strangers all over the country.

'Good afternoon, may I please speak to Steve?'

'Speaking.'

'Hi, Steve! My name's Danny, I'm calling from 2evolve on behalf of the Red Cross. How are you today?'

'Oh . . . good, I guess.'

'That's good! Look I'm just calling for a quick catch up, can you spare a couple of minutes?'

'Yeah make it quick.'

'Of course! So I'm calling for a couple of reasons – firstly, I'd just like to extend a *huge* thank-you for supporting the Red Cross in the past! It's because of people like you that we can help local and overseas communities, so thanks a lot for that!'

'OK.'

'And if I may ask, do you remember what *inspired* you to give your support in the first place?'

'No. It was a long time ago.'

'No worries! And have you had a chance to keep up to date with the work we've been doing lately?'

'No not really.'

'That's OK! So look you may be aware that the Red Cross plays a vital role in times of crisis and emergencies that affect thousands of people around Australia. I'm sure you've heard all about the Queensland and Victorian floods, for example?'

'Yeah.'

'Now the Red Cross is committed to helping communities as disaster strikes, and thereby enabling victims to rebuild their lives. For example, *over $16 million* was paid out to households damaged in the Victorian floods! But even though great work is being done, thousands of people are still in need. Your support would make a big difference Steve, so what we'd like to do today is kindly invite you to re-join us as a Regular Giver and help transform the lives of thousands of people in need. Does this sound like something you might be able to do today?'

'No not today sorry.'

'That's alright, mate. Well nonetheless thanks a lot for your support in the past, and best of luck for the future.'

'Thanks, bye.'

I'd then write down the time I called Steve on a piece of paper, circle "NEGATIVE" next to his name, put it in the ever-growing "REJECTED" pile, and then dial the number on the next piece of paper.

It was so wearisomely tedious, so mind-numbingly boring, having to repeat the same thing over and over and over again, in the same fake upbeat tone, always putting emphasis on the same old words. Then there was my supervisor always breathing down my neck, demanding that I put more pressure on the person to donate: *'you can't let them off the hook so easily'; 'you've got to rephrase the way you ask them'; 'you've got to sweet talk them more'*. Blah fucking blah. I hated it so much. The whole time I was on the phone I'd be watching the clock – literally – just willing the time to pass faster. And then at the end of my second week, on the long bus ride home at half-past nine at night, an anxious fear took hold of me as the cold hard reality set in:

My novel isn't published.

I'm broke as fuck.

I don't have a girlfriend.

I'm 23 years old and I live with my parents.

I spend my days working a mundane, minimum wage, dead-end job that I hate.

It had started off so romantically, writing all day and living the dream. When I was doing what I loved and when I got on a roll, it was easy to see myself succeeding; it was easy to see myself in the future as a published author with bestsellers to my name and a loving, supportive family by my side. But working at the call centre had given me a preview of my future if I never in fact made it:

> *I'm 40 years old and living in a one bedroom shithole downtown. I'm still working mundane, minimum, dead-end jobs during the day to scrape by while I bust a gut writing all night, only to see my manuscripts get rejected again and again and again. I'm still single – after all, what do I have to offer a woman? – and when anyone thinks of me, it'll be as someone for whom life held so much early promise, but who in the end amounted to nothing. They'll all say, 'Danny Baker – what a gigantic waste'. And the worst part is that I'll agree with them. I'll be plagued by that thought every day of my life.*

And on that particular day, exhausted after another horrendously monotonous eight hours at work, the only future that seemed possible was the one where I didn't make it. All I could see myself amounting to was that lonely, unfulfilled, miserable man and it scared the fucking shit out of me.

The next day

Dear Danny,

I can see that a lot of work has gone into this draft, and while the second half of the book is now less dark and you've made an obvious effort to bring the love story more to the fore, there is still another draft required.

The opening couple of chapters of the novel still aren't up to scratch. You still need to do a better job of setting the scene, and on second reading, I also think you need to develop Jimmy's character better in these chapters too. We need to know Jimmy's thoughts and feelings earlier on so that we know what's driving him – so that when he falls into depression later on we understand why. At the moment we learn it too late – by which time the reader has started questioning the character and doubting his authenticity. So you need to beef the start up a lot. Slow it down, insert key scenes here and there to allow us to understand Jimmy earlier.

Like I said in my last report the middle of the book is in good shape and has some very powerful sequences, but I still think the "love" element of the story could be structured better. Some of the interplay between Jimmy and Olivia is a bit repetitive, and a couple of the incidents were non-events that didn't change the dynamic of their relationship or push the story to a new height. You need to make these occurrences more extreme to heighten the drama – you're still writing a little conservatively. Use your imagination a bit more.

I also think the ending still needs work. At the moment, it doesn't pay off on the story you've built up. It lacks real incident or punch – when I got there I didn't feel there was a proper climax to Jimmy's illness and his relationship with Olivia. You need to finish on a bang – leave the reader wanting more.

Keep at it, Danny. You have a great product here, but it still needs more work to reach its full potential.

Good luck,

Nick.

The first thing I felt when I read Nick's review was shock. I was hoping I'd fixed most of the problems with the previous draft, but now I could see that my novel was nowhere near as developed as I'd thought. As opposed to closing in on the finish line, I was still stumbling around the middle.

Then gradually, the shock wore off, and all the anxiety, all the fear that I'd felt the previous night tightened its grip around my throat, and I was once again strangled with a flurry of doubt.

Was I an idiot for bailing on such a safe, lucrative career?

Did I really make the right decision?

Was I wrong in thinking that I'm good enough to make it as an author?

I tried to fight it but the questions kept coming as the anxiety, the fear, grew stronger and stronger. I tried to picture myself achieving my dream, tried to envision the great big smile spread across my face and the tears of joy streaming down my cheeks in the moment of being offered a contract; I tried to envision myself as the happy 40 year old – as the successful author surrounded by the loving, supportive family. But just like the previous night the picture was a blur. Every day it seemed less and less attainable, and the image of that lonely, unfulfilled, miserable man became more and more vivid in its place.

~~~

A few years beforehand, the fear that I was feeling then would've plunged me into an alcohol-fuelled tailspin. It would've plummeted me into an almost suicidal depression, one that would've almost certainly culminated in another trip to the psych ward. Then again, maybe even that's giving myself too much credit – a few years beforehand, I would've never had the courage to take the risk that I was taking then. In my first few years of uni my self-worth was predicated on being a scholarship-holding Commerce/Law student, destined to have a house on the harbour, to drive a Porsche and to take the pretty wife and kids overseas every year. There was no way in hell I could've ever given that up.

But I'd come a long way since then. By 2012, not only could I take that fear on, but through all the therapy and self-analysis I'd done, I also had the skillset to be able to stare it down and stop it from crippling me. To once again use my war metaphor, I now had enough men guarding my fortress to prevent depression's army from re-attacking my brain.

So after breakfast the next day, I sat down comfortably on my bed and took a long, deep breath. I continued breathing, in . . . and out . . . in . . . and out, gradually calming myself down as I reminded myself of the premise upon which I based my confidence, of the reason why I believed I'd be able to make it as an author.

I have the right attitude to succeed, I said out loud. *I'm so determined, so self-motivated, so disciplined. And I'll never, ever, ever quit. And with this attitude, it's only a matter of time before I produce a novel that's ready to be published. And after that, I trust God that I'll get the break I need to achieve my dream.*

Working at the call centre and then getting a disappointing book review has made me lose sight of this lately, and that's what's allowed all the fear to shoot through. And from time to time, that's going to happen. I'm travelling a difficult road, and I'm going to have setbacks. There are going to be times when I feel scared. There are going to be times when the future I want seems far from attainable. But whenever that happens, I need to remind myself that I've got everything it takes to achieve my dream. I need to remember to have faith in myself, to have faith in God, and know that so long as I do, I can make it come true.

I spent all day on my bed, repeating the same thing over and over and over again. And gradually, the fear began to fade. My confidence started to return. And even though I was in the same position I was in 24 hours previously, by the end of the day, I felt refortified. I felt optimistic. I felt ready for the challenge.

I'm going to do this, I told myself. *I don't know when it's going to happen, but I am going to do this eventually.*

Once again, I tried to picture myself in the moment of being offered a publishing contract, with that huge smile spread across my face and tears of joy streaming down my cheeks – where I'm so suffused with happiness that I can't even talk.

For the first time since I started working at the call centre, it felt real, again.

May, 2012

In its first six months of operation, Open Skies raised over $13,500 for the greenhouses project in Peru, and started funding the women's centre project in Cambodia to teach impoverished mothers how to weave products they could sell for a profit in local markets. I was really happy with our progress, and it felt great to finally be making a difference after spending two years setting the organisation up. Raising nearly $15,000 in our first few months was a hell of an effort, and it would certainly go a long way to helping those in need.

Succeeding with Open Skies also gave me an extra shot in the arm of confidence to succeed with my writing. It reinforced the idea that if I worked hard and believed in myself, then I really could achieve what I was going for. Not a day went by where I wouldn't picture my deliriously overjoyed self in the moment of being offered a contract, and I knew that I could be that person if I just kept having faith.

And at some point in May, that was the message I got tattooed across my arm:

Faith Conquers.

~~~

I saw my psychologist for my regular monthly check-up.

'How've you been doing?' Dr Gregor asked.

'Pretty well, on the whole. I quit my job at the call centre and I'm back to writing full-time again. I'm really enjoying it, and most of the time, I'm confident I'll succeed.'

We kept on talking.

'Do you still get days when you feel scared?' he asked. 'Do you still get days when you feel terrified that you're never going to get your novel published and that you'll end up a broke, lonely, miserable 40 year old?'

I nodded solemnly.

'Yeah. Sometimes.'

We explored the issue further before Dr Gregor offered me some advice.

'I think you need to focus more on the journey you're on, and less on the end outcome,' he said. 'It's going to be a while before your novel is completely finished and ready to try and publish, so there's no need to think about what's going to happen then until the moment's upon you. Right now, just enjoy yourself. After all, you're writing full-time – right now, you're *already* living your dream! Experience it to the full. Be wholly present in the moment. Enjoy it for what it is instead of fretting about whether or not you'll get published and what may or may not happen if you don't. Whenever you do stress about all that, you're only taking away from your enjoyment of this exciting journey that you're embarking upon. Later on, if you do end up getting rejected by every agent and publisher in the business, you can worry. But right now – just forget about it.'

July, 2012

My novel still wasn't published, I was still flat broke, I still didn't have a girlfriend, I was still living with my parents, and all those scholarship holders that I used to beat my brains out competing with back in the day had expense accounts and were getting paid $100,000 salaries while I barely scraped by tutoring high school and uni students.

But ever since I started living more in the moment and enjoying my journey for what it was, I was the happiest I'd been since high school.

The Bhagavad Gita, an ancient Indian Yogic scripture, says that it is better to live your own destiny imperfectly than to live an imitation of somebody else's life with perfection. And as imperfect as it may have seemed, I could definitely say that I was living my destiny.

No wonder happiness was seeping back into my life.

October, 2012

On the first Wednesday evening of October, I was peacefully reading a novel on the couch in the kitchen when I heard my phone go off.

It was an email from Nick.

I was confident yet nervous. I really did feel like I'd gotten it right this time. But then again, it wouldn't have been the first time I'd been wrong about that.

I opened the email apprehensively, my whole body tingling with anticipation.

You're nearly there, bar a few final fix-ups.

I released a huge sigh of relief. I'd done it. I'd finally done it. It'd taken me six long, hard years, but at last I'd produced a novel that was (nearly) ready to be published. I was thrilled. Completely over the moon. My dream felt so close. So close that I could almost taste it.

November, 2012

It's time I told you how I came up with the idea for the Depression Is Not Destiny Campaign.

In August, I started watching *The X Factor*, which for those who don't know is an amateur singing competition were thousands of people across the country battle it out for a record deal. I was only peripherally interested at first, but I got really hooked when I heard the story of one of the contestants, Samantha Jade. When she was 15, she got signed by Jive Records in the States, the same label as Britney Spears, Pink and Justin Timberlake. She too seemed on her way to stardom, but unfortunately things didn't quite pan out for her and after several years of setbacks, she left the singing industry. Before she auditioned for *The X Factor* in the "Over 25s" category, Sammi was working in a factory counting stock.

'I see this as my last chance for music,' she said at her audition.

I was drawn to her right away. Although our plights had been far from similar, I felt like I could really relate to her struggle – that of having a dream you put your soul into and going through hell to try and make it come true. Knowing how it feels to want something that much, whenever I'd hear her sing, all I could think was, *she is so talented. It is a joy to watch her perform. She more than anyone deserves to have her dream come true.* I'd think the same thing when I was at work, too – coincidentally at that point in time at a factory as well: *she deserves to be on the radio I'm listening to at the moment, she deserves to be on stage at her own concert – not counting stock in a factory like this.* I just wanted the best for her. I really wanted to see her succeed.

Sammi made it through to the Top 12, from which point the artists were to sing a song each week and get eliminated one by one until only the winner was left standing. For her debut, Sammi sung *Wide Awake*, which judge Ronan Keating said she sung better than Katy Perry had sung the original. But unfortunately, the public voted her into the bottom two, and it was only by the judges' vote that she got through to the next round.

Over the next few weeks I thought Sammi was magnificent – I couldn't take my eyes off her when she was on stage, and the song she'd sing would often be stuck in my head for the rest of the night. But in the fifth and seventh rounds she found herself in the bottom two again, each time just scraping through to see another day. She admitted that coming so close to being eliminated had left her feeling "very defeated", particularly since she'd had a history of setbacks and as a result of which, was already low on confidence. Testing her resolve further still was all the unwarranted hate she was receiving over social media, saying that she couldn't sing and was only on the show because she was friends with judge Guy Sebastian; the vitriol was so intense that she was even receiving death threats. It was a time when a lot of people would've collapsed and folded, but being the fighter Sammi is she kept soldiering on, kept listening to the judges and trying to get better.

'You're a great singer, but you need to connect with the viewers more,' they said. 'You need to show your personality more. You need to be a little edgier.'

She took it all on, and as the competition progressed she went from strength to strength, and Australia got to realise how nice, how genuine, how truly loveable she really was. Her confidence seemed to gradually come back, and from the semi-finals on there was no stopping her – she was absolutely spellbinding – and in late November, Australia voted her the winner. In that moment, the emotion in her face was haunting, one of the most beautiful expressions of joy I've ever seen in my life. I literally had goose bumps just looking at her. As an artist I was deeply inspired by her triumph after everything she'd been through, and as a person I was flushed with pure and utter happiness for her. It couldn't have happened to a more deserving girl, and I'm really glad I was there to witness it.

After the finale, I found myself musing about *The X Factor* in general:

It's obviously great for Sammi and the other top contestants who'll surely go on to get record deals, but to say that it only benefits the singers isn't doing it justice. On top of being a talent show, The X Factor *is a treasure trove of uplifting individual tales that transcend all realms of life, and by providing a forum for the contestants to tell their story, and for the country to then be able to follow their journey and watch them beat their demons and succeed,* The X Factor *gives hope and inspiration to viewers who need it.*

Thinking about *The X Factor* in that way then got me thinking about my own story:

If people currently suffering from depression knew what I went through and then saw me in my ardently happy moment when I've achieved my dream, then wouldn't they be inspired too? Wouldn't it give them hope that they could also recover and go on to live a happy, healthy life?

And so, the Depression Is Not Destiny Campaign was born.

EPILOGUE

October, 2013

I never thought the first few years of my adulthood would turn out the way they have. When I was 18 at the scholarship dinner, I was sure that I'd finish my Commerce/Law degree and by now be making six figures at a management consulting firm or an investment bank. Never did I think I'd fall victim to depression, become an alcoholic, found a charity, develop bipolar disorder from a doctor's negligence, go to a psych ward, write a second book, quit law, return to the psych ward, un-enrol from honours and at 24 end up a philanthropist, a mental health advocate and an aspiring author who's still broke and living with his parents. It's been a strange ride, and at times an extremely painful one, but the truth is that I wouldn't change any of it, because it's brought me to the wonderful place that I'm in right now: I'm helping impoverished communities through my foundation; I'm about to launch a mental health campaign that I hope will inspire thousands of people; and with a bit of luck, I'll soon achieve my dream of becoming a published author. Above all else, however, I am finally happy, and I can't ask for anything more than that. At last, I have enough armed men stationed outside my fortress to prevent depression's army from being able to get through again. It still tries to – I'm often getting tested by the inevitable frustrations and disappointments of life – but I now understand myself so well and my coping mechanisms are so refined that these days, I can handle all the tribulations that used to rip me to shreds.

'How did you recover?' is the most common question I'm asked.

I get the feeling that half the time the person's expecting me to have some wild, crazy explanation they've never heard of before, as if how to beat depression is one of the eternal mysteries of life. But at the end of the day, how I recovered was very simple: I never gave up on happiness, I never stopped fighting my illness, and most importantly, I got the help I so desperately needed. And if I had to identify the biggest problem surrounding the mental health industry right now, I'd probably say that it's the fact that so many sufferers fail to seek help. In all my interaction with victims in group therapy sessions, psych wards, mental health forums, charity functions and even in day to day life, I've heard a million and one reasons for why people don't get help. Sometimes it's financial, which is tragic (and even then there are alternatives), but often money's got nothing to do with it.

A lot of the time it's stigma:

'If I see a psychologist, take medication or read self-help books, then people might judge me – so no way!'

Nearly as often it's pride:

'I refuse to "get help" because I want to sort my problems out for myself. "Getting help" is weak, and if I "got help", then I'd feel like a failure.'

And of course there's also fear – of facing your demons, of going down a path unknown.

It's hard for me to relate to such lines of thinking, because I never had any of these hang-ups. I just wanted to get well again – plain and simple. If that meant seeing a psychologist, then I saw a psychologist. If that meant taking medication, then I took medication. If that meant checking into a psych ward, then I checked into a psych ward. Stigma, pride and fear never came into it – and logically speaking, it shouldn't for anyone else either. As many professionals in the field say:

'If you had a broken leg, would you get help?

If you had diabetes, would you get help?

If you had cancer, would you get help?

Of course you would.

So you need to get help if you have a mental illness, too.'

So if there's one thing I can say to the 350 million people on this planet that are estimated to have depression – and to everyone else who suffers from another form of mental illness – it is that: abandon all your hang-ups and get the help you need. I did, and it saved my life. And it can save yours, too.

Yet in saying that, I also understand that I was extremely fortunate to receive the treatment I did. My parents were very supportive from day one, and could afford to pay for my medical and psychological bills. And when I think of my experience with mental illness as a whole, it's this good fortune that really comes to mind. To the best of my recollection, at no point did I ever think of myself as unlucky for having suffered so severely. Quite the opposite – I've always thought of myself as extremely blessed to have received the help I did to beat my illness. And it's this good fortune that's motivated me to start the Depression Is Not Destiny Campaign.

'Aren't you going to find it hard?' my mum often asks. 'You'll be spilling your soul to the entire world. You'll be opening yourself up for everyone to see some of the most private, intimate moments of your life. Not to mention that mental illness still carries such a stigma – by being so open about your experiences with it, you're going to cop all sorts of criticism from all the ignorant Tom, Dick and Harrys out there. Hell, Samantha Jade was receiving death threats, and what you're doing is more controversial than singing! I do think you have the chance to help a lot of people, but you're also exposing yourself to a hell of a lot of abuse from any person with internet access.'

She's right – I'm sure I will find it hard at times. Contrary to how it may appear, I'm actually a very private person. Aside from Sylvia back in 2008 and 2009, I've hardly discussed my struggles with anyone except for my family and my medical team. Even my closest friends have no idea what I've been through – they'll read this book and be shocked as hell. So I'm sure I will find being so open quite challenging. But that doesn't mean that I'm going to let it stop me.

'You're right, Mum,' I always reply. 'But I'll take that on. The way I see it, if it wasn't for the support you and Dad have given me and for all the treatment I've received, I have no idea where I'd be right now. Maybe I'd be in a psych ward. Maybe I'd be homeless. Maybe I'd be dead. So the way I see it, I'm lucky just to be here. I'm really, really lucky just to be here. So if there's anything I can do to help someone who's in the same position I was in – particularly someone who isn't as fortunate to receive the help that I got – then I'm sure as hell going to do it.'

As Mr Williams once said to me:

'To whom much is given, much is expected.'

This Is How You Recover From Depression

Book #2 in the *Depression is a Liar* series

PROLOGUE

When I graduated from high school in 2006, I was on top of the world. I'd been offered a scholarship to study Commerce/Law at Australia's most prestigious university, begun writing my first novel, had a great group of friends, and was going through a flattering phase of being approached by modelling scouts on the street on a monthly basis.

However, over the next couple of years, my world began to crumble, and I fell victim to a crippling depression. I grew sicker and sicker as the months wore on, and by April of 2010, my illness had suffocated the life out of me – as you can see from this excerpt from my memoir *Depression is a Liar*:

> *The days dragged along. This was the worst I'd ever felt. Period. There was no relief from the ceaseless dread. I could barely function. Paying attention in class was almost impossible. Studying was too overwhelming. I'd fallen absurdly behind. I hadn't touched my novel in days. I'd quit my part-time job at the law firm, too—needed all my free time to try and catch up on uni. But there was never enough time. I was constantly exhausted. Drained of life. Depression sucked at my soul. My spirit withered. My goal for the day got broken down even further:* just survive the next six hours, *I'd tell myself.* The next four hours. Hold off killing yourself until then. *[At which point, I'd tell myself the same thing over again].*
>
> *I'd previously thought I'd get better. I'd always thought it true that hope and depression were bitter rivals until one inevitably defeated the other, and I'd always thought that hope would win out in the end. But for the first time in my life, I was void of hope. I honestly believed that being depressed was just the way I was, and that being depressed was just the way I'd be, for the rest of my life. And because I was so convinced that I'd never get better, there seemed no point in fighting my illness. Instead of willing myself to*

"hang in there" because I believed that my suffering was temporary and that everything would be better one day, I comforted myself with the knowledge that human beings are not immortal. That I would die, one day. One special, glorious day. Then I could spend the rest of eternity moulding in a grave, free from pain. You might be wondering why I didn't just kill myself if I wholeheartedly believed that my future consisted of nothing more than excruciating misery. Well, first of all, I still was not a quitter. But more importantly, I didn't want to hurt the people that loved me.

It's not fair to commit suicide and ruin their lives, *I thought.* So I have to hold on. No matter how much it hurts me I have to hold on.

Hence why I drew comfort from the thought that one day I'd die and finally be free.

When you're that depressed, that insanely and utterly depressed that you genuinely believe you'll suffer that acutely for the rest of your days, life seems to lack all purpose.

After all, *I remember thinking,* what's the point in working, fighting, striving for a better life if I'm sentenced to one of chronic anguish and despair? There is no better life. There is no life outside of pain. So what's the point in doing anything but waiting until death finally arrives on my doorstep and whisks me away to the Promised Land?

I was still studying, and I still planned on finishing my novel and trying to get it published, but it was more out of force of habit than anything else. My passion had been drained. My zest for life asphyxiated. I was like a ghost, just drifting through the ghastly days.

'Shit! What's wrong, mate?' an old friend once said when I ran into him at uni. 'Perk up, brother!'

I was shocked. One of the most well-known attributes of depression is that it is entirely possible – and very common – to suffer horrifically without anybody knowing. But somehow without realizing it, I'd crossed the line from a place where I was able to put on a front and fool people into thinking I wasn't depressed to a place where I was so sick that it was obvious to people I hadn't even seen for a year. When I got home I looked in the bathroom mirror, and realized that I was staring back at a man whose eyes were exhausted slits, whose whole face shrieked of agonizing misery. I was staring back at a man whose spirit had been broken, whose soul had been destroyed. I was staring back at a man who, for all intents and purposes, was already dead.

As you can see, I was so convinced I'd never get better. I was 100% sure of it. But over the next two years, I learned – with help from doctors, therapists, family members, friends and strangers alike – how to recover from my depression and find the happiness that had been eluding me. My last episode was at the very beginning of 2012, and ever since then, I've been feeling great.

How this book will work

Recovering from depression and finding happiness again is one of the hardest things I've ever done, yet what I came to realise is that the process for doing so is relatively straightforward. In fact, I believe it can be broken down into three logical steps – and it's according to these three steps that this book will be structured.

Step 1: Understanding what is causing our depression

Depression is always caused by something – or a combination of things – and the first step in beating our illness is to understand exactly what's causing it.

In this part of the book, I'll tell you exactly what I did to work out what the causes of my depression were, and show you how you can do the same.

Step 2: Learning how to deal with the underlying causes of our depression so that they no longer depress us

In this section, we'll talk about how we can deal with some particularly common causes of depression, including spending too long doing things that we don't enjoy, loving ourselves for unhealthy reasons, holding onto anger, victimising ourselves, spending too much time with toxic people, being prisoners of what other people think of us, living an unbalanced life, perfectionism, living an unhealthy lifestyle, negative thinking, worrying about things that are out of our control, and several more.

Step 3: Learning how to handle a relapse

What I eventually learned is that if we're having a relapse, it means that right now, we're not yet able to manage the causes of our depression to an extent so masterful as to prevent them from depressing us. For this reason, if we experience a relapse, we need to go back and repeat steps one and two – i.e. we need to put more work into understanding what is causing that particular episode of depression, and then put more work into learning how to deal with that cause so that it no longer has the power to trigger our depression.

If you repeat steps one and two every time you have a relapse, then like me, your relapses will gradually become less and less intense, and fewer and farther between. And in time, you can stop having relapses all together.

To quote a metaphor from *Depression is a Liar*:

> *It's as if there's a fortress surrounding our brains that's there to protect us from getting depressed, and every time we repeat steps one and two, another armed guard gets posted outside it. If depression's army still gets through from time to time, then it just means there aren't enough guards defending it yet. But if we keep repeating steps one and two, we will eventually have so many guards protecting us that depression's army will be shut out for good. It'll have no way of getting through.*

And it's because of this reason that if you follow this three step blueprint, then you really can recover from depression over time. It won't be easy, because you'll have to be proactive when you feel exhausted, you'll have to fight when you feel like giving up, and you'll have to remain hopeful when depression is doing everything in its power to break your will. But if you follow this three step process, you can get there in the end, because while it's hard for a person to beat depression, it's even harder for depression to beat a person who never gives up.

Step 1: Understanding what is causing our depression

CHAPTER 1

As you may already know, clinical depression can be caused by one or more of the following things:

- A chemical imbalance in our brains;
- Our behaviours (for example, spending time with toxic people);
- Our circumstances (for example, doing a job we don't enjoy);
- Our thought processes (for example, concluding that we're unattractive and unlovable if someone says "no" to going on a date with us);
- Life events (for example, going through a messy break-up).

And, like we've said, in order to recover from depression, we need to figure out precisely what's causing it. Trying to recover without taking the time to do so is analogous to trying to stop a ship from sinking when we've got no idea where the water's getting in from. Try all we want, but we're going to keep sinking.

To help us understand what might be causing our depression, we can do the following.

See a psychiatrist (or a good GP)

Like we've said, depression can sometimes be caused by a chemical imbalance in our brains. In the case of unipolar depression, this is due to a lack of serotonin, dopamine, adrenalin or noradrenalin. Alternatively, depression can often be part of another illness that involves a different sort of chemical imbalance, such as bipolar disorder (depression coupled with mania). Either way, one of the most important things to do if we suffer from depression is to see a psychiatrist (or if that isn't feasible, a good GP). Their job is to correctly diagnose us, and if they then deem it appropriate, to prescribe us medication to manage our chemical imbalance.

Seeing a psychiatrist and taking medication was crucial to my recovery. For the record, I was diagnosed with bipolar disorder at the end of 2010, and medication helped keep me on the straight and narrow until November of 2014, when my psychiatrist said I no longer needed to take it.

See a therapist

The reason why it's so important to see a therapist is because part of their role is to determine the behaviours, circumstances, thought processes and life events that may be causing our depression.

Seeing a therapist is crucial to recovering from depression, but a lot of people don't see one – often because they think that seeing a doctor and taking medication will be enough. But as we've intimated, the role of a doctor and a therapist are *not* the same. Again, a doctor's role is to accurately diagnose us, and if necessary, to prescribe us medication to balance the chemicals in our brains; on the other hand, a therapist's job is to analyse our behaviours, circumstances, thought processes and the events that have taken place in our lives to work out what may be causing our depression, and then to teach us how to deal with these underlying causes. *So if we see one but not the other, we're missing out on some vital treatment that is crucial to our recovery.*

Start keeping a mood diary

Before you go to bed every night, take note of what you did that day, and rank how you felt that day out of 10 – with 10 being very happy, and one being suicidally depressed. For example:

Activity	Time
Sleeping	12:00am – 8:00am
Having a shower	8:00am-8:15am
Having breakfast with my wife	8:15am-8:45am
Travelling to work	8:45am-9:30am
Working by myself at my desk	9:30am-11:30am
Having coffee with Bob	11:30am-12:15pm
Work meeting with Jeff	12:15pm-1:30pm

Having lunch with Jane	1:30pm-2:15pm
Work meeting with Phil	2:15pm-3:15pm
Working by myself at my desk	3:15pm-4:15pm
Work meeting with Brad	4:15pm-4:45pm
Working by myself at my desk	4:45pm-6:00pm
Travelling home reading a book	6:00pm-6:45pm
Going for a run	6:45pm-7:45pm
Eating dinner with my family	7:45pm-9:00pm
Watching TV with my wife	9:00pm-10:00pm
Listening to music	10:00pm-11:15pm
Getting ready for bed	11:15pm-12:00am
How I felt today	**8/10**

After a while, you'll notice that days when you feel depressed correlate to you doing certain activities – or not doing certain activities – and this can help you work out what may be causing your depression.

For example, when I used to keep mood diaries, it helped me work out that drinking alcohol really triggered my depression. Over time, I noticed that if I went out on a Saturday evening for a big night, I'd often find myself feeling down on Tuesday, Wednesday or Thursday. After noticing this trend, I decided to significantly reduce how much alcohol I drank on weekends, and low and behold, I began noticing an upward trend in my mood on Tuesdays, Wednesdays and Thursdays. I thus concluded that drinking too much alcohol contributed to me feeling depressed – something I may not have worked out if I hadn't kept a mood diary.

In terms of how to logistically keep a mood diary, I recommend using a regular diary to record what you're doing each day, and <u>Mood Tracker</u> to document your mood. This tool's graphical feature shows your daily mood level, as well as how many hours you slept that night and what dosage of medication you're taking (if any). In addition to being a handy mood tracking tool, it also has a public forum where you can share your mood chart and medication records with other people going through similar things as you. Moreover, you can schedule text messages or emails to be periodically sent to you to remind you to take your medication.

Talk to someone we're close with about what they think makes us depressed

If we spend a lot of time with someone, then sometimes they will notice a lot about our mood that we don't always pick up on, and these insights can be really valuable in helping us understand what's causing our depression. For example, our partner may notice that when we don't get a good night's sleep, we're really cranky and crabby the next day. Similarly, our kids might notice that we're tense and irritable if we don't exercise for a week.

Key takeaways from this chapter

In order to determine what's causing our depression, we want to:

1/ See a doctor (preferably a psychiatrist);

2/ See a therapist;

3/ Keep a mood diary;

4/ Talk to someone we're close with about what *they* think makes *us* depressed.

Each of these things is worth doing. If we only do one or two of them, then we're likely to miss out on identifying a couple of the things that cause us to feel depressed. This is really going to slow down our recovery, and if it's a particularly key cause, the reality is that it's likely to keep us trapped in depression forever.

Step 2: Learning how to deal with the underlying causes of our depression so that they no longer depress us

CHAPTER 2

Common Cause of People's Depression #1:

Spending too long doing things that we don't enjoy doing

Have you ever watched the movie *Dead Poets Society*? If not, I'd highly recommend it, because its plot can give you powerful insight into the human psyche, and the kind of things that can trigger your depression.

The main character, Neil Perry, wants to be an actor, but he knows his father will disapprove. Without telling him, he auditions for the role of Puck in Shakespeare's *A Midsummer Night's Dream*, and he gets it. To cut a long story short, his father finds out, and demands that Neil withdraw from the play. When Neil doesn't, he tells his son that he is going to enrol him in a military school, after which Neil would go to Harvard to study medicine. Unable to face such a prospect, Neil then gets his grandfather's gun, and kills himself.

A tragic story, no doubt, and one that raises a very, very important point: a big trigger for a lot of people – including myself when I used to suffer from depression – is spending lots of time doing things that don't make us happy, and very little time doing things that do make us happy.

During my interaction with thousands of people who suffer from depression, I've noticed that this generally occurs for four main reasons:

1/ Many of us just don't know what makes us happy and what doesn't make us happy;

2/ Even if we do know what makes us happy and what doesn't make us happy, many of us aren't good at structuring our lives in such a way that we maximise the time we spend doing things that make us happy and minimise the time we spend doing things that don't make us happy;

3/ Like our friend in *Dead Poets Society*, many of us don't do what we enjoy doing because of pressure from others to do something else;

4/ Sometimes our inflexible circumstances make it difficult for us to do a lot of what makes us happy.

Let's now deal with each of these four issues in turn.

What makes us happy?

In order to figure out what makes us happy, there are a number of things that we can do.

Set aside some time to identify our core values

When I say "identify our core values", what I mean is identifying those things that mean the most to us in the world.

Ask yourself, *what gets me excited?*

What inspires me?

What gives me a buzz?

What am I thinking about during those times when I'm lying in bed and I feel so alive that I can't fall asleep? (I know if you're suffering from depression then this may be difficult to remember, but really try. Really try to think about what gets you going).

Is it helping people?

Is it making money?

Is it spending time with your friends and family?

Is it being artistic – like playing a musical instrument, singing or writing a book?

Is it travelling?

Is it sport?

I could go on and on, but what I'm saying is that we all need to be in touch with our core values, because once we're in touch with them, we can then go about restructuring our lives so that we spend as much time as possible doing things that satisfy our core values. And it's when we're doing this that we'll be our happiest selves.

For example, two of my primary core values are being creative (by writing books) and helping people. However, when I was at university I studied Commerce/Law – a degree which would've led to a career in law, investment banking, or management consulting. Those sorts of careers are much more congruent with satisfying a core value along the lines of "making lots of money", as opposed to satisfying the core values of being creative or helping people. As a result, I was miserable studying Commerce/Law, and the mere idea of going into that line of work would make me feel suicidal – much like a career in medicine did for Neil Perry in *Dead Poets Society*. Now, I'm certainly not knocking being a lawyer, an investment banker or a management consultant – they're great jobs if they satisfy *your* core values. But, they didn't satisfy *my* core values, and as a result, pursuing such a career didn't make me happy. For no other reason, I eventually quit my Commerce/Law degree at the start of 2012, and as soon as I did, and as soon as I started focusing on satisfying my core values of being creative and helping people, I started feeling much, much happier. In fact, I haven't had a depressive episode ever since.

Talk to someone we're close with about what they think makes us happy

The second thing we can do to try and work out what makes us happy is to talk to someone we're close with about what *they* think makes *us* happy.

For example, my brother loves food. I mean, he *really* loves food. If we go out for a really tasty breakfast in the morning, he'll be on a high all day – seriously, he'll be significantly more elevated, inspired and vibrant after he's had a nice meal. After we'd been backpacking around Asia for a couple of months together, I started to pick up on this trend, and I asked him:

'Mat, do you notice that whenever you eat a meal you really enjoy, you're so much more lively for the rest of the day?'

'No,' he replied, 'I'd never noticed that before. But you're right – I *am* always in a particularly good mood after I eat a nice meal'.

This insight helped my brother better understand what makes him happy, and from that moment on, he's been able to use this information to make decisions that have led him to be happier. For example, he now makes a thoughtful effort to eat an enjoyable meal whenever he can afford it – as opposed to wasting his money on something else that doesn't impact him in as positive a way.

Expose ourselves to new activities

The third thing we can do to try and work out what makes us happy is to expose ourselves to new activities with the hopes of finding a new hobby and to meet new groups of people. Here are some tips to help us do so:

1/ **When considering a new hobby, we need to think about what's feasible for our lifestyle and budget.** For example, if we live 500 kilometres inland, then surfing isn't a suitable hobby – but keeping a garden might be.

2/ **Go back to our core values.** Whether it's making money, spending time with loved ones or doing something creative, thinking about the things that mean the most to us can help us identify potential new hobbies.

3/ **Go back in time.** Most of us have things that we loved doing when we were younger, but then at some point life got in the way and we stopped doing them. If we're looking for new hobbies now, however, then it's a good time to revisit those things.

4/ **Join a friend.** Next time one of our friends is going somewhere to pursue one of their hobbies, we can tag along with them.

To give you a few ideas to think about, I've put together the following list of potential hobbies, organised into various categories. It's by no means exhaustive, but it should serve as a starting point to get your mind ticking:

- **Something creative:** writing, painting, drawing, singing, dancing, playing a musical instrument, sculpting, pottery, origami, calligraphy, scrap-booking or jewellery making.
- **Something intellectual:** reading, learning another language, philosophy, history, taking an open university course or studying part-time.
- **Something active:** playing a sport, running, going to the gym, swimming, rock climbing, cycling, skiing, snowboarding, bodybuilding or martial arts.
- **Something extreme:** skydiving, bungee jumping, base jumping, motor cycling, hangliding or white water rafting.
- **Something outdoors:** kite flying, camping, snorkelling, scuba diving, gardening, fishing, bush walking, caving, bird watching, star gazing, hiking, paintball, photography, sailing, noodling, restoring old cars, horse riding, canoeing or kite surfing.
- **Something spiritual:** yoga or meditation.
- **Something social:** hanging out with friends, listening to live music, going to the movies, going to trivia nights, getting involved in local events, or wine tasting.
- **Something indoors:** puzzles, card games, board games, dominoes, video games, museums, art galleries, darts, billiards, fantasy sports or woodwork.
- **Something financial:** investing, share trading or building financial models.
- **Volunteer work:** founding a charity about a cause you care about, doing volunteer work for an existing charity, organising a fundraiser or coaching a local sports team.
- **Start a collection:** of stamps, postcards, antiques, trading cards, coins, rocks or minerals.
- **Travelling.**
- **Get a pet.**

Keep a mood diary

The fourth thing we can do to try and work out what makes us happy is to keep a mood diary. This is a concept that we talked about earlier on in the context of trying to figure out what's triggering our depression, but keeping a mood diary is also an invaluable exercise that can help us figure out what makes us happy.

To refresh your memory about how a mood diary works, before you go to sleep every night, write down everything you did that day, and rank your mood out of 10 – 10 being very happy, and one being miserably suicidal. After a while, you'll notice that days when you're in a good mood correlate to you having done – or not having done – certain activities, and days when you're depressed correlate to you having done – or not having done – other activities.

For example, one of the things I identified from keeping a mood diary was that days I spent in the sun were days when I was in a better mood. When I noticed this, I raised it with my psychologist.

'That's not surprising,' he said. 'We get Vitamin D from the sun, and Vitamin D increases our serotonin levels.'

Ever since making this observation, I've thus made a deliberate effort to do most of my writing outdoors, and I'm in a really great mood whenever I do so. This is another example of how knowing what makes us happy allows us to then take deliberate actions that will lead us to be happy.

On the other hand, however, if we don't know what makes us happy, then it's really difficult to make the decisions that we need to make or to take the actions that we need to take in order for us to be happy. Or, put another way, it's really *easy* for us to make decisions and take actions that will lead us to be *unhappy* – or even worse, that will lead us to be depressed.

Let technology help us!

The great thing about living in the 21st century is that there are apps and tools (most of which are free) that can help us do plenty of the things that we want to do – including determining what makes us happy. One app I'd particularly recommend is the <u>Happy Habits</u> app. This app features a 119 question quiz covering 14 factors that affect your mood, and based on your answers, Happy Habits will provide suggestions to create more happiness in your life. The app also includes a "happiness journal" for you to record affirmations and positive events, in addition to articles about cognitive behavioural therapy and happiness.

Another really helpful app is <u>Secret of Happiness</u>. Every morning for 30 days, the app asks you to think of a reason to be happy, and every night, it asks you to think about something you did that day that made you happy. The creators of the app believe that by training your mind in this way to be more aware of what makes you happy, you may find that at the end of 30 days, you know the secrets to your happiness.

How to structure our lives in such a way as to maximise our happiness

If we take the time to identify our core values, talk to people close to us about what *they* think makes *us* happy, expose ourselves to knew activities, keep a mood diary, and use a cleverly developed happiness app or two, then after a while, we're going to really understand what makes us happy. However, this knowledge is next to useless if we don't then use it to structure our lives in such a way that we maximise the time we spend doing things that make us happy, and minimise the time we spend doing things that don't make us happy.

I've noticed that the main reason we often struggle with this implementation process is because we can be prone to putting up roadblocks that stop us from actually making the changes that we need to make in order to be happier.

Let's talk about some of those roadblocks now.

Saying we don't have time

Let's be perfectly honest with ourselves: what we *really* mean when we say that we "don't have time" to do something is that we're choosing not to make that something a priority. Let's look at a really common example of going to the gym. Literally speaking, we *all* have time to go to the gym – there are 24 hours in a day, and going to the gym takes around an hour. Yes, we have a bunch of other things that we need to do in those 24 hours too, but that's my point – when we say that we "don't have time" to go to the gym one day, what we're really saying is that for that 24 hour period, we're prioritising doing 24 hours' worth of other things over going to the gym.

The reason I make this point is that in order to recover from depression – and in order to be happy in general – we can't afford *not* to prioritise doing things that make us happy. Put another way, in order to be our happiest selves, we need to make sure that we are allocating as many of our 24 hours as possible to activities we enjoy.

In my experience, the easiest way to prioritise the things that make us happy is to set aside a dedicated block of time for them in our schedule. Then, all we have to do is stick to our timetable. I do this with reading, for example. It's something I absolutely love to do, but I find that it's one of those things where, if I don't set aside blocks of time to do it, then other things come up and it often falls by the wayside. For this reason, I set aside an hour every morning to read, and that's how I make sure I find time to do it.

In order to help you prioritise your time, I recommend using the Way of Life app. Marketed as the "ultimate habit maker and breaker", this app helps you set goals and then track whether or not you're achieving them on a daily or weekly basis. Alternatively, you might like to use the Daily

Routine app, which is designed to keep busy people on task. This app will keep track of your schedule and send you notifications about what you should be doing and when. You can schedule routines for specific days of the week or month, and have special reminders sent to you for tasks you're worried you might forget. The app also syncs with your online calendar, to include new events as they are scheduled.

Fear

Fear of change is another thing that can be an impediment to us restructuring our lives so that we're doing more of what makes us happy and less of what doesn't make us happy. For example, I used to study Commerce/Law as you know, and as a result, I know a lot of people who followed the path of becoming lawyers or investment bankers or management consultants. Unfortunately, I also know for a fact that a lot of them hate their jobs. They've told me things like, 'instead of being a lawyer, I wish I was a journalist'; or 'I wish I could teach scuba diving instead of being a management consultant'.

'Mate, you could still be a journalist,' I've said to them before 'You're only 24! You still have the opportunity to do pretty much anything you want to!'

'No, I don't,' they'd reply. 'I've spent close to a decade working my ass off to become a lawyer. I can't give up on that now.'

I can relate to that line of thinking, because it held me back for a long time as well.

I've spent five or six years building up my career, I remember thinking. *I've studied so hard and put so much effort into padding my resume with work experience and other extracurricular activities to get one of those top corporate jobs . . . am I really going to throw all of that away now? And particularly since I'm getting so close to graduating?*

The prospect of giving up everything I'd worked so hard for was terrifying, but what scared me even more was knowing that if I continued along the path I was on – that of becoming a lawyer or an investment banker or a management consultant and completely ignoring my core values of being creative and helping people – then I would never be happy. So I made a huge career change, and I've never regretted it since.

If you're in a similar position with respect to your career, your relationship, or in another area of your life, then I encourage you to think about taking a similar sort of leap. I know change can be scary as hell, but ask yourself: is it scarier than the prospect of being unhappy for the rest of your life?

Wasting time on things that don't make us happy

A few months ago on my Facebook fan page, I asked everyone:

What do you think is the biggest impediment to making you happy?

To my surprise, one of the most common responses was "wasting time" on things that at the end of the day, "don't contribute much to making us happy". This included, to quote the responses, "spending time on Facebook", "watching the news or mediocre television shows", "browsing the internet", or "reading trashy magazines".

If we find ourselves in this position, then we need to remind ourselves of all the things we have in our lives that do make us happy, and make a determined effort to do those things. Like we've said, scheduling those activities into our days is a good way to make sure that we'll have time to do them, and if it's distracting websites that's causing us to waste time, then a solution we haven't mentioned yet it using the SelfControl app. This app lets you block access to websites of your choice for a pre-defined period of time, thereby forcing you to focus on something else.

Pressure from other people

The scenario in *Dead Poets Society* is not an uncommon one, and it doesn't just happen in the parent/child context. For example, often it's our partners that pressure us to enter or stay in a career that we really don't like, just because it's more financially attractive than the one we'd prefer.

This is a really tough situation to be in, and I don't think there's an easy way out of it. In my opinion, if we find ourselves in such a position, then the first step we should take is to sit down with the person who's pressuring us and try to explain to them that we don't like what we're doing and that we'd much rather do something else. It's best to be really open, honest and genuine here, because I've found that if we are, then there's a good chance that the person will understand, and stop pressuring us into living a life we don't want. After all, our loved ones don't like to see us suffering, do they?

However, there are times when the other person just won't budge. I've heard people say to their children and partner things like "until you retire, you don't have time to be happy – you have to build your career and make as much money as possible"; and, I've had people look at me like I was from outer space when I told them that I was going to quit Commerce/Law to pursue my dream of becoming an author. People who think like this will in all likelihood never understand us if we tell them that we want to pursue a different path in the name of happiness. And when we're dealing with these people, we have a couple of choices.

Firstly, we could give in to their pressure and just keep doing what we're doing. Sometimes circumstances dictate that we have to do this – such as if we need to keep our high-paying-but-uninspiring job because we have a mortgage to pay off (see next section). However, I wouldn't recommend doing this if it is possible not to. If we find ourselves in such a position, there's a reason why treading the path we're on is making us miserable, and that's because it's not the right one for us. Continuing to stumble down it might preserve our relationship with those people who are pressuring us to do so, but it will just make us more and more unhappy.

Alternatively, we could begin to distance ourselves from these people – which is the option that I personally took and the one I'd recommend insofar as it is possible. The way I saw it, anyone who valued my happiness so minimally that they'd rather see me be miserable than pursue something I enjoy is not someone I consider a good influence on my life. And secondly, anyone who would rather me pursue something I hate as opposed to something I enjoy has an entirely different set of values to me – in the dropping-out-of-Commerce/Law scenario, this was the prioritising of money over more or less everything else – and, as we'll talk about later on, we're unlikely to have happy, healthy relationships with people who have vastly different values to us anyway.

What if our inflexible circumstances make it difficult to do what makes us happy?

Like we just alluded to, there are times when we may be forced to continue doing something that we don't particularly enjoy because of less than flexible circumstances – the most common example being sticking with an unenjoyable but well-paying job to pay off the mortgage or the school fees. While we may not be able to change our job in such a scenario, there are a number of things we can do to make it more bearable.

1/ **Remind ourselves of the reasons why we're doing it.** Ask yourself, *what's the reason I'm making this sacrifice?* Then, remind yourself of it every single day. Focusing on the fruits of our labour can make the labour itself a whole lot more tolerable.

2/ **Make sure we enjoy the fruits of our labour.** For example, if the reason we're working an unenjoyable but high-paying job is to put our kids through a private school, then we can make a point of getting involved in our children's school activities. Doing this helps us focus on the reason why we're making the sacrifice that we're making, which like we've said, can make our job itself more endurable.

3/ **In our *free* time, make a point of maximising the time we spend on enjoyable activities and minimising the time we spend doing**

unenjoyable activities. Like we've said, this is something that everybody ought to do, but it's even more important if we're forced to do a job we don't particularly like. In such a case, if we're at least spending our leisure time doing things we find pleasurable, then it can help sustain us during our working hours.

4/ **Make our unenjoyable job as enjoyable as can be.** We might not be able to quit our job, but in many cases, there are things we can do to make it more enjoyable. For example, getting involved in inter-office social activities, changing projects, or changing departments.

Key takeaways from this chapter

1/ If we can structure our lives in such a way that we maximise the time we spend doing things that make us happy and minimise the time we spend doing things that don't make us happy, then we will take gigantic strides towards recovering from depression and returning to living the life we want.

2/ We can understand more about what makes us happy by:

a) Identifying our core values;

b) Talking to people we're close with about what they think makes us happy;

c) Exposing ourselves to new activities;

d) Keeping a mood diary;

e) Using nifty apps and tools like Happy Habits or Secret of Happiness.

3/ There are five common obstacles that often prevent us from implementing the changes that we need to make in our lives in order to maximise the time we spend doing the things that make us happy and minimise the time we spend doing the things that don't make us happy. These include:

a) Saying we don't have time;

b) Fear;

c) Wasting time on things that don't add to our happiness;

d) Pressure from other people;

e) Inflexible circumstances.

4/ We can do the following to help us overcome such obstacles:

a) Schedule time to do the things that make us happy, and be disciplined about following that schedule.

b) Acknowledge that while change can be scary, continuing down a path that we know is making us miserable is pretty damn scary too, and that for this reason, perhaps change is actually the lesser of two fears.

c) Have an honest, open-hearted talk with the person who is pressuring us to do something that we really don't like doing. If they listen and understand, they're likely to ease up on us; however, if they don't listen or understand, then we may want to consider distancing ourselves from that person.

d) If we're somewhat shackled by inflexible circumstances, we can make the best of our situation by reminding ourselves of the reasons why we're making the sacrifices we're making, by ensuring that we enjoy the fruits of our labour, by making sure we do what we enjoy in our leisure time, and by making our unenjoyable job as enjoyable as can be.

CHAPTER 3

Common Cause of People's Depression #2:

Loving ourselves for unhealthy reasons, or not loving ourselves at all

Many of us who suffer from depression do not love ourselves. Or, even if we do love ourselves, it's entirely possible that the love we have for ourselves is based on a foundation that's relatively unstable; this in turn means that *we* will be relatively unstable, which makes us an easy target for Depression (and he's a hell of a good shooter). If you've read my memoir *Depression is a Liar*, you'll know that loving myself for unhealthy reasons was one of the biggest, if not *the* biggest cause of my depression. Learning how to love myself for healthy reasons was thus crucial to my recovery, and for this reason, this particular chapter is one that's very close to my heart.

We'll start by talking about some of the really "healthy" reasons why we can love ourselves. Then, we'll go on to talk about some of the really "unhealthy" reasons why people love themselves, and demonstrate how basing our love for ourselves on one or all of these reasons can lead us to become extremely unstable – and thus extremely depressed.

Healthy reasons to love ourselves

Healthy reasons to love ourselves can be divided into two categories:

1/ Our skills – i.e. things that we're good at;

2/ Our personal qualities and characteristics.

These "reasons to love ourselves" are healthy because they are:

1/ In our control;

2/ Independent of what other people think of us;

3/ Independent of circumstances.

As I've said, loving myself for healthy reasons is something I really used to struggle with, but over the years, it's a skill I've worked very hard to master. In the course of doing so, I once wrote down the following list of healthy reasons to love myself, which I used to read through all the time so that they'd become ingrained in my mind.

- *I love myself because I'm a kind person – someone who always tries to treat other people with respect.*
- *I love myself because I'm an honest person who acts with integrity.*
- *I love myself because I have the determination and the work ethic to pursue my dreams through to completion.*
- *I love myself because I have the courage to face my problems and deal with them, instead of denying that they exist.*
- *I love myself because I'm a compassionate person who helps other people.*
- *I love myself because I'm intelligent.*
- *I love myself because I'm a good writer.*
- *I love myself because I'm a fighter – because I had the strength to turn my life around and transform myself from the extremely suicidal person I was into the extremely happy person that I am today.*

These are all healthy reasons to love myself, and because my love for myself is based upon reasons that are healthy – i.e. reasons that are in my control, independent of circumstances, and independent of what other people think of me – I am an emotionally stable person, which contributes to me being very happy.

How does loving ourselves for healthy reasons lead us to be emotionally stable?

Let's say that, for example, a girl I ask on a date turns me down. In such an instance, I would feel disappointed, of course. However, because I love myself for healthy reasons, I wouldn't then conclude that I'm "unattractive", "ugly", "unlovable" or anything else of the sort, nor would I go to pieces and spiral into depression. On the contrary, my self-esteem would remain high, and I'd still feel emotionally stable.

Why?

Because a girl turning me down for a date has no impact on the reasons why I love myself.

Let's return to my list.

I love myself because I'm a kind person – someone who always tries to treat other people with respect.

Does a girl turning me down for a date mean that I'm no longer a kind person? Or that I no longer treat other people with respect? No, it doesn't mean that at all.

Next reason: *I love myself because I'm an honest person who acts with integrity.*

Does the fact that a girl turned me down for a date mean that that's no longer true? Of course not.

Third reason: *I love myself because I have the determination and the work ethic to pursue my dreams through to completion.*

Once again, a girl turning me down for a date has no impact on this reason why I love myself. After all, despite being turned down, I am still a determined person who works hard.

Fourth reason: *I love myself because I have the courage to face my problems and deal with them, instead of denying that they exist.*

Once again, does a girl turning me down for a date change that? Does it mean that I no longer have the courage to face my problems and deal with them instead of denying that they exist? Not at all.

I can go through this analysis for each of the reasons on my list and arrive at the same conclusion every time – because as we've said, each of the reasons on my list are *healthy* reasons to love myself. For this reason, if a girl turns me down for a date, instead of falling apart, I can instead think:

OK, a girl turned me down . . . that's disappointing, but at the same time, I still know I'm a good person. I know I still have a lot to offer a girl. And, even though this particular girl didn't want to get to know me better, I know there's another one out there who will.

Let me give you another example. Let's say that someone disagrees with an article I write about depression, and they decide to send me an email saying that it's terrible and that I'm an idiot and that I have no idea what I'm talking about. If this happened, I wouldn't exactly be jumping up and down, but at the same time, it's not going to shatter my self-esteem or cause me to go to pieces. In reality, it's going to have very little effect on me. Why? Because once again, it has no impact on the reasons why I love myself – and because it has no impact on the reasons why I love myself, I still love myself just as much as I did before that person sent me an abusive email.

The running theme is this: I love myself for reasons that I am in control of, that are independent of what other people think of me, and that are independent of circumstances. For this reason, no-one can take them away from me – not a girl, not someone who disagrees with something I write, not anyone. I don't need them – or anyone else – to validate my own love for myself. And this is critically important, because it means that when something goes wrong or when I'm facing adversity, my self-esteem remains high, and I don't go to pieces.

What happens if our love for ourselves is based on unhealthy reasons?

Now let's talk about what happens if our love for ourselves is based on what I like to call "unhealthy" reasons. For example:

1/ If we were to love ourselves because our partner loves us;

2/ If we were to love ourselves because our boss likes the job we do at work;

3/ If we were to love ourselves because our business is going well.

Now you may ask: *why are these "unhealthy" reasons to love ourselves?*

And my answer is this: the reason that these reasons to love ourselves are unhealthy is because they are *not* in our control, they are *not* independent of circumstances, and they are *not* independent of what other people think of us. This is very dangerous, because it leaves us extremely vulnerable to falling victim to depression – as we can see in each of the following examples.

If one of the fundamental reasons why we love ourselves is because our partner loves us, then imagine how we're going to feel if that person breaks up with us. Firstly, just like someone who loves themselves for healthy reasons will be, we're going to be heartbroken. However, *unlike* someone who loves themselves for healthy reasons, we're also likely to think all sorts of thoughts like:

Wow, my partner broke up with me . . . that must mean that I'm unlovable . . . and if I'm unlovable, then that must mean that no-one will ever love me again . . . and if no-one will ever love me again, then that must mean that I'll never find another partner . . . and if I never find another partner, then that means I'm going to spend the rest of my life miserable and alone.

If we love ourselves because our partner loves us, then we're likely to catastrophize the break-up like so, which is going to destroy our self-esteem and plunge us into an awful spell of depression.

Let's take another example: we love ourselves because our boss likes the work we do, but then we get a new boss who doesn't particularly appreciate our input. If this happens, then just like someone who loves themselves for healthy reasons will be, we're going to feel disappointed. However, *unlike* someone who loves themselves for healthy reasons, we're also likely to catastrophize the situation and think all kinds of poisonous thoughts like:

Oh, my new boss doesn't appreciate my work . . . that must mean I'm a terrible worker . . . and because I'm a terrible worker, I'm probably going to get fired soon . . . and because I'm a terrible worker, I'll probably never be able to get another job once I get fired . . . so I'm probably going to be unemployed for years on end.

Once again, catastrophizing this issue like so is going to cripple our self-esteem and trigger our depression.

Last example: we love ourselves because our business is doing well, but then the economy crashes and our business goes with it. Again, just like someone who loves themselves for healthy reasons, we're going to feel absolutely shattered. However, *unlike* someone who loves themselves for healthy reasons, we're also likely to catastrophize the situation and think things like:

My business crashed because I'm an idiot . . . and because I'm an idiot, I'll never be able to start another business again . . . and because I'll never be able to start another business again, I'll always be broke . . . and because I'll always be broke, I'll always be miserable . . . and because I'll always be broke and miserable, I'll never be able to attract a partner . . . which means I'll never be able to have a family . . . which means I'm going to die broke, miserable, and all alone.

The running theme is this: when we base our love for ourselves on what other people think of us or on circumstances that are out of our control, we give those people and those circumstances so much power over our own happiness. And because we can't control those people or those circumstances – they can change at any minute – it means that when adversity strikes us, we're going to catastrophize everything that's going wrong and completely fall to pieces. And that's a big reason why a lot of us suffer from depression.

Homework

What I'd really encourage you to do now is to come up with a list of reasons to love yourself that are in your control, independent of circumstances, and independent of what other people think of you. As we've said, it's very important to be extremely mindful of the reasons why you ought to love yourself, because it will contribute to you being much better able to cope with adversity and to prevent it from plummeting you into depression. So set aside some time to create this list, and then keep reading and re-reading it so that you train your brain to love yourself for those healthy reasons.

Key takeaways from this chapter

1/ "Healthy" reasons to love ourselves include:

    a) Our skills – i.e. things that we're good at;

    b) Our personal qualities and characteristics.

2/ These reasons to love ourselves are healthy because they are:

    a) In our control;

    b) Independent of what other people think of us;

    c) Independent of circumstances.

3/ Similarly, "unhealthy" reasons to love ourselves are reasons that are:

    a) *Not* in our control;

    b) *Not* independent of what other people think of us;

    c) *Not* independent of circumstances.

4/ When we love ourselves for healthy reasons, we are much better able to weather adversity than we would be if we loved ourselves for unhealthy reasons.

CHAPTER 4

Common Cause of People's Depression #3:

Anger

If you've read my *Depression is a Liar*, then you'll be very familiar with a girl called Chanel. We dated for four or five months, over which time my feelings for her grew to the point where I envisioned marrying her one day and spending my life with her. But we broke up when I realised that the whole time we'd been going out, she'd been cheating on me with one of my best friends. When I found out, I was furious. I was heartbroken. And to make matters even worse, I later heard that she began spreading the lie that I'd raped her.

In the aftermath of all this, I was not only very hurt, but also enraged. Remember in the previous chapter, where I said that one of the reasons why I love myself and one of the things that I take a lot of pride in is the fact that I'm kind to people, that I'm compassionate, and that I act with integrity? Well, to hear all of that being called into question . . . to hear someone say that I'd been acting in such a vile and despicable way – particularly somebody who I loved and who I thought felt the same way about me, and somebody who had already betrayed me by cheating on me with one of my best friends – it was absolutely devastating. I was horribly distraught. And like I've said, above all else, I was disturbingly mad.

To be completely honest with you, I was so angry with her that I wanted to kill her.

Of course, I did no such thing. I knew that the best revenge in such cases is living well, and I knew that I needed to forget about Chanel and move on in order to do so, because as we opened this chapter by saying, holding onto anger is like drinking poison and expecting someone else to die. The only person it hurts is us.

And for this reason, it is in *our* best interest to forgive those who have done harm to us.

Why should we forgive someone who's hurt us badly?

I understand if you're objecting to this notion right now. I understand if you're thinking:

I don't want to forgive the people who've wronged me! They really screwed me over! I hate them! The last thing they deserve from me is forgiveness!

I get it. I've felt that way too. But what I learned in time was that the reason why it's in our best interest to forgive the people who've wronged us is because it gives *us* peace – and this is exactly why I chose to forgive Chanel. Did she deserve it? I don't know, and I don't care. Whether or not she deserved it is completely irrelevant. Again, I chose to forgive her so that I could gain closure and move on with my life, because I knew that if I didn't – if I instead held onto the anger that I was feeling for her forever – it would just continue to poison me. And after all, Chanel had already hurt me once . . . I didn't want to give her the power to hurt me again.

The second point I want to make about forgiveness is that when we choose to forgive someone, it doesn't mean that we're all of a sudden condoning what that person did to hurt us. Again, we're forgiving them because it gives *ourselves* peace – and it's entirely possible to do so while at the same time holding the belief that what that person did to us was terribly wrong.

The third point I want to make is that choosing to forgive someone doesn't mean that the pain and anger we feel towards that person is going to immediately disappear. It takes time for anger to fade and for our pain to heal. However, when we forgive the people who have wronged us, it allows the healing process to finally begin.

Lastly, I'd like to stress the point that forgiveness does not have to lead to any sort of reunion with the person who's wronged us. In fact, I think that often the best way to forgive someone is to do so privately in our head. For the record, I never told Chanel that I forgave her. In fact, I haven't spoken to her since a couple of days after I caught her cheating on me, way back on New Year's Eve of 2007. I think there are some people like Chanel that we're better off without – but that doesn't mean that we can't forgive those people to free ourselves from the anger we feel toward them.

I'll close this chapter by saying that I know the act of forgiving someone who's wronged us is difficult. I know it may seem counterintuitive. And, I know that it's often the last thing in the world that we feel like doing. But I can promise you from experience that if you choose to do so, you are going to feel infinitely better as a result. You are going to feel so much more at peace with yourself, and so much more at peace with the world. You're going to feel as if a huge weight has been lifted off you. And as a result, you're going to feel much less depressed.

Key takeaways from this chapter

1/ Holding onto anger is like drinking poison and expecting someone else to die – the only person it hurts is us. For this reason, it is in our best interest to forgive all the people who have wronged us.

2/ Whether or not a person who has wronged us deserves our forgiveness is irrelevant. It's in our best interest to forgive such people because doing so gives us peace, and allows us to move on with our lives.

3/ Choosing to forgive someone who has wronged us does not mean that we condone what they did to us.

4/ Choosing to forgive someone who has wronged us does not mean that the pain and anger we feel toward that person is going to immediately disappear. However, choosing to forgive that person will allow the healing process to begin.

5/ Forgiving someone who has wronged us does not need to lead to a reunion with that person. Often the best way to forgive someone is to do so privately in our head.

CHAPTER 5

Common Cause of People's Depression #4:

Not allowing gratitude to co-exist with our pain

When I say that a common cause of depression is not allowing gratitude to co-exist with our pain, I'm definitely not implying that we're not entitled to suffer from depression because there are people worse off than us, or that if we just realised how lucky we were, we wouldn't be depressed. No-one has the right to diminish or trivialise any pain we may be feeling, and just because someone may be worse off than us, it certainly doesn't mean that we're not allowed to hurt or suffer from depression ourselves. What I *am* saying, however, is that in order to recover from depression, it's extremely important to maintain an accurate perspective, and feel gratitude *in addition* to any pain we may be feeling.

How having gratitude saved my life

In hindsight, having gratitude was such a driving force in my recovery from depression because it gave me *perspective*. And we need to have perspective for two very important reasons:

1/ When we have perspective, we appreciate everything much more than someone who doesn't. As a result, we're much less depressed.

2/ Perspective gives us the positive attitude we need to be able to navigate our way through our depression and find the light at the end of the tunnel.

Let me now illuminate these two points by talking about how I personally came to be so conscious of what I'm grateful for, and how having gratitude quite literally saved my life.

When I finished high school at the end of 2006, I was lucky enough to be offered a scholarship to study Commerce/Law at Sydney University, and as such, found myself one evening at the scholarship presentation dinner. A couple of my high school teachers were invited to attend, and at some point, one of them said to me:

'You've been blessed with so much, Danny. You've been brought up in a wonderful neighbourhood; you're surrounded by a loving, supportive family; and you've got the opportunity and the ability to do anything you want to in life.'

Mr Williams then paused for a moment.

'I hope you use your blessings for good,' he said. 'I hope you always do charity work, and I hope you always try to help people. Remember, Danny: to whom much is given, much is expected.'

That notion really stuck in my mind, and in time, inspired me to volunteer for a month at an underprivileged school in Cusco, Peru. At that point, I was amidst the thick of my depression, having been suffering for six months or a year; but when I arrived in Cusco and started witnessing some of the tragedies that were taking place there, it made me realise how lucky I truly was. To quote a section from *Depression is a Liar:*

> *Before I went to Cusco, I'd never been to a place where 56% of the population lived on less than US$1 a day, where 85% of children never attended high school, where the school dropout rate was 40%, where the unemployment rate was 42%, where the underemployment rate was 74%, where the literacy rate was 18%, where the infant mortality rate was 5%, and where the average life expectancy was 41 years.*

I'd never met any children who wore the same World Vision clothes to school every day.

I'd never been to a school where not a single kid was fat, nor had I ever been called fat by anyone else, which is what some of the children thought the volunteers were because we weren't bone-skinny.

I'd never had 10 year olds try to sell me cigarettes on the street at two in the morning on a school night to help support their family.

I'd never been too embarrassed to tell someone I had a swimming pool in my backyard, like I was when my host family – who lived in a flat barely larger than my living room – had asked me to describe my home to them.

I'd never lived in a place where only ice-cold water came out of the taps, meaning that I had to heat it with a kettle and use a bucket and cup to shower.

I'd never seen villages of houses that didn't have any windows and were made out of mud bricks, much less had I helped build chimneys out of bamboo for said houses so that smoke wouldn't suffocate the air when the families cooked over a fire.

I'd never been to a place where all the adults looked 20 years older than their actual age, and where people as young as 30 had dry and wrinkled skin.

I'd never met a kid who grabbed other peoples' crotches and stuck his fingers up their bums during a school yard game of dodge ball.

'Why does he do that?' one of the volunteers asked.

'Because . . . he gets sexually abused at home.'

'By who?'

The volunteer manager released a painful sigh.

'By his father.'

We were all flabbergasted.

'How come . . . how come no-one's reported it?'

'We have.'

'And?'

He sighed again.

'The police . . . it's not like in your country. There's so much corruption . . . it's not like in your country.'
'But surely something can be done about it?'
'I'm afraid not.'

Seeing this poverty, this exploitation, this corruption, this perversion; waking up every morning and staring it in the face . . . it helped me think about my own set of worries in a different light.

Yeah, I do suffer from depression, I remember thinking, *but I'm still really lucky. I'm so fortunate to live in a safe country, to be surrounded by a supportive family, and to have the opportunity to do whatever I want with my life. So while I'm not without my problems, I'm also not without some incredible blessings.*

Having such a high degree of gratitude sitting beside my pain helped give me a different perspective about my depression, and this perspective continued to develop in the months and years that followed. When I got back to Sydney, I started volunteering with a charity that supported battered women, and learning about the hardship that they go through further reinforced my belief that while I did have depression, I was still an extremely lucky person in many other ways. This gratitude then led me to co-found The Open Skies Foundation at the start of 2010, a non-profit organisation that aimed to create sustainable change in Third World Communities.

'But Danny, you're deeply suffering yourself right now,' the people close to me would say. 'You're going through one of the worst bouts of depression you've ever been through. Why would you now, of all times, decide to found a charity?'

And they were right – I *was* going through an awful time myself. Yet in spite of that, I still felt immensely fortunate for all the *good* things that I knew existed in my life alongside my despair – and this gratitude ignited an urge in me to want to help others who weren't bestowed with the privileges that I'd always known. And perhaps ironically, it was this commitment to helping other people that ended up saving my life several months later – as you can see from this passage from *Depression is a Liar:*

Woke up feeling ghastly. Dad drove me to uni for my exam. Silence all the way.

He dropped me off. I dragged myself to the exam room in a soulless, debilitated shuffle. When I got there I fell to the floor, sat slumped against the wall. My classmates talked to me, asked me questions, but still . . . nothing.

We got called in.

'Ten minutes reading time, starting now,' the announcer said.

I tried to read. I understood the words on their own, but put together they made no sense. I flicked through the exam. Not much of it did.

The exam itself began. I reread questions I knew I'd studied for, but in the moment the answers were a blur. I felt like I was in a trance. The world seemed a black hole. A vacuum of agony. I couldn't see any escape. The only possible salvation seemed death.

I scribbled down a few answers before the end of the exam.

'How did you go?' one of my friends asked. But I just shook my head and shuffled spiritlessly away.

I pulled myself into the streets. It was pouring down with rain. I had no idea what to do next. Should I go home? Go back to uni and study? Go to a coffee shop? Call a friend? Get smashed at a bar? Every possibility seemed brutally unbearable. The only one that didn't was killing myself. As you know, I'd always thought suicide was selfish, because even though it might've given me peace, I knew it would've left my family in ruins. But right then, on what was, unquestionably, the worst day of my life to date, I started to think that maybe I was wrong. I started to think that perhaps I'd been too narrow-minded.

Because I swear, *I vividly remember thinking,* if my family knew how depressed I am right now . . . if they could comprehend the gut-wrenching severity of the pain I'm in . . . I swear they'd want me to put myself out of my misery. I swear they'd want me to end it all and finally be free.

It was a dangerous revelation.

Does this mean I can die now? *I thought.* Guilt-free and with my family's blessing?

I stopped walking, let the rain pound down on top of me.

Can I do it? Can I really kill myself? Jump in front of a speeding car and join the rest of the road toll casualties?

I stood at a right angle to the road, watched the cars zooming by.

Is this really it? Can I really end it all right here?

My mind was a warzone. So much conflict. But eventually there emerged a definite answer.

No.

I can't do it.

It's the answer I'd always reached, but this time, the reason was different.

It wasn't for me.

It wasn't even for my family.

It was for those less fortunate than me.

Regardless of how depressed I feel right now, *I thought,* I know that I've been tremendously blessed: with a loving, supportive family; with First World privileges; and with the opportunity and the ability to do whatever I want to in life. Regardless of how I feel right now, I have had a lot bestowed upon me, and I have to use my good fortune to help others who aren't as immensely privileged as I am. If I kill myself, Open Skies will disband. All the charity work I'd planned on doing will never get done. I'd be abandoning all the people I have the capacity to help. And no matter how much pain I'm in I just can't do that. To whom much is given, much is expected. I can't kill myself. Not now, not ever.

I felt it so strongly, with such paramount force that it couldn't be doubted. It was as if it was a calling, a message from God in my hour of need:

I put you on this earth for a reason, Danny. You can't leave it. There's so much work that you need to do . . .

So I stepped away from the road. I called my mum.

'Hello?'

'Ma . . .' I croaked.

'Danny? Are you alright?'

I murmured something inaudible.

'Danny?' she panicked. 'Is everything OK?'

'Come and get me . . . please. Wynyard.'

I met her there, crawled into the car, muttered in broken sentences what happened.

'Danny, we would never want you to kill yourself!' she stressed. 'Never, ever, ever, ever! Suicide is a permanent solution to a temporary problem! You know that, don't you?'

I eventually managed to nod my head. From the corner of my barely opened eye, I saw Mum fighting back tears as she tried to drive through the rain. At some point she pulled over to call my dad. She talked to him while I sat motionless in the front seat.

After a long time, she finally hung up.

'Danny . . .' she murmured. 'Danny we think . . . we think it's time you be admitted to hospital.'

She paused solemnly.

'What do you think?'

I just wanted to get better. I was so tired of feeling sick and I just wanted to get better.

'OK,' I managed to say. 'I'll go to hospital.'

As you can see, gratitude really did save my life, because if it wasn't for being so conscious of how lucky I really am, then I may not have had anything else to stop me from jumping in front of those speeding cars.

Since that day, I've done a lot more charity work through Open Skies, various other organisations, and most recently, as a mental health advocate – and in the course of doing so, I've seen some absolutely heartbreaking things.

I've met seven year old Cambodian girls who have to beg on the streets to get their food because their parents are too busy gambling and getting high to feed them. Sometimes they also have to beg to get food for their parents, and if they don't get enough, their parents beat them.

I've met girls who started being sexually abused when they were three.

I've met refugees as young as 10 who've lost their entire families at sea when they tried to come to Australia.

I've met suicidal 14 year old kids who've been kicked out of home and forced to live on the streets because their parents "don't believe in mental illness" and are sick of them being "drama queens".

This is just the tip of the iceberg – I could go on forever with these stories – but the point to note is that witnessing all of these tragedies has helped me realise how fortunate I really am, and filled me with gratitude for all the privileges that I've been blessed with. Like I've said, having such a high degree of gratitude is the reason I'm still alive today, because it prevented me from jumping in front of those speeding cars; however, it's also been the saving grace of my life for two other very important reasons.

Firstly, it kept me positive throughout my entire fight with depression, which allowed me to navigate my way through it and beat it in the end.

Secondly, not only did it lead me to beat my depression, but it also led me to be happier than I ever thought I could be, because it's made me really, truly appreciate my life. As a result, I now get so much more enjoyment out of everything than I otherwise would.

For example, because I know how lucky I am to be able to walk peacefully down the street without having to worry about being assaulted or shot – something that's commonplace in many war-ravaged countries – I can derive a lot of pleasure, enjoyment and appreciation from an act that's often taken for granted like strolling down the road to a coffee shop. It's the same with other simple pleasures like having lunch at a nice café with a friend, flicking on the T.V. and watching a basketball game, or lying in the sun at the beach – because I'm cognisant of how lucky I am to be able to do seemingly little things like this when so many other people in the world can't, I can really appreciate them, and thus get so much more enjoyment out of them than I otherwise would.

I'm telling you: the more gratitude you have in your life, the happier you will be, because you're going to appreciate everything so much more than you otherwise would.

And you *do* have reasons to be grateful.

I don't know anything about you, but since you have access to a computer and can afford to buy this book, you have a lot more than hundreds of millions of people in the world.

Just to reiterate, I'm not saying this to belittle any pain you may be feeling or to make you feel guilty for suffering from depression. Like I said at the start of this chapter, just because there may be people in the world who are worse off than you, it certainly doesn't mean that you're not entitled to your grief. Instead, what I'm saying is that in order to beat your depression and become the happy person that you want to be, it's vital that you maintain an accurate perspective about your life, and allow an appropriate level of gratitude to co-exist with your anguish.

What can we do to have more gratitude in our lives?

Having gratitude is so central to being happy that it's become a field of study in and of itself, leading to books and articles being written, studies being undertaken and apps being developed to help us become more grateful and conscious of all the beauty, joy and pleasure that exists in our lives. Having been a student of gratitude for several years now, I'd like to share with you some of the things that have helped me become more grateful over the years, and some of the tips, tools and tricks I know have worked for others.

Help someone less fortunate than ourselves

Like I've said, the main reason I'm so grateful is because I've done so much volunteer work, and have thus met countless people whose lives are much more trying that mine. If you're in a position to do so, I recommend travelling to a Third World country to do some too, and to witness how people much less fortunate than ourselves live. If that's not feasible, then I'd recommend doing something more locally – like volunteering at your local homeless shelter or at your closest children's hospital. Not only will this help give you perspective and cause you to feel more grateful about all the positive things in your life, but there are also few things in the world that are more uplifting and more rewarding to do than to offer your time to help other people less fortunate than yourself. It's such a wonderfully gratifying thing to do – just watching a little kid's face light up when you give them a yoyo, or having someone reach for your hand and say "thank-you, you've helped me, you've had a positive impact on my life" is one of the most beautiful feelings you can experience.

If you don't have the time to do volunteer work but you do have the money to be able to help someone less fortunate than yourself, then becoming a donor – regardless of how much or how little you donate – can make a huge difference to someone's life and heighten your gratitude for your own good fortune. You could do something like sponsor a hungry child through World Vision, or, if you have a soft spot for mental health, you could donate to an organisation like NAMI, SANE or Beyond Blue.

Keep a gratitude journal

Every night before you go to bed, write down five things that you're grateful for – either things that you're thankful that you were able to do that day, or things that you're thankful for in general. For example:

- I'm grateful for having been able to eat my favourite meal for dinner tonight.
- I'm grateful for being able to spend time with my family today.
- I'm grateful for living in a safe, beautiful country.
- I'm grateful that today was a sunny day, and that I got to enjoy it by being able to take a stroll in the park.
- I'm grateful for my partner.

See how easy it is? It doesn't take long, and it can really help you focus on all the positive things in your life. In fact, studies have shown that gratitude exercises such as this result in increased alertness, enthusiasm, determination, optimism and energy, in addition to – you guessed it – decreased levels of depression.

I've personally found it immensely beneficial to keep a gratitude diary in this way, however leading gratitude researcher Robert Emmons suggests in his book Gratitude Works! that there's an even more effective way to keep a gratitude journal: instead of picking five things that you're grateful for each day, pick one thing and write five reasons why you're grateful for it. For example, I'm grateful for my brother because he:

- Makes me laugh.
- Is always honest with me.
- Always makes the most of the time we spend together.
- Is always there when I need him.
- Helps me relax and enjoy my life.

I like both methods, so these days, I mix it up – sometimes I do one and sometimes I do the other. I'd recommend giving both a try and seeing what works best for you.

Lastly, in terms of how to logistically keep your gratitude journal, you can of course use a regular diary, or, you can use the immensely popular Gratitude Journal app.

Key takeaways from this chapter

1/ Being grateful for all the wonderful things in our lives is very important because it gives us perspective, which is essential to our wellbeing because:

a) When we have perspective, we appreciate everything so much more than we otherwise would;

b) Perspective gives us the positive attitude we need to be able to navigate our way through our depression, and find the light at the end of the tunnel.

2/ A great way to inject more gratitude into our lives is to:

a) Do volunteer work;

b) Keep a gratitude journal.

Chapter 6

Common Cause of People's Depression #5:

Victimising ourselves

This is a really important topic, because unfortunately, many people I interact with who suffer from depression constantly victimise themselves. It's a very human thing to do. Whenever something goes wrong in our lives, often our natural reaction is to think:

Why is this happening to me? Nobody else I know has to deal with this! I'm a good person . . . I don't deserve this! This is so unfair! Why do bad things always happen to me and me only?

However, while it's easy to do, victimising ourselves is a very unhealthy habit to get into, because if we do victimise ourselves, it's almost impossible to recover from depression.

Here's the cold hard reality: bad things happen, and feeling sorry for ourselves won't get us anywhere. When we are struck by adversity or when we suffer from depression, instead of complaining and acting like a victim, we need to confront our problems, resolve them, and then move on from them.

When I say this, please understand that I'm not trying to be dismissive of your hardship or to trivialise it in any way, nor am I coming at this from the perspective of a person who's never experienced anything painful or heartbreaking. I've been through my fair share of problems, too. I haven't told you before, but when I was 15, my dream was to be a professional basketball player. I was pouring everything I had into achieving it, but then I severely injured my knee, and whatever chance I had was gone. A couple of years later, I had that disastrous relationship with Chanel, and then a few months after that I started suffering from depression, which over the next four years led to alcoholism, drug abuse, medicine-induced psychosis, near-suicide attempts and multiple hospitalisations. No matter what I was going through, however, I made a point of never victimising myself, because I knew that doing so would lead me to feel bitter, spiteful and even more miserable. Instead, I chose to face my problems, resolve them, and then move on from them – and it's this approach I really believe we need to take if we don't want our *temporary* problems to turn into *permanent* problems.

At the end of the day, this is exactly what victimising ourselves does: turn adversity that we can overcome in time into adversity that will plague us forever, by changing our focus from *what can I do to resolve my problems?* into *Why do bad things always happen to me? Life is so unfair! I don't deserve this at all!* And the problem with this latter approach is that it doesn't lead us to take the proactive steps that we need to take in order to overcome our hardship. Rather, it leads us to wallow in our misery, and wallowing in our misery is a sure-fire way to stay trapped in depression forever.

What can we do to feel less like a victim?

Each of the following practices are ones I commonly employ to this day to help prevent me from feeling sorry for myself whenever something in my life doesn't go according to plan.

Focus on moving forwards

Like I've said, when adversity strikes us, I firmly believe that the best thing we can do for ourselves is to confront our problems, resolve them, and then move on from them. If this is out mindset, then when we fall on hard times, we're so busy trying to deal with our problems and move on from them that we don't have time to feel sorry for ourselves.

Take responsibility

When something goes wrong in our lives, I also believe it's in our best interest to analyse the situation, take responsibility for all the mistakes we've made, and learn as much as we can from the experience to try and prevent it from ever occurring again. This approach is the opposite of the "blaming everybody else" approach, which is so often at the root cause of self-victimisation.

Let go of anger

Taking the steps that we need to take in order to let go of anger once again shifts our approach from "blaming everybody else" to being focused on moving forwards. Looking back, I can see that it's because I worked so hard to forgive Chanel that I didn't victimise myself when everything went awry with her.

Gratitude, gratitude, gratitude

When I injured my knee, one of the main things that stopped me from victimising myself was reminding myself of all the blessings in my life, even though my dream was shattered. Because I had gratitude sitting beside my pain, I was able to say to myself:

OK, this is really heartbreaking, but on the bright side, I'm still only 15 years old. What happened is devastating, yes, but it hardly means my life is over. I'm fortunate enough to go to a very good school where I'm able to receive a great education, so even though I can no longer be a professional basketball player, if I make the most of the wonderful opportunities still available to me, I'll be able to recover from this setback, and go on to live a happy life.

Key takeaways from this chapter

1/ Victimising ourselves turns our *temporary* problems into *permanent* problems, since it changes our focus from *what can I do to resolve this problem?* to *Why do bad things always happen to me? Life is so unfair! I don't deserve this at all!* This latter approach doesn't lead us to take the proactive steps that we need to take in order to overcome our hardship. Instead, it leads us to wallow in it, and wallowing in our problems is a sure-fire way to stay trapped in our depression.

2/ When we're hit with adversity, we can take various steps to reduce and eliminate the "I'm a victim" feeling by:

    a) Focusing on moving forwards;

    b) Analysing what went wrong, taking responsibility for any mistakes we may have made, and learning what we can from the experience so that we can minimise the chance of it happening again;

    c) Working to let go of the anger that we feel towards the situation;

    d) Working at being more grateful for all of the good things that exist in our lives – even though we're going through adversity at the moment.

CHAPTER 7

Common Cause of People's Depression #6:

Not being surrounded by the "right" people . . . or even worse, being surrounded by "toxic" people

Author and motivational speaker Jim Rohn once remarked that we are the average of the five people who we spend the most time with. And I think he's right. As you've probably experienced yourself, who you surround yourself with affects the way you think, the way you feel, and the decisions you make.

For this reason, in order to recover from depression and become the happy people that we want to be, it's critically important that we surround ourselves with the "right" people and distance ourselves from the "wrong" people.

However, this then raises the question: *How are we supposed to know who the "right" people and who the "wrong" people are?*

This is something I really used to struggle with, so I asked a psychologist for his advice. Below is an exercise he taught me to do which, despite its simplicity, really worked wonders. I'll lay it out like a high school science experiment, just for a bit of fun.

Aim

To figure out who the "right" people and who the "wrong" people to surround ourselves with are.

Materials needed

- An A4 piece of paper;
- A pen;
- A person who's ready to learn and improve their surroundings (that's us!).

Method

1/ Draw a mind-map connected to a centre circle that asks, "what do I value in a friend?"

2/ Around the circle, write down the characteristics or personality traits that you appreciate in a friend. For example, loyalty, kindness, or someone who's down to earth. Let me emphasise that it is very important that you don't rush this part. Make sure you really think about what you value in a friend so that what you write down accurately reflects your true feelings. The benefits of this exercise is in getting this section "right" – so if you rush it and jot down characteristics or personality traits in a friend that *don't* correctly reflect your true feelings, then this exercise won't help you achieve the results that it can.

Conclusions

1/ Everyone who possesses the characteristics and personality traits that we've identified as valuing in a friend are the "right" people for us to surround ourselves with. As a result, we want to make a deliberate effort to surround ourselves with these people, because we're in all likelihood going to have really positive, healthy relationships with them.

2/ On the other hand, those who do not possess the characteristics and personality traits that we've identified as valuing in a friend are the "wrong" people for us to surround ourselves with. For this reason, it's in our best interest to distance ourselves from such people, because we're in all likelihood going to have negative relationships with them.

~~~

I know this exercise sounds simple. I know this exercise may sound corny. But it can really work if you take the time to do it properly. Like I said, the value of it comes in taking the time to identify what you truly desire in a friend, because it's this level of self-awareness that is ultimately going to lead you to make good, healthy decisions about who you choose to spend your time with.

Toxic people

Another thing that's worth noting is that there are certain traits that make up some people which are outright toxic, and if we surround ourselves with people who have such characteristics, it's likely to compromise our happiness. Over the years, I've talked to thousands of people who have depression, and one of the biggest triggers for many sufferers is that they have toxic people in their lives who exhibit some of the following traits.

1/ **They're judgmental.** Instead of being supportive, some people are critically judgmental. For example, if you suffer from depression, then choosing to see a therapist is an excellent decision to make. However, a judgmental person may condemn you for that. They may think, *oh, so-and-so is seeing a psychologist . . . that means they must be really weird! That means they must be crazy!* And we never want to be surrounded by people like that.

2/ **Jealousy.** Supportive people will celebrate with us when we have a success, but jealous people are likely to try and drag us down instead. Those are people we're definitely better off without.

3/ **People who don't believe in us.** Again, people who don't believe in us are the opposite of supportive, and it's not in our best interest to surround ourselves with such people.

4/ **People who take their anger and frustration out on us when something goes wrong in their life.** There are certain people who will constantly treat us like garbage whenever something is bothering them, even if what's bothering them has nothing to do with us. We deserve better.

5/ **People who bring out the worst in us.** For example, if you're a recovering alcoholic and you're trying to stop drinking, then a supportive person will respect your decision and encourage you to lay off the bottle. On the other hand, a toxic person will suggest that you go to the pub together and "just have a few rounds".

6/ **People who try to change us from the person we are into the person that they want us to be.** We are all unique, and if someone tries to trample on our individuality and turn us into someone we're not, then they're not a good person for us to be around. It's really hard to be happy when someone's forcing their beliefs about how we should look, act or think down our throats.

What if we're still not sure about a particular person?

We can use everything we've learned so far in this chapter to help us figure out who the "right" and who the "wrong" and/or "toxic" people to surround ourselves with are. However, there may be times when we're still not quite sure about a particular person, which can sometimes happen when they possess a few of the characteristics we value in a friend, but they also possess some of the toxic traits we want nothing to do with. In such an instance, it helps to ask ourselves the following question, which can serve to give us a definitive answer.

After I've spent time with that person, how do I feel?

If you feel in a positive mood after you see them, then that's a "good" person for you to spend your time with. However, as you probably know from experience, there are certain people who will repeatedly leave you feeling down after you've engaged with them. Maybe you find that your confidence is lower because they don't believe in you. Maybe you feel exhausted because they dump their problems on you all the time. Maybe you feel angry because every time you have some good news, instead of celebrating it with you, they are jealous, spiteful, and try to minimise your success. Whatever it may be, here's the critical point to note: if you continuously feel down after spending time with someone, then it's not in your best interest to be around that person.

As the saying goes, throughout our lives, we will constantly meet angels and devils, and we only know who is who *after* we've met them.

What if the toxic person in our lives is a family member? Or, someone we've known for a really long time?

Being family does not preclude someone from being a toxic person. Just because someone is a parent, sibling, in-law, cousin, aunt or uncle, it doesn't strip them of their power to have a very negative impact on our lives. Accordingly, if we have a family member who either exhibits a lot of the toxic traits we've talked about or who does not have the characteristics that we value in a friend, then I think it behoves us to distance ourselves from that person. I know it can be difficult. I know it's not always practical to cut them completely out of our lives. However, I still think it's worth putting as much space between them and us as we can. At the end of the day, our happiness is too important to have them compromise it.

The same goes for someone we've been friends with for a very long time. They can be toxic too, and sometimes there comes a time in our relationship with that person when we have to move on. Once again, our happiness is too important to have them poison it.

Key takeaways from this chapter

1/ People who possess the characteristics and personality traits that we value in a friend are the "right" people for us to surround ourselves with, because we're likely to have very positive, healthy relationships with those people. On the other hand, people who do not possess the characteristics and personality traits that we value in a friend are the "wrong" people for us to surround ourselves with, because we're likely to have very negative, toxic relationships with those people.

2/ People who are judgmental, who are jealous, who don't believe in us, who take their anger and frustration out on us when something doesn't go right in their life, who bring out the worst in us, who try to change us, and most importantly, who leave us feeling down after we've spent time with them are toxic people for us to surround ourselves with.

3/ Just because someone is family or someone we've known for a very long time, it does not preclude them from being a toxic person.

CHAPTER 8

Common Cause of People's Depression #7:

Being a prisoner of what other people think

Judging by all the emails I get, I know that being held captive by what other people think is a huge trigger for a lot of people's depression. Now, I would never say that we should completely ignore what everyone else thinks and never take into consideration anything they say, because it's undoubtedly good to listen to others and be mindful of their thoughts. However, I do believe that we should stop short of becoming *prisoners* of their opinions, because that can lead us to do things against our better judgment, or to do things that aren't in our own best interest – and this can certainly lead to depression.

In what ways is it possible to be prisoners of what other people think of us?

We can be held captive by what other people think of us in two main ways.

1/ By defining ourselves by what others think of us

Remember when we talked about the importance of basing our love for ourselves on reasons that are *in our control*, that are *independent of what other people think of us*, and that are *independent of circumstances*? And, remember when we said that when we *don't* do this – i.e. when we instead base our love for ourselves on what other people think of us – then we give those people so much power over our happiness?

Speaking from the heart, I truly believe that one of the reasons why I'm so happy today is because I really don't mind what other people think of me. And if you remember from earlier on, this is because I don't base my love for myself on what other people think of me. If people think I'm a freak because I used to suffer from depression, then I don't mind. If they don't like something I write somewhere, I don't mind. I don't need their validation to be able to love myself, because I have a whole bunch of reasons to love myself that are *independent* of what other people think of me. And this is really important, because when we love ourselves for reasons that are independent of what others think of us, we can free ourselves from their opinions, and as a result, greatly ease our depression.

2/ By letting what others think of us govern the decisions we make

We are also prisoners of what other people think of us when we allow them to govern the decisions we make, which can be a major problem for people with depression. For example, I've spoken to countless people who've told me something along the lines of:

'I know that seeking help is a good idea, but what will everyone think of me if I do? They might think I'm crazy . . . and that scares me. So I haven't sought help.'

In this case, letting what other people may think of us dictate the decisions we make is having a detrimental effect on our health and happiness, since seeking help is vital to recovering from depression (just for the record by the way, chances are that not many people – if anyone – are going to think you're "crazy" for seeing a psychologist).

Letting what other people think of us govern the decisions we make can also harm us in many other aspects of our lives. For example, it can cause us to pursue a career we don't really enjoy, get romantically involved with someone we don't really love, end a romantic relationship with someone we *do* really love, waste money on something that we don't really want, or cause us to make practically any other bad decision you can think of.

I understand how scary it can sometimes be to follow our hearts and go against what other people may think of us, but the truth is that if we don't, then we will end up being the person that *other people* want us to be, instead of the person that *we* want to be.

You might be thinking:

OK, I get that in theory, and I agree, but how do I actually go about emotionally freeing myself from what other people think of me so that I'm then able to make decisions that aren't dictated by what they think?

Well, here's a notion that's always helped me.

When trying to free ourselves from what other people think of us, it helps to remember a line from Dr Seuss: *"those who matter don't mind and those who mind don't matter"*.

I really do believe this. The "right" people are going to be supportive of the decisions we make, and if someone's not, then like we said in the previous chapter, they're probably not a person we want to spend time with anyway. In fact, this is something I can specifically recall my psychologist explaining to me before I released my memoir *Depression is a Liar* in 2013.

'So Danny, how've you been feeling?' he asked when I arrived.

'Yeah, really good on the whole. But I've been a bit nervous lately about publishing my memoir. I mean, hardly anyone knows that I used to suffer from depression . . . so what are they going to say when they find out I used to? And what are they going to say when they find out that it led to alcoholism, drug abuse, medicine-induced psychosis, near-suicide attempts and multiple hospitalisations? What if some of my friends read my book, conclude that I'm a freak, and then decide they don't want to be friends with me anymore?'

'I don't think anyone is going to think that,' my psychologist said. 'But even if a few people do, I don't think it really matters.'

I was shocked.

'Huh? How can you say that it doesn't matter?'

My psychologist smiled at me gently.

'When you release your memoir, Danny, there are going to be a lot of people who find it inspiring, uplifting and encouraging – and dare I say it, I think there are going to be some people who find it life-saving. However, you may also get some people who can't deal with it, and for that reason, choose to distance themselves from you. But let me ask you this: if someone chooses to distance themselves from you because they don't like your past or because they think you're a "freak", as you put it, then do you think you'd ever be able to have a good relationship with that person anyway?'

I thought about it for a few moments.

'No,' I eventually said. 'I guess not.'

'Would you even want to be friends with them?'

I considered that question for another few moments before shaking my head.

'No.'

'So then why would you care if a few people think like that after reading your memoir? Those who matter don't mind, and those who mind don't matter, remember?'

I really took that advice to heart, and ever since that conversation, I've never worried about what people think of me (just for the record, though, almost everyone I know was really supportive when they read my memoir – no-one called me a "freak" or anything like that, and I realised that I needn't have worried so much about people judging me).

Key takeaways from this chapter

1/ When we become prisoners of what other people think of us, it hurts us in two main ways:

    a) By leading us to do things against our better judgment;

    b) By leading us to do things that aren't in our own best interests.

2/ To free ourselves from what other people think of us, we want to:

    a) Make sure that we love ourselves for reasons that are *independent* of what other people think of us;

    b) Remember that those who matter don't mind, and those who mind don't matter.

CHAPTER 9

Common Cause of People's Depression #8:

Forgetting that we're only a part – and often only a very small part – of everyone else's world

Let me start this chapter by asking you a very important question:

When you have an interaction with someone that doesn't go according to plan, do you automatically assume that it's "your fault", or a consequence of one of your "personal failings"?

For example, you give your boss what you feel is a really good piece of work, but your boss isn't particularly enthusiastic about it – and as a result, you jump to the conclusion that your boss doesn't value your contribution at all, and that you're the weak link in the team.

Another example: your partner says they're not in the mood to have sex, and you jump to the conclusion that they're losing interest in you.

A third example: you go on a date with someone, and they don't call you for a second date – or, when you call them, they turn you down; as a result, you then jump to the conclusion that you're boring and unattractive.

Have you ever done something like this before?

I know I have. I've definitely exacerbated my depression in the past by convincing myself that the way someone else reacts to something I've done is a direct reflection on me.

But what I eventually learned is that when we think like this, what we're doing is completely ignoring the fact that the way someone reacts to us is not only a reflection on us, but also a reflection on *them* and *their* circumstances.

Let's go back to our examples.

Firstly, you give your boss what you feel is a really good piece of work, but they aren't enthusiastic about it – and as a result, you jump to the conclusion that your boss doesn't value your contribution, and that you're the weak link in the team. But, isn't it also possible that your boss was just in a bad mood because of something else that's entirely unrelated to you, and that their less-than-enthusiastic response to your work was just a projection of their prior irritation? And, if you're honest with yourself, haven't you done this before? Hasn't there been a time when your partner or your friend or your son or your daughter has come to you with something they're really excited about, but you brushed them off because you were angry or upset about something else?

Now let's turn to our second example, where your partner says they're not in the mood to have sex, and you then jump to the conclusion that they're losing interest in you. Now, anything's possible – maybe your partner *is* losing interest in you. But, isn't it also possible that they're just tired and not in the mood? Isn't it also possible that they're stressed out about something else, and for that reason, don't want to have sex? Isn't it also possible that they have something on early the next morning and just want to get some sleep? Aren't any of these reasons possible – in addition to a bunch of other reasons? And, hasn't there been a time when you've done the exact same thing yourself? Haven't you turned down having sex with your partner before not because you were no longer attracted to them, but because of some other reason that's completely unrelated to them?

What about our third example, where a first date with someone doesn't lead to a second, so you jump to the conclusion that you're boring and unattractive. But let me ask you: isn't it also possible that the reason that person decided against going on a second date with you is not because they think you're boring and unattractive, but because they have a fear of commitment? Or because they met someone else? Or because they're coming off a recent break-up and on second thoughts, aren't ready to start dating another person yet? And again, haven't you at some point decided not to go on a second date with someone for a reason that has absolutely nothing to do with that person?

Here's the point: just because somebody has a
less than positive response to something we do,

we can't jump to negative conclusions about ourselves. When we do this, we are completely ignoring the fact that we are only a part – and often only a very small part – of that person's world. They – like us – have got a million things going on in their head that influence their decisions and their responses to certain events, and for this reason, it's entirely possible that when they have a less than positive reaction to something we say or do, that it has absolutely nothing to do with us.

Knowing this, and being conscious of it, can be a very powerful, soothing concept that can eliminate a lot of our stress and significantly ease our depression.

Key takeaways from this chapter

1/ Just because somebody has a less than positive response to something we say or do, we can't jump to negative conclusions about ourselves. Doing so completely ignores the fact that we are only a part – and often only a very small part – of that person's world.

2/ For this reason, it's entirely possible that when someone else has a less than positive reaction to something we say or do, that it has absolutely nothing to do with us.

CHAPTER 10

Common Cause of People's Depression #9:

Living an unbalanced life

In order for us to live a balanced life, we need to:

- Make sure that we're bringing in enough money to live off;
- Take care of our bodies by eating well, sleeping well and exercising frequently;
- Satisfy each of our core values (to refresh your memory, our core values are the things that mean the most to us in the world).

Sometimes it's OK to be temporarily unbalanced – for example, a student studying for his final year exams may choose to bury himself in his books and not see his friends for a few months, or pull an all-nighter cramming just before a test. However, if the student constantly lives this way – and if any of us continuously live an unbalanced life – it's likely to seriously trigger our depression.

What can we do to live a more balanced life?

Add structure to our days

It's certainly possible to live a very *un*structured yet balanced life, but it's been my observation that most of us are better at maintaining a balance when we make a point of scheduling time to do all the different things that we want to do. For example, if we don't set aside time to exercise, it often doesn't get done. However, if we schedule in our diaries to go to the gym at 6pm every Monday and Thursday, it's much more likely that we'll actually go.

Listen to our mind and body

If we're not doing enough of one thing or overdoing another, our mind or body will usually tell us. For example, if we constantly feel tired, then our body's trying to let us know that we need to sleep more. If we're feeling mentally drained and exhausted, then our mind's trying to warn us that we're working too hard.

Listen to our loved ones

For example, if our partner's complaining that we're always at work and never home, then they probably have a point.

Establish boundaries between "work time" and "leisure time"

It's good to work hard while we're in the office, but in the interest of living a balanced life, it's best if we leave our work at work. If we're always bringing files home or checking our smartphones to see if our boss has emailed, then we're making it very hard for ourselves to "switch off" and achieve a desirable work/life balance.

Let technology help us!

Because living a balanced life is something that so many of us struggle with, there are an abundance of apps that have been developed to help us do it. I recommend using one or more of the following, all of which are free or only cost a few dollars:

1/ **iPlanSuccess:** By allowing you to define your values, strengths and the ways you deal with being busy, this clever app helps you set realistic goals in order to achieve a better balance between your work and personal life.

2/ **Cozi Family Organiser:** This app lets you keep track of your family members' schedules so that you can know when they're free and thus set aside time to spend with them.

3/ **SelfControl:** This app lets you block access to distracting websites, your mail servers, or anything else on the internet for a pre-defined period of time. In addition to being a great productivity app, it will help you achieve a more balanced life by forcing you to take a time-out from work and do something else.

4/ **Timer+:** Like we've said, it's much easier to live a balanced life when we make a point of setting aside time to do each of the things that we want to do. This app helps you do that by allowing you to set a time limit on what you're doing so that you don't run over time and miss out on doing something else. Multiple timers can be set at once, and alerts can be sent out even when the timer's running in the background.

5/ **CrunchTime**: The aim of this app is to provide busy users with an improved knowledge of how they spend their time, and to help them achieve a better balance between all their activities. Similar to the iPlanSuccess app, CrunchTime lets you set work-life balance goals in the areas of hours worked, sleep time, overtime worked, mood, weight and vacation taken, and awards you with an achievement badge every time a goal is met.

6/ **Balanced**: This app allows you to track the things you wish you did more often, and helps motivate you to do them again. Balanced will acknowledge when you achieve a goal by giving you positive feedback, will allow you to prioritise your activities in order of importance, will give you a list of 50 uplifting activities that you can do to improve your life, and much more.

7/ **Life Balance**: Marketed as personal coaching software, Life Balance dynamically adjusts your to-do list as you check off completed tasks to help you manage your time more efficiently.

8/ **Wonderful Life Plan**: This app allows you to set short, medium and long term goals and helps you keep track of whether or not you're achieving them.

If we suffer from depression, we also need to set aside time to …

We said before that in order to be happy and to live a balanced life, we need to make sure that we're satisfying each of our core values, in addition to making sure that we're bringing home enough money to live off, and that we're taking care of our bodies by eating well, sleeping well and exercising frequently. This is 100% true, but if we suffer from depression, there's also one other critically important thing that we need to make time for in our lives.

> If we're suffering from depression, then part of living a balanced life involves doing the things that we need to do in order to recover from depression – such as seeing a therapist, reading self-help books such as this one, keeping mood diaries, and anything else that will help us understand what is causing us to feel depressed or help us to deal with that underlying cause.

While I haven't said this explicitly, it's certainly been implied that recovery from depression does *not* happen by being passive. It happens by confronting our demons, and then fighting like hell to try and beat them. Accordingly, in order to recover from depression, we need to make time to do whatever it takes for us to recover. We can't afford to be "too busy" to do such things.

Taking this into account, an amended list of things we need to do to live a balanced life if we suffer from depression would thus be:

- Making sure that we're bringing in enough money to live off;
- Taking care of our bodies by eating well, sleeping well and exercising frequently;
- Satisfying each of our core values;
- Doing whatever we need to do in order to recover from depression.

Key takeaways from this chapter

1/ In order to live a balanced life, we need to make sure that we're making enough money to live off; taking care of our bodies by eating well, sleeping well and exercising frequently; and satisfying each of our core values.

2/ To live a balanced life, it helps if we do the following:

   a) Structure and plan our days;

   b) Listen to our mind and body;

   c) Listen to our loved ones;

   d) Establish boundaries between our "work" time and our "leisure" time;

   e) Use one or more of the many apps that exist for just this purpose.

3/ If we suffer from depression, then we also need to set aside time to do the things that we need to do in order to recover.

CHAPTER 11

Common Cause of People's Depression #10:

Perfectionism

There's a lot to be said for being a perfectionist, as it pushes us to strive for excellence and to reach our true potential. However, it can also be a double-edged sword, which I learned at 19 when my perfectionism plunged me into depression. After two miserable years, I wound up in a psych ward, and quickly discovered how prevalent a problem it really was. Out of the 20 or so group therapy sessions I attended during that particular two week stay, the one on perfectionism drew by far the biggest crowd – the room was so packed that people had to bring in extra seats from their bedrooms, and latecomers had to sit on the floor. At the time, I was shocked. I had no idea that perfectionism was an Achilles heel for so many people. It always seemed to me to be such a good trait to have, so how was it that it had affected so many people so negatively?

As the session progressed, there emerged three main ways in which perfectionism seemed to harm people. We'll hash each of them out below, and talk about how we can stop these tendencies from triggering our depression.

Perfectionism can lead us to measure our self-worth in terms of how "perfectly" we achieve our goals – which can lead us to feel worthless, inadequate, like a failure, and to hate ourselves

This was one of the main causes of my depression. Below is an excerpt from my memoir *Depression is a Liar*, where my psychologist summarised how my perfectionism triggered me and explained what I had to do to manage that trigger.

'You relentlessly seek excellence, Danny, and you always set extremely challenging goals and then throw yourself into achieving them. Being perfectionistically goal-driven like this is fine in and of itself, but the problem with you is that you measure your self-worth entirely in terms of whether or not you achieve these goals. If you don't achieve a goal that you set out to achieve- like getting a High Distinction average at university or getting your novel [that I'd been working on] published by a particular point in time, you hate yourself. You feel worthless and inadequate. You feel like a failure. And you feel this pain so intensely that you become suicidal.

'You're human, Danny, and humans, by our very composition, are not perfect. Humans make mistakes. Humans don't always achieve their goals. You need to accept this, and not be so hard on yourself. You need to accept this, and be able to love yourself regardless. You need to be able to love yourself regardless of how you go in your uni exams and no matter what happens with your novel. Even if you fail every exam for the rest of your degree and your novel never gets published, you should still be able to love yourself. You should be able to find elements of yourself that you love that will be there no matter what. That will let you love yourself no matter what.'

He paused for a moment.

'If you can do this, then I think you'll go a long way towards conquering your depression.'

Over the next week or so, I battled to find things about myself that I liked. To find reasons that weren't related to "success" or "achievement" or anything of that nature was very hard for me, because they weren't ideas I'd ever considered before. All that had ever mattered to me was whether or not I was achieving my goals. If I was, or was on track to, then I loved myself. If I hadn't, or was not on track to, then I hated myself. The concept of loving myself regardless of whether or not I succeeded was completely foreign to me. But after a long time pondering, I finally managed to write the list that I included in the earlier chapter about learning how to love ourselves for healthy reasons. And when I focused on those healthy reasons, I could actually see that there really was a lot to love about me.

I actually am a good person, I remember thinking. *And this really is true, regardless of what my marks are at university or whether or not my novel ever gets published. These are the reasons why I can love myself, and whether I succeed or fail has nothing to do with it.*

This was such an empowering revelation, and once I'd made it, I took a huge step forward in conquering my depression.

If you too pin your self-worth to how well you achieve your goals, then I'd recommend writing a similar list of your own. Doing so, and having a revelation comparable to the one I had, doesn't mean you stop striving to achieve your goals – rather, it just means that you stop hating yourself when you don't fulfil them.

Being perfectionistic can cause us to be neglectful

Because being perfectionistic leads us to be goal-orientated and pushes us to do our best in everything we do, it can sometimes lead us to neglect other things that matter – like our family or our health. For example, if we're always working late, then we may climb the corporate ladder quickly – but if we sacrifice exercising, then our health is going to suffer, and if we never socialise, then so will our relationships. Because of our hard work, we may well speed up the ranks – but is it really worth it if our partner leaves us? Or if we put on 60 pounds and develop diabetes?

One approach that's helped me keep things more in perspective is making a conscious effort to focus more on trying to be "happy" as opposed to trying to be "successful". They both certainly overlap to some degree, but I think the former is a vastly more well-rounded approach to life, and ever since adopting it, I've been much happier and healthier.

Perfectionism can lead us to procrastinate things or never get them finished

Doing things perfectly – or at least, to the very best of our ability – can be much more time consuming than just doing things well. And because us perfectionists are aware of this, we can often fall into the trap of putting off doing certain tasks altogether, because we can't find the time to do them "perfectly". Alternatively, we can spend so long trying to do something perfectly that we end up spending too long on it or never getting it finished (I've found this to particularly be the case with projects that don't have a time deadline per se, such as writing my first novel or designing a website for my charity). In such cases, and in the cases where perfectionism leads us to procrastinate, I think it's important to remind ourselves that a job well done – albeit not a job perfectly done – is still better than a job not done at all.

Keep sharpening the good side of the sword, but try to blunt the bad side, too

We started this chapter by saying that perfectionism has a lot of positive aspects to it. This is definitely true, and for this reason, we certainly don't want to throw the baby out with the bath water just because it has the potential to lead to problems down the line. In my opinion, the best thing for us perfectionists to do is to just be mindful of the ways it may be hurting us, and if we find that it is, then take the necessary steps to correct it. On the whole, perfectionism is a great quality to have – we just have to make sure that it isn't triggering our depression and destroying our life.

Key takeaways from this chapter

1/ Being perfectionistic is a good thing, because it pushes us to strive for excellence and to reach our true potential. However, it also has its downfalls when it:

    a) Leads us to measure our self-worth in terms of how "perfectly" we achieve our goals – which can lead us to feel worthless, inadequate, like a failure, and to hate ourselves;

    b) Leads us to neglect some of life's most important aspects, such as our health and our relationships;

    c) Leads us to procrastinate things or never quite finish them.

2/ We can prevent our perfectionistic tendencies from triggering our depression by:

    a) Loving ourselves unconditionally.

    b) Focusing on trying to be "happy" as opposed to being "successful".

    c) Reminding ourselves that a job well done – albeit not a job perfectly done – is still better than a job not done at all.

CHAPTER 12

Common Cause of People's Depression #11:

Living an unhealthy lifestyle

Seemingly trivial things like eating well, sleeping well and exercising are easy things to forget about when we're trapped in the throes of depression. After all, when we're in that place, usually the last thing we want to do is go for a run. However, it's undeniable that if we do make the effort to live a healthy lifestyle, then it will significantly spur on our recovery. We'll talk about how we can do so in this chapter, with an emphasis on eating well, sleeping well and exercising frequently.

Eating well

The dietary guidelines for adults in Australia, as developed by the National Health and Medical Research Council, suggest that we should:

- Eat lots of vegetables, legumes and fruits;
- Eat plenty of cereals, including breads, rice, pasta and noodles (ideally of the wholegrain variety);
- Eat lean meat, fish, poultry and/or alternatives;
- Eat milks, yoghurts, cheeses and/or alternatives (ideally reduced fat substances, where possible);
- Drink lots of water;
- Limit saturated fat intake;
- Lean towards foods that are low in salt;
- Consume only moderate amounts of sugar;

- Minimise how much alcohol we drink.

Tools to help us eat healthily

Like we've said, when we suffer from depression, we're often so consumed with pain that we find it difficult to get anything done, including taking care with our diet and ensuring that we're eating healthily. However, this list of apps will make life easier:

1/ Swap It Don't Stop It: Developed by the Australian government, this app will help you make healthier food choices by showing you how to swap less nutritional foods for more nutritional substitutes, how to save calories, and much more. It's also possible to track your progress and set reminders to inform you when it's time to "make a swap".

2/ Fooducate: This app helps you make healthier choices when grocery shopping by illuminating the quality of calories in each item of food, and suggesting similar yet healthier alternatives.

3/ LoseIt: If it's a weight loss plan you're after, this app can customise a plan for you that will suit your life. You can even start head-to-head, team- and group-based challenges with other people.

4/ HealthyOut: Tell this app your dietary restrictions and nutritional needs and it will suggest what you should eat at your restaurant of choice.

5/ ShopWell: Just by scanning the barcode, this app can tell you which foods at your supermarket meet your dietary needs based on your age, gender, health goals, diet needs, and ingredient and nutrition preferences.

6/ Zipongo: This app helps you eat healthily on the cheap, by letting you know about weekly sales at supermarkets in your area, and digital coupons that can save you money. It also contains lots of healthy eating tips and recipes.

7/ My Diet Coach: This app helps keep you motivated when you start a new weight loss plan by allowing you to upload photos and notes that inspire you, set reminders about what you want to eat and avoid, and make weight loss and fitness goals. You can even keep a food and exercise journal, and receive virtual prizes when you meet your targets.

8/ Calorie Counter and Tracker: Tell this app your age, gender and weight loss goals and it will help you reach them in your desired time frame. It also allows you to keep a food diary and keep track of how much exercise you're doing.

9/ Lifesum: If you prefer counting your kilojoule intake (as opposed to your calorie intake) then this app will help you do it. It also allows you to upload a "before healthy eating image" and helps you keep track of your weight so that you can reach your goals.

10/ Traffic Light Food Tracker: This app helps you compare packaged food products by entering the amount of salt, fat, saturated fat and sugar they contain per 100g. It will then display a traffic light for each nutrient: red indicating "high", yellow indicating "medium", and green indicating "low".

11/ MyFitnessPal: Enter your own recipes into this app and have MyFitnessPal calculate its nutritional information.

Are you drinking too much alcohol?

Like we've said, part of eating healthily involves limiting how much alcohol we drink. I know how tempting it can be to try and drown our depression in booze – being a recovered alcoholic, I've done it countless times myself. However, I can tell you from experience – and there are numerous studies to back me up – that drinking can significantly exacerbate our depression over time. Alcohol is a depressant after all – and, because of this, using it as an escape from our depression creates a devastatingly vicious cycle: we feel depressed, so we drink to feel better, which ultimately leads us to feel more depressed, which leads us to drink more, which leads us to feel even more depressed . . . and so the cycle goes, accelerating quicker and quicker since alcohol is also addictive. When we try to make ourselves feel better like this, we truly do become dogs endlessly chasing our tails.

As it always is with prevention, the less you drink, the better. However, below are some tell-tale signs that you may be hitting the bottle too hard.

1/ You go out with the intention of only having a couple of drinks, but you end up getting drunk;

2/ Your tolerance for alcohol has been increasing;

3/ You start to crave alcohol;

4/ Your drinking interferes with your day-to-day life because you're too drunk or hungover to get what you need to do done;

5/ You frequently go out with the objective of getting drunk;

6/ You continually find yourself in precarious situations while being under the influence;

7/ Your friends and family are hinting – or flat out telling you – that you're drinking too much;

8/ You've started drinking alone;

9/ Whenever something goes wrong or you're having a bad day, one of your first thoughts is, *I need a drink*;

10/ You don't know how to relax without alcohol;

11/ You aren't comfortable in social situations without alcohol;

12/ You plan your social and work calendar around alcohol;

13/ You hide the amount you drink from others;

14/ You've changed your drinking patterns to get drunk quicker (for example, by switching from wine or beer to spirits on the rocks);

15/ You've tried to quit drinking before but you haven't been able to.

If you found yourself relating to a lot of these scenarios, then chances are that your drinking is excessive enough that it's contributing to your depression (and quite possibly creating a number of other problems in your life, too). I'd strongly recommend significantly reducing how much alcohol you drink, and if that idea scares you, or if you've tried to cool it for a while and you haven't been able to, then it's worth seeking professional help.

What about drugs?

This almost goes without saying, but abusing illicit substances, just like drinking too much, will drastically undermine any attempt we make to recover from depression. Just like alcohol, it might help us escape our pain temporarily, but in the long run, it will keep us trapped in it forever.

Exercising

I know exercise is usually the last thing we feel like doing when we're suffering from depression, but if we give ourselves a push and do it, then we're going to enjoy the fruits of our labour. According to numerous studies, regular exercise can increase our level of brain serotonin and brain endorphins, both of which have "mood-lifting" properties. And, luckily for us, research also suggests that exercise doesn't have to be overly rigorous to be effective, with even a brisk walk said to make a noticeable difference.

Tools to help us exercise

This list of apps will help you create, strive for and reach your exercise goals:

1/ Cody: This app connects you with a fitness community where you can share and discover workouts complete with video, photo, and text instructions. Your friends are able to like and comment on your workout activity to help keep you motivated, and you can use the app's detailed statistical timeline to track your progress.

2/ Fitness Fast: This app provides instructions for a range of exercises targeting key muscles for pre-loaded or personally customised workouts. It also number-crunches a bunch of stats and other workout-related information, and offers a community forum for you to share and receive fitness information from others.

3/ Pact: This app uses financial incentives to encourage you to exercise. Each week, you'll pledge a set number of hours that you plan on exercising, and pledge a set amount of money that you'll pay up if you don't hit your target. If you do fulfil your pledge, however, then you'll get paid! If you like the sound of this, then you can also use this app to enter into nutritional pacts, where you'll pay up if you don't achieve your healthy eating target, and get paid if you do.

4/ EveryMove: This rewards-based app lets you earn rewards points with different retailers when you exercise.

5/ Moves: This app calculates how many calories you're burning when you're running, walking or cycling.

6/ The Walk: Make exercise fun by turning a routine stroll into an incredible adventure! This app tracks how long and how far you've walked while you participate in games where your mission is to save the world. Before you begin your walk, you can choose an episode. The longer you walk, the more clues are revealed to help you in your quest.

7/ SecondsPro: This app allows you to create an extremely detailed, customised timer to help you complete your workouts. Even better, it can integrate with your I-pod, allowing you to assign playlists or tracks to individual timer intervals.

8/ Spring Moves: This app will scientifically create a personalised playlist for you based on your running rhythm!

9/ Strava Cycling: This app allows you to connect with other cyclists and challenge them to riding races. It also lets you and your friends support one another in each of your quests to achieve your cycling goals.

10/ <u>Charity Miles</u>: With this app, each mile you run, walk or cycle raises money for different non-profit organisations.

11/ <u>Fitness Builder</u>: This app gives you access to a library of over 5,600 exercise images and videos, and even gives you the option of picking a personal trainer's brain for advice.

12/ <u>Daily Workouts</u>: Perfect for busy people trying to squeeze in a workout on the fly, this app allows you to choose how long you want to exercise (10, 15, 20, 25 or 30 minutes) and which area of your body you want to focus on. It then suggests an exercise for you to do, and shows you exactly how to do it.

Sleeping well

Depression is notorious for disrupting our sleep, but that doesn't change the fact that in order to recover, it really helps to get an average of seven or eight hours of sleep every night. To help you do so, I encourage you to use one or more of the following apps:

1/ <u>SleepCycle</u>: This app will analyse your sleep patterns and, within a desired interval, wake you up when you're in your lightest sleep phase so that you can start your day feeling more refreshed and energised. It can also map your sleep patterns over time to show how factors such as alcohol or exercise affect your rest.

2/ <u>Sleep</u>: This app plays soothing sounds, gentle lullabies and tranquil music to relax you in preparation for a good night of shuteye.

3/ <u>Insomnia Cure</u>: Containing hours of audio content and 40 pages of insomnia tips and learning tools, this app can finally help you get a good night's sleep.

4/ <u>Nature Sounds Relax and Sleep</u>: Whether it's a crackling campfire, songbirds, or the roar of the ocean surf that you find most relaxing, this app will help you unwind so that you fall asleep. All soundtracks are also accompanied by calming images.

5/ <u>Long Deep Breathing</u>: This app will teach you mindful breathing techniques that you can use to relax and help you fall asleep naturally.

6/ <u>SleepBot</u>: This app uses motion and sleep tracking capabilities to help you understand your sleep patterns, which can then help you make better decisions to improve your sleep habits. It's also got an extensive database of sleep resources to teach you about good sleep hygiene, and allows you to keep track of your sleep history by date, sleep time, wake time, hours of sleep, or amount of sleep lost.

Key takeaways from this chapter

1/ In order to recover from depression, it's critical that we live a healthy lifestyle. This includes:

a) Eating well;

b) Laying off drugs and alcohol;

c) Exercising frequently;

d) Sleeping well.

2/ When we suffer from depression, living healthily can seem an overwhelming and sometimes impossible task. However, if we use a few of the countless apps that have been specifically developed to help us take better care of ourselves, then it will become a whole lot easier.

CHAPTER 13

Common Cause of People's Depression #12:

Having too many negative thoughts and not enough positive thoughts

It's no secret that when we have a negative thought, it can have a negative impact on our mood.

For example, thinking "nobody likes me" can cause us to feel sad.

Thinking that our partner is about to break up with us can make us feel scared and depressed.

Thinking that we're inadequate can make us feel jealous of other people.

Not only that, but studies have shown that when we have a negative thought, the left pre-frontal cortex part of our brain ("LPC") will then begin looking for examples in our lives that validate that negative thought.

For example, if we think the thought that "nobody likes me", then our LPC will automatically be steered towards finding more and more evidence to reinforce the belief that no-one likes us.

If we think that our partner's about to break up with us, then our LPC is going to go crazy looking for all sorts of signs to confirm the belief that we're about to get dumped.

And, if we think that we're inadequate, then our LPC is going to be focused on looking for more and more reasons to suggest that we're not as good as everybody else.

Due to the way our left pre-frontal cortexes work, negative thoughts set into motion a very poisonous cycle: the more negative thoughts we have, the harder our LPCs work to validate those thoughts . . . and the harder our LPCs work to validate those thoughts, the more negative thoughts we have . . . etcetera, etcetera, etcetera. As a result, one negative thought sets off a chain reaction of even stronger negative thoughts – negative thoughts that are so strong they can plunge us into depression.

Accordingly, in order to recover from depression, it's vital that we learn how to deal with those negative thoughts.

How can we manage our negative thoughts?

The following practices will help prevent us from experiencing negative thoughts, or help us deal with them when we do.

Challenge our negative thoughts

Our brains are great at playing tricks on us, often causing us to view our circumstances through pessimistic lenses. For this reason, in order to perceive our circumstances accurately and not allow our negative thoughts about those circumstances to trigger our depression, we need to challenge the rationality of our negative thoughts by asking ourselves the following questions:

- **What evidence is there to suggest that this thought is true? What evidence is there to suggest that it's false?** Remember how our left pre-frontal cortexes work? By looking for all the evidence they can to validate our negative thoughts? For this reason, when we take a step back and examine the evidence that is contrary to what our negative thoughts are telling us, we often end up with a much more accurate perception of our circumstances, and realise that they aren't as dire as we originally thought.
- **Is there a more positive, accurate way that I could be viewing this situation or circumstance?** In most cases, there usually is.
- **What would I tell my friend if they came to me saying that they're thinking this negatively about something in their life?** Asking ourselves this question has the effect of distancing ourselves from our circumstances and looking at them from a different, more objective angle.

Avoid "black or white" thinking

When we think in terms of "black or white", everything is either good or bad, a success or a failure – there's nothing in between.

For example, *I'm not as well prepared for this exam as I'd like to be, so instead of acing it, I'm going to flunk.*

I know I don't look my best because I only had two minutes to get ready, so I must look terrible.

I said one silly little thing in my job interview today, so the whole thing was a complete disaster.

Thinking in this way can trigger our depression, because it leads us to conclude that just because something didn't – or isn't likely to – turn out perfectly, then it must be – or will be – an unmitigated catastrophe.

However, when we think of our circumstances in such a rigid way, what we're not doing is acknowledging that in reality, there are many shades of grey, and that even though things may not turn out perfectly, they can still turn out OK.

Avoid making everything "about us"

Remember: if someone has a negative reaction to something we say or do, we can't jump to negative conclusions about ourselves. Doing so completely ignores the fact that we are only a part – and often only a very small part – of that person's world.

Avoid "filter thinking"

"Filter thinking" is when we filter out all the praise that is coming our way and instead only listen to the criticism. For example, our university professor returns our essay – it gets 90% and receives lots of positive feedback, but our professor also offers some constructive criticism and suggestions for improvement – however, instead of focusing on all the good things we did, we completely block them out, and only focus on what we didn't do well. As a result, we conclude that we're not very clever, and begin to feel depressed.

To avoid "filter thinking", it helps to get a piece of paper and make two columns – one for the positive feedback we received, and one for the not-so-positive feedback. Then, we want to write down all the feedback we received in their respective columns. If we're thinking with a filter, we'll soon realise that we're blowing the negative feedback we received out of proportion.

Minimise the time we spend doing things that trigger negative thoughts

We can reduce the number of negative thoughts we have by figuring out what causes us to think negative thoughts, and then making a determined effort to minimise – and ideally eliminate – the time we spend doing such things.

For example, I find the news very negative, because in Australia at least, most of what's shown on the news is bad news. I'm not denying that bad things happen in the world, but beautiful, miraculous, unbelievably positive things occur every day as well – and yet for some reason, it's usually only the tragedies that hit the air. Accordingly, I find the news to be a skewed portrayal of life, and in the vast majority of cases, anything but uplifting. Consequently, watching the news leads me to have negative thoughts. Whenever I used to watch it, I'd find myself thinking,

Wow, there really are a lot of bad things happening in the world! It's all just one heartbreaking incident after another. How come nothing good ever happens?

And when I had these thoughts, my LPC would then look to further validate them by finding all the evidence it could to support their premise. Accordingly, I'd find myself zeroing in on all the sad and devastating things that were happening in the world, and completely ignoring all the good things that were simultaneously occurring. As a result, my mood would nosedive.

For this reason, part of my recovery from depression involved – as silly and as trivial as it sounds – me deciding to quit watching the news. And ever since I've stopped doing so, I've felt a whole lot better.

In terms of *how* we can figure out what's causing us to think negative thoughts, we can keep a thought diary. Similar in concept to keeping a mood diary, taking note of all the things that cause us to think negative thoughts can help us figure out what we're doing that is causing us to think so negatively. After we've pinpointed those causes, we can then take steps to minimise the time we spend on them.

Avoid trying to predict the future

Sometimes when something hasn't worked out well in the past, we convince ourselves that that something's destined never to work out in the future as well. But if we learn everything we can from the experience the first time something goes awry, then we'll be much more prepared the next time to ensure a better result. Primarily for this reason, history does not have to repeat itself. If we can remember this, and learn to take things on a case-by-case basis, then we can eliminate a lot of our negative thinking, and be all the happier for it.

Distinguish our thoughts from reality

Instead of saying, for example, "no-one likes me" and accepting it as reality, it can help to instead say, "I'm having the thought that no-one likes me". Although this may seem like a trivial distinction, doing this gives us distance from our thoughts, and helps us realise that that's all they are – thoughts – as opposed to cold, hard, irrefutable facts.

Avoid toxic people

Toxic people certainly have the power to cause us to think negative thoughts, and the sooner we distance ourselves from them, the less negatively we'll think.

Do our minds work the "other way", too?

When I first learned about how our negative thoughts affect our mood and about the power of our LPCs to contribute to our depression by looking for evidence to verify our negative thoughts, I immediately wondered if our brains also worked the "other way", too.

If I have a positive *thought,* I remember thinking, *then does that mean that our LPCs will look for evidence to validate that thought too, and as a result, contribute to putting us in a positive mood?*

And the answer, I was pleased to find out, is yes! That's exactly how our LPCs work!

For example, when we have a positive thought like "my life is good", our LPCs will get to work trying to find all the evidence they can to validate the notion that we have a really good life. As a result, we're likely to find ourselves in a pleasant mood, because we're going to be highly mindful of and focused on all the reasons why we have a good life – as opposed to the reasons that lead us to believe that our life isn't so good.

> For this reason, in order to recover from depression and start living the happy life we want, it's critical that we not only take steps to minimise how many negative thoughts we have, but that we also take steps to *maximise* how many *positive* thoughts we have.

What can we do to have more positive thoughts?

Below is a list of things we can do to have more positive thoughts. You'll notice that we've talked about many of them in different contexts before.

- **Spend more time outdoors.** This may sound frivolous, but exposure to the sun increases the amount of serotonin (AKA the "happy chemical") in our brain.
- **Maximise the time we spend doing things we enjoy.**
- **Surround ourselves with the "right" people for us.**

- **Practice gratitude.**
- **Live healthily – i.e. eat well, sleep well and exercise frequently.**

Key takeaways from this chapter

1/ Our thoughts control our moods, and due to the way the left prefrontal cortex part of our brain works, one negative thought can set off a chain reaction of even stronger negative thoughts, which can have the power to trigger our depression.

2/ We can reduce or eliminate our negative thoughts by challenging their validity, avoiding "black or white" thinking, not making everything "about us", avoiding "filter thinking", minimising the time we spend doing things that trigger negative thoughts, reminding ourselves that the future doesn't have to be the same as the past, distinguishing our thoughts from reality, and avoiding toxic people.

3/ We can have more positive thoughts by spending more time in the sun, reading positive affirmations, maximising the time we spend doing things we enjoy, surrounding ourselves with the "right" people for us, practising gratitude, and exercising.

CHAPTER 14

Common Cause of People's Depression #13:

Worrying

When I suffered from depression, this was something that I used to do all the time. Whenever I had an exam at university for example, I remember worrying that I wouldn't study for something that would surprisingly be on the test, and that I'd end up doing badly as a result; I'd worry that I'd misread the exam details and turn up to the wrong room; or, I'd worry that I'd oversleep my alarm and not turn up at all. Worrying can be beneficial when it galvanises us to do what's necessary to solve a problem, but if we're obsessing over "what-ifs" and worst-case scenarios like so, then it can significantly trigger our depression.

What can we do to stop worrying so much?

What my psychologist taught me is that when we find ourselves worrying, the first thing we want to do is stop and take a few minutes to *dissect* our worry. Specifically, we want to ask ourselves the following question:

Is there something I can do to fix the problem that's troubling me? Or, is what I'm worrying about out of my control?

Now, if there's something we can do to fix the problem that's troubling us, then we need to turn our attention to doing everything we can to fix it.

However, if we find that we're worrying about something that is out of our control, then it means that our worrying is unproductive, and is doing nothing more than stressing us out and igniting our depression. For this reason, it's vital that we stop worrying about whatever we're worrying about. The following suggestions can help us do this.

Challenge our worry

Similar to when we're thinking negatively, when we're jumping to conclusions, fretting over "what-ifs" and going crazy thinking about all the worst possible scenarios that could ever take place, what we're usually doing is viewing our circumstances in a much darker light than they really are. Such pessimistic thinking can often come very naturally to us, but in order to prevent our worry from destroying our lives, we need to retrain our brains to think about our circumstances more realistically – i.e. in their proper, brighter light.

In order to do this, we need to start by zeroing in on our worrying thought. Then, instead of accepting it as gospel, we must challenge its validity by asking the following questions (a few of which will sound familiar):

- **What evidence is there to suggest that this thought is true? What evidence is there to suggest that it's false?**
- **Is there a more positive, accurate way that I could be viewing this situation or circumstance?**
- **Realistically, what is the probably that what I'm stressing out about will actually take place?** Studies indicate that 85% of what we worry about never happens. In all likelihood, what we're worrying about is much less likely to occur than we think.
- **If what I'm stressing out about does take place, does it mean that my life is over? Or, will I be able to cope with it and recover in time?** Studies also indicate that even if what we're

worrying about does occur, then 80% of us handle it better than we originally thought we would. We need to give ourselves credit for being stronger than we think, and acknowledge that even if something bad does unfortunately take place, that we have the strength to survive it and overcome it in time.

- **What would I tell my friend if they came to me saying that they're worrying about this problem?** When I ask myself this question, most of the time I envision myself saying to my friend, "just try to relax . . . everything is going to be OK". And when I imagine myself saying this, I realise that my worrying is nothing more than over-reacting, and then I'm able to let it go.

Tolerate uncertainty

After I'd quit Commerce/Law to pursue my dream of becoming an author, there were times when I'd worry that my novel would never get published and that instead of achieving my dream, I'd wind up a broke, lonely, miserable old man. But then my psychologist offered me some advice that has stuck with me ever since.

'I think you need to focus more on the journey you're on, and less on the end outcome,' he said one day when I expressed my concerns to him. 'It's going to be a while before your novel is completely finished and ready to try and publish, so there's no need to think about what's going to happen then until the moment's upon you. Right now, just enjoy yourself. After all, you're writing full-time – right now, you're *already* living your dream! Experience it to the full. Be wholly present in the moment. Enjoy it for what it is instead of fretting about whether or not you'll get published and what may or may not happen if you don't. Whenever you do stress about all that, you're only taking away from your enjoyment of this exciting journey that you're embarking upon. Later on, if you do end up getting rejected by every agent and publisher in the business, you can worry. But right now – just forget about it.'

Accordingly, one of the most important steps I took in reducing how much I worried was learning to accept and tolerate uncertainty. Once I'd accepted that it was an inherent part of my life and detrimental to my happiness to worry about, I naturally started focusing more on enjoying the present, and stopped stressing so much about "what-ifs" and worst-case scenarios.

Keep a worry diary

Similar in concept to keeping a mood- or a thoughts diary, taking note of all the things that cause us to worry over time can help us figure out the sources of our worry. We can then take steps to eliminate those sources, and thus become much more at peace with the world.

Keep repeating what we're worried about until we accept it

If we repeat something that we're worried about again and again and again, we'll gradually come to accept that something as a possibility that may occur, and in the course of doing so, it will begin to lose its ability to worry us. For example, if I'd have kept saying to myself, "my novel may never get published, my novel may never get published", then such a notion would have eventually lost its power to scare me.

Write down what we're worrying about

Studies suggest that writing down our worries can help us come to terms with them, and similar to the way repeating them over and over again does, rob them of their power to worry us.

Meditation

Studies indicate that meditating can lower our anxiety levels and greatly reduce how much we worry.

Distract ourselves by doing something enjoyable

If we can lose ourselves in something pleasurable, then we'll be too busy having fun to worry about whatever it is that we shouldn't be worried about.

Exercise

Getting our heart rate up is a great way to relieve our stress and forget about our problems for a while.

Key takeaways from this chapter

1/ When we catch ourselves worrying, we need to stop and ask ourselves the question: *Is there something I can do to fix the problem that's troubling me? Or, is what I'm worrying about out of my control?* If there's something we can do to fix it, then we should try to fix it. However, if there's nothing we can do, then our worrying is unproductive, and it's vital to our mental health that we cease doing so.

2/ We can stop worrying about things that are out of our control by challenging our worry, tolerating uncertainty, keeping a worry diary, keep repeating what we're worrying about until we accept it, writing down what we're worrying about, meditating, distracting ourselves by doing something enjoyable, and exercising.

CHAPTER 15

Common Cause of People's Depression #14:

Struggling to trust someone again after we've been hurt in love

Have you ever been through one of those terrible relationships or break-ups that leave you doubting whether or not you'll ever be able to trust someone again?

I have. And so have countless other people.

In fact, fear of trusting someone again is such a common reaction to being hurt in love that it has its own name: *pistanthrophobia*.

As any of us who've been there will agree, it's an extremely difficult thing to get over. However, if we want to be in a happy, healthy relationship again, then we do need to overcome it. The four suggestions below helped me, and if pistanthrophobia is triggering your depression, then I think they'll also help you get past some of the things that are holding you back from a brighter future.

Don't assume the future will be the same as the past

As you know, my first proper relationship ended when I found out that my girlfriend was cheating on me with one of my best mates; then afterwards – perhaps to get back at me for breaking up with her – I heard that she'd been spreading the (extremely false) rumour that I'd raped her. I was shattered. Combined with some of the other things that were taking place in my life at the time, the experience plunged me into a crippling and near fatal depression, and my ability to trust another girl was destroyed.

Over the next few years, I brought my pistanthrophobia with me on every date I went on, and suffice it to say, there weren't a lot of second dates. My inability to trust another girl was ruining any chance I had of being in a functional relationship, and I wondered if I'd ever be able to overcome it and make things work with a woman.

Eventually however, I started seeing a therapist for my depression. Everything that happened with my ex inevitably came up, and my psychologist gave me a piece of advice that helped me immensely:

Don't cast dispersions on the entire female population because of one bad experience with one bad girl.

I think casting such dispersions is the root cause of the vast majority of people's pistanthrophobia; because we've been hurt by one person – or in some cases, a number of people – we become conditioned to believing that the next person will hurt us too. But projecting this assumption onto the next person isn't being fair. Unless that person has done something to make us wary of trusting them, then they deserve to be given an open-minded chance. It's important that we start each relationship with a clean slate, and not let it be poisoned by our past.

Learn from the past: what were the warning signs that our ex was untrustworthy?

In my case, my ex would constantly break promises, lie, say one thing then do something else, and continuously do things that she knew would bother me. With the benefit of hindsight, it's not surprising that she ended up seriously hurting me. People who have certain self-centred, manipulative and malicious traits are not worthy of our trust. If we can learn from our past relationships to identify such traits and the types of people who aren't to be trusted, then we'll be better at picking a lover the next time around – and knowing that we're wiser and more likely to pick a better lover will make us less scared of getting hurt.

Learn from the past: what were the things that we could have done differently?

The way my ex used to look at my mate, the amount they used to talk to each other on the phone, the amount of time they'd always spend together . . . I was always suspicious that something was going on. But whenever I'd bring it up with her, she'd always stress that they were just friends, and feeling guilty for raising it, I'd let the matter drop – even though my gut was telling me that something wasn't right. In the end of course, I ended up being correct.

The key lesson I learned from this was to trust my instincts. Where there's smoke there's often fire, so if something seems off to us, then it probably is. Part of the lesson I learned is that my girlfriend should have addressed my fears and not dismissed them. As a result of learning this lesson, I now have confidence in myself that should a similar situation present itself, I won't make the same mistake. And once we trust ourselves to be able to make better decisions in the future, it becomes much easier to trust somebody else.

Give ourselves time to heal

After a difficult break-up, I think it's extremely helpful to take a timeout from dating and try to grow in our pain. I personally rushed back into things when in hindsight I wasn't ready, and all it did was lead to more failed relationships, which led to more heartache, which led to more pistanthrophobia, which led to more failed relationships, which led to more heartache, which led to more pistanthrophobia . . . etcetera, etcetera, etcetera. Instead, I think it's better to learn everything we can from our previous relationships, and work to arrive at a place where we feel that if we were to meet someone else that we're interested in, we'd be able to start fresh. Once we've done that, then we're ready to start dating again.

The best revenge is living well

As the saying goes, once we're bitten, we're twice shy. The natural intention is to put up barriers around us and try to protect ourselves by refusing to open up and trust anyone again. But if we do that, we could miss out on the joy of spending our lives with someone great. And we should try our damnedest not to let that happen. An ex's deceitfulness does not have to have a permanent impact on our ability to trust another person, and it doesn't have to destroy our future relationships.

After all, our ex has already hurt us enough. We don't want to give them the power to hurt us anymore.

Key takeaways from this chapter

1/ Fear of trusting someone again can be very difficult for us to recover from, but if we want to be in a happy, healthy relationship again, then we *do* need to overcome it.

2/ The four suggestions that helped me recover from my pistanthrophobia were:

- a) Not making the assumption that the future will be the same as the past;
- b) Understanding the warning signs that my ex was untrustworthy, which will protect me in the future by helping me recognise similar signs in another person who may also be untrustworthy;
- c) Learning what I can do differently to prevent a similar heartbreak from occurring in the future;
- d) Giving myself time to heal from my pain.

CHAPTER 16

What steps can we take to learn how to deal with any causes of our depression that weren't discussed in this book?

In chapters 2-15, we covered a bunch of particularly common causes of people's depression and talked about how we can deal with them. But of course, we didn't cover *every* possible cause, because unfortunately, there are just too many of them. If one or more of the causes of your depression weren't analysed in this book, then I recommend taking the following steps to learn how to deal with them. In fact, I strongly encourage you to take the following steps anyway, even if *all* the causes of your depression were covered in this book, because doing so will give you additional insight and help you deal with them at an even quicker rate.

See a therapist

Like we said way back in chapter 1, this is part of a therapist's job – to teach us how to deal with the underlying causes of our depression. The way I always thought of it was like this: a person with depression has a broken brain, and they need therapy to mend it – in the same way that a person with a broken leg needs surgery to fix it. And, in the same way that a broken leg will never heal without surgery – or, at the very best, not heal properly – a broken brain will never heal properly – or at all – without therapy. Seeing a therapist gave me my life back, and I really, really recommend that you see one too.

Read self-help books

Another thing we can do is read self-help books about how to recover from depression. The best ones are written by some of the most respected psychologists and psychiatrists in the world, and can be immensely valuable resources – particularly if we don't have access to one-to-one therapy. Books I recommend in particular are:

- *Feeling Good* by Dr David D Burns;
- *Authentic Happiness* by Dr Martin E. P. Seligman;
- *The Mindful Way Through Depression* by Mark Williams, John Teasdale, Zindel Segal and John Kabat-Zinn.

Of course, there are also self-help books written about specific causes of depression. Whether it's a lack of self-esteem that's at the root of your depression, a fear of intimacy, difficulty being assertive or something else, you can be sure that there's been a book written on the topic by a renowned psychologist or psychiatrist that you can find on Amazon.

Do online therapy . . . for free!

Given that many people with depression don't have access to private therapy, the availability of free online therapy programs is something that isn't publicised anywhere near enough. There are some great programs out there run by some of the best universities in the world, and building this type of therapy into our day is likely to do wonders over time. The one I recommend using is MoodGYM, which is run by the prestigious Australian National University. To quote their website:

MoodGYM is an innovative, interactive web program designed to prevent depression. It consists of five modules: an interactive game, anxiety and depression assessments, downloadable relaxation audio, a workbook and feedback assessment.

Using flashed diagrams and online exercises, MoodGYM teaches the principles of cognitive behavioural therapy – a proven treatment for depression. It also demonstrates the relationship between thoughts and emotions, and works through dealing with stress and relationship break-ups, as well as teaching relaxation and meditation techniques.

The Australian National University has also recently brought out <u>E-couch</u>, their newest online program for preventing and coping with depression, generalised anxiety disorder, and social anxiety disorder. Like MoodGYM, it's also free.

A final note on dealing with the causes of our depression

After reading the last hundred or so pages of this book, I hope you can see how vital it is to your recovery to learn how to deal with the causes of your depression.

And it really is vital, because here's the reality:

Most of our triggers will never go away.

Let's take my perfectionism as an example. For the rest of my life, there are going to be times when I don't achieve a goal that I set out to achieve. And, if I'd never learned how deal with this cause of my depression, then I'd always feel depressed every time I didn't achieve one of my goals. But since I now know how to deal with it – along with the other causes of my depression – I have recovered from my illness, and now live a very happy, healthy life.

If we can learn how to deal with all of the causes of our depression so that they no longer cause us to feel depressed, then we can recover from depression. But if we don't learn how to deal with them, the sad reality is that we'll probably battle depression for the rest of our lives.

Key takeaways from this chapter

1/ Three things we can do to learn how to deal with the causes of our depression that haven't been covered in this book include:

 a) Seeing a therapist;

 b) Reading self-help books;

 c) Doing free online therapy at MoodGym.

2/ If we learn how to deal with the underlying causes of our depression, then we can recover. However if we don't, then we'll probably suffer from depression for the rest of our lives.

Step 3: Learning how to handle a relapse

CHAPTER 17

Like we've been saying throughout this book, when we're suffering from depression, we want to work through the first two steps we outlined – i.e. we want to figure out what's causing our depression (Step 1), and then we want to figure out how to deal with the underlying causes of our depression so that they no longer cause us to feel depressed (Step 2). Once we've done this, we'll recover from that particular episode of depression. However, in the future, we may experience a relapse.

For many people, experiencing a relapse is a huge cause for concern. It used to be for me, too.

How the hell could I feel so good, feel so certain that I'd conquered my demons, only to feel depressed again a short while later? I used to think.

And then came the most terrifying thought that a person with depression can possibly have:

Will I always feel this way? Is this just the way I am? Will I forever be condemned to a life of insufferable pain and despair?

I get it. However, what I eventually realised is that what having a relapse means is that at the point in time we're having one, we're not yet able to deal with the causes of our depression to an extent so masterful as to prevent them from depressing us.

That's such an important point that I'm going to say it again.

What having a relapse means is that at the point in time we're having one, we're not yet able to deal with the causes of our depression to an extent so masterful as to prevent them from depressing us.

So what do we do then?

When we experience a relapse, then instead of panicking, we want to repeat steps one and two – i.e. we want to put more work into understanding what is causing that particular bout of depression, and then put more work into learning how to deal with that cause so that it no longer has the power to trigger our depression.

We can repeat steps one and two by, for example:

- Going back and re-reading the relevant chapters in this book to better deal with the causes of our depression;
- Going back to see our therapist if we've stopped, or start seeing them more regularly if we haven't;
- Going back to our doctor to see if there's a more effective medication and/or dosage we could be taking.

I'm telling you, if you repeat steps one and two every time you experience a relapse, then your relapses will gradually become less and less intense, and fewer and farther between – and eventually, you can stop having relapses altogether.

To quote a metaphor from my memoir *Depression is a Liar:*

> *It's as if there's a fortress surrounding our brains that's there to protect us from getting depressed, and every time we repeat steps one and two, another armed guard gets posted outside it. If depression's army still gets through from time to time, then it just means there aren't enough guards defending it yet. But if we keep repeating steps one and two, we will eventually have so many guards protecting us that depression's army will be shut out for good. It'll have no way of getting through.*

And it's because of this exact reason that if you follow this three step approach, you really can recover from depression eventually. It will be extremely difficult, because you will have to be proactive when you feel exhausted, you will have to fight when you feel like giving up, and you will have to remain hopeful when depression is doing everything in its power to break your will. But if you follow this three step process, you can get there in the end, because as I like to say, while it is hard for a person to beat depression, it's even harder for depression to beat a person who never gives up.

Hold On, Pain Ends

Book #3 in the bestselling *Depression is a Liar* series

PROLOGUE

Hey there,

My name's Danny Baker, and if you suffer from depression, I just want to say that you are not alone.

Like you, I know how painful depression is. I know how difficult it is to get out of bed some days. I know how depression can suck the pleasure out of everything. And worst of all, I know how it can trick you into believing that your despair is permanent, and that it's destined to oppress you for the rest of your days.

Of course, because I've suffered from depression myself, I also know how helpful it can be to receive some additional support and encouragement throughout your day. For this reason, I've put together *Hold On, Pain Ends* – the third book in my bestselling *Depression is a Liar* series – which is comprised of 365 supportive, uplifting quotes to help you start each morning of the year off in a positive mood and help you cope with your depression as the day wears on. If you'd prefer, you can also re-read your favourite quotes throughout the day, or read through all 365 of them in one hit when you're going through a particularly hard time and need all the help you can get to keep your depression at bay.

No matter which way you choose to read this book, however, I truly hope that these quotes bring as much comfort to you in your time of need as they brought to me during mine.

All my love,

Danny.

~~~1~~~

"On those really difficult days when it seems impossible to go on and you feel like giving up, just remind yourself that you've been there before and you've survived every time, so you can survive this time, too."

~~~2~~~

"Even the darkest hour only has 60 minutes."

~~~3~~~

"Perhaps the butterfly is proof that you can go through a great deal of darkness yet become something beautiful again."

~~~4~~~

"Always try to end the day with a positive thought. No matter how hard things are, tomorrow is a fresh opportunity to make everything better."

~~~5~~~

"We do not heal the past by dwelling there.
We heal the past by living fully in the present."

Marianne Williamson

~~~6~~~

"The World Health Organisation estimates that 350 million people suffer from depression worldwide.
I know it may not seem like it, but you are NOT alone."

~~~7~~~

*"The greater part of our happiness or misery depends on our disposition,
and not upon our circumstances."*

Martha Washington

~~~8~~~

*"Holding onto anger is like drinking poison and expecting someone else
to die.
The only person it hurts is you."*

Buddha

~~~9~~~

*"Don't hate yourself for everything you aren't. Instead, love yourself for
everything you are."*

~~~10~~~

*"Some people find reaching out for help hard. Maybe it is, but suffering
from depression for the rest of your life will be a whole lot harder."*

~~~11~~~

"Running away from your problems is a race you'll never win."

~~~12~~~

*"Don't let your struggle become your identity.
You are so much more than just your illness."*

~~~13~~~

*"On your good days, write down your reasons to keep on fighting.
Then on your bad days, read over your list to give you strength."*

~~~14~~~

"Pain is real but so is hope."

~~~15~~~

*"Be proud of who you are, instead of ashamed of how someone else sees
you."*

~~~16~~~

*"Crying doesn't mean that you're weak. Since birth, it's always been a
sign that you're alive."*

~~~17~~~

"Do not let the behaviour of others destroy your inner peace."

Dalai Lama

~~~18~~~

*"Don't dwell on those who hold you down.
Cherish those who hold you up."*

~~~19~~~

*"Our lives become much brighter when we stop complaining about all
the troubles we have and offer thanks for all the troubles we don't have."*

~~~20~~~

"Depression is a LIAR.
Speaking from experience, there IS light at the end of the tunnel."

Danny Baker

~~~21~~~

"Don't compare your life to others'.
It is not a race.
Live it at your own pace."

~~~22~~~

"Tough times never last, but tough people do."

Robert H Schuller

~~~23~~~

"Healing doesn't mean the damage never existed.
It just means that it no longer controls your life."

Akshay Dubey

~~~24~~~

"Being able to say 'I had depression, but I fought it and won' is one of
the best feelings you'll ever experience."

~~~25~~~

"Worry is a down payment on a problem you may never have."

~~~26~~~

"Never, ever, ever, ever, ever give up on yourself. As long as you keep on fighting, then you can beat your depression."

~~~27~~~

"Sometimes being self-reliant involves recognising that you need help and then going out and getting it."

~~~28~~~

"Set happiness as your highest goal and organise your life around it."

Brian Tracy

~~~29~~~

"Recovering from depression always starts with the decision to try. If you don't try to get better, you never will."

~~~30~~~

"Forgive yourself for not having the foresight to know what now seems so obvious in hindsight."

Judy Belmont

~~~31~~~

"Having a bad day does not mean you have – or will have – a bad life."

~~~32~~~

"You're imperfect, and you're wired for struggle, but you are worthy of belonging."

Brené Brown

~~~33~~~

"What doesn't kill you makes you stronger."
(A cliche, yes – but that doesn't make it any less true)

~~~34~~~

"Nobody can go back and start a new beginning, but anyone can start today and make a new ending."

Maria Robinson

~~~35~~~

"One small crack does not mean you are broken. It means you were put to the test and you didn't fall apart."

Linda Poindexter

~~~36~~~

*"Alcohol may numb the pain temporarily, but being a depressant, it only exacerbates depression in the long run.
Instead of drinking, it's best to seek help."*

~~~37~~~

"Small daily improvements are the key to staggering long-term results.
Stay strong.
Keep fighting."

~~~38~~~

"Choose the positive. After all, you have choices – you are the master of
your attitude. So choose the positive, choose the constructive, because
optimism is a faith that leads to success."

Bruce Lee

~~~39~~~

"Worrying does not take away tomorrow's troubles.
It takes away today's peace."

~~~40~~~

"Hope is one of the most powerful emotions a person can have.
Combine it with determination and there's no stopping you."

~~~41~~~

"I only have time for things that will affect my life in a positive way."

Dylan Smith

~~~42~~~

"In any given moment, we have two choices: to step forward into growth,
or step backwards into safety. Stepping backwards may make us feel
better in the short term, but stepping forwards will undoubtedly make us
feel better in the long term."

~~~43~~~

"Surround yourself only with people who are going to lift you higher."

Oprah Winfrey

~~~44~~~

"There are seven days in the week, and 'someday' isn't one of them. If you suffer from depression, then seek help NOW."

~~~45~~~

"Instead of wiping away your tears, wipe away the people who made you cry."

~~~46~~~

"Just because somebody is worse off than you, it doesn't mean that you're not entitled to your pain."

~~~47~~~

"It's your road, and yours alone. Others may walk it with you, but no one can walk it for you."

Rumi

~~~48~~~

"One of the bravest things you can do in life is continue to live even when you want to die."

Juliette Lewis

~~~49~~~

"Never put the key to your happiness in someone else's pocket."

~~~50~~~

"Just because you're going through a rough patch, doesn't mean you always will be.
Recovery is possible.
I promise you."

~~~51~~~

"You're problems always feel lighter when you're not carrying them alone."

~~~52~~~

"Just because you have a mental illness, it doesn't mean that you are that illness.
You're still a person – just like everybody else."

~~~53~~~

"Recovery is a process.
It takes time.
It takes patience.
It takes hard work.
It takes everything you've got.
But it IS possible."

~~~54~~~

"Sometimes you just need to cry your eyes out to be able to keep going.
And that's OK."

~~~55~~~

*"Listen to positive people and ignore negative ones.
People who doubt, judge and disrespect you are not worth your energy."*

~~~56~~~

"It's not selfish putting your recovery first. If you don't prioritise it, then who will?"

~~~57~~~

*"It's hard for a person to beat depression,
but it's even harder for depression to beat a person who never gives up."*

Danny Baker

~~~58~~~

*"You are not what happens to you.
You are what you choose to become."*

Carl Jung

~~~59~~~

*"You are not crazy.
Some people are just prejudiced."*

~~~60~~~

"It's better to be single and waiting for the right person than to be in a relationship that makes you miserable all the time."

~~~61~~~

"Recovery is a process, not an event.
Give it time.
Good things happen to those who never give up."

~~~62~~~

"Don't get so busy trying to make a living that you forget to make a
life."

Dolly Parton

~~~63~~~

"At times we get too comfortable and ask our demons to pull up a chair,
when we should be pulling it away before they get a chance to sit down."

Rachel Wolchin

~~~64~~~

"Be gentle with yourself.
After all, you're doing the best you can."

~~~65~~~

"I know drinking alcohol is enjoyable, but if you suffer from depression,
then it will only make things worse."

~~~66~~~

"It is necessary, and even vital, to set standards for your life and the
individuals you allow in it."

~~~67~~~

"Mental illness is NOT a life sentence."

~~~68~~~

"Don't be upset and caught up with things or people you cannot change. Instead, move on, let go, and concentrate on what you can change."

~~~69~~~

"Believe with all your heart that recovery is possible and you're halfway there."

~~~70~~~

"It's not happiness that makes us grateful, but gratefulness that makes us happy."

David Steindl-Rast

~~~71~~~

"Choose carefully which battles you want to fight. After all, sometimes it's better to be at peace than to be right."

~~~72~~~

"Next time someone says your depression isn't real, tell them that it's much more real than their imaginary medical expertise!"

~~~73~~~

"Today, do one little thing to take better care of yourself. Then, do it again tomorrow."

~~~74~~~

"Don't let people who do so little for you control so much of your mind, feelings, and emotions."

~~~75~~~

"Learning to ignore things is one of the most effective ways of achieving inner peace."

~~~76~~~

"Our greatest weakness lies in giving up. The most certain way to succeed is always to try just one more time."

Thomas Edison

~~~77~~~

"Make sure everyone in your metaphorical boat is rowing instead of drilling holes in it."

Trent Shelton

~~~78~~~

"When you're suffering from depression, living a balanced life involves setting aside time to do the things you need to do in order to recover – such as seeing your therapist or reading self-help books. You can't afford to say 'I don't have time'."

~~~79~~~

"When something goes wrong, take a moment to be thankful for all the things in your life that are going right."

~~~80~~~

"Relapse is part of recovery.
Don't let it destroy you.
Instead, learn from it and let it strengthen you."

~~~81~~~

"You're been criticising yourself for years and it hasn't worked. For once, try approving of yourself and see what happens."

Louise Hay

~~~82~~~

"Often what hurts the most is pretending that it doesn't hurt at all."

~~~83~~~

"No one ever injured their eyesight by looking on the bright side."

~~~84~~~

"Don't do something permanently foolish just because you're temporarily angry, tired, stressed, scared or depressed."

~~~85~~~

"You're allowed to scream.
You're allowed to cry.
You're allowed to fall apart.
But you are not allowed to give up."

~~~86~~~

"Sometimes it's better to break down in tears than to bottle everything up inside and not tell a soul."

~~~87~~~

"Worrying won't stop the bad stuff from happening – all it will do is stop you from enjoying the good."

~~~88~~~

"Never lose yourself in your search for acceptance by others."

~~~89~~~

"Scars tell where we have been. They do not have to dictate where we are going."

~~~90~~~

"Seek help for your depression immediately, because life is much too short to spend any more time at war with yourself."

~~~91~~~

"Happiness is not something you postpone for the future. It's something you design for the present."

Jim Rohn

~~~92~~~

"Remember, breakdowns can create breakthroughs. Sometimes, things fall apart so that other things can fall together."

~~~93~~~

"Most fears of rejection rest on the desire for approval from other people. Don't base your self-esteem on their opinions."

Harvey Mackay

~~~94~~~

"The worst thing about depression: it hurts like hell.
The best thing: it is temporary. So keep fighting, get help, and you can beat it in the end."

~~~95~~~

"Sometimes you have to fight through your worst days to earn the best days of your life."

~~~96~~~

"The longer we dwell on our misfortunes, the greater is their power to harm us."

Voltaire

~~~97~~~

"Worry about loving yourself, instead of loving the idea of other people loving you."

~~~98~~~

"Aim to learn from your depression so that one day, you can say to yourself:
Dear Past: Thank-you for the lessons.
Dear Future: I am ready."

~~~99~~~

"Your time is limited, so don't waste it living somebody else's life."

Steve Jobs

~~~100~~~

"Remember that life's greatest lessons are usually learned at the worst times and from the worst mistakes."

~~~101~~~

"Suicide doesn't end the pain – it just gives it to somebody else."

~~~102~~~

"You might be sad because you've been through a lot, but you should also be proud of yourself for being strong enough to make it through everything you've been through."

~~~103~~~

"When you say you suffer from a physical illness, you get sympathy. When you say you suffer from depression, you sometimes get blamed. I know it sucks, but at the very least, please take solace in the fact that you are not alone – as evidenced by the fact that 350 million people in the world suffer from depression."

~~~104~~~

"Don't be afraid to give up the good to go for the great."

~~~105~~~

"The struggle you're in today is developing the strength you need for tomorrow.
Keep going.
Don't give up."

Robert Tew

~~~106~~~

"Don't fake being OK, because ultimately, you'll only hurt yourself.
Instead, give yourself a chance to recover by opening up and asking for help."

~~~107~~~

"Breathe.
It's just a bad day, not a bad life."

~~~108~~~

"Being defeated is a temporary condition,
but giving up is what makes it permanent."

~~~109~~~

"Therapy + (possibly) medication + reading self-help books + exercise
+ healthy eating + a regular sleep pattern
= recovery from depression."

~~~110~~~

"Sometimes the people around you won't understand your journey.
But, remember that they don't need to.
After all, it's not for them."

Joubert Botha

~~~111~~~

"We cannot start over, but we can begin now and make a new ending."

Zig Ziglar

~~~112~~~

"Respect yourself enough to walk away from anything that no longer
serves you, grows you or makes you happy."

Robert Tew

~~~113~~~

"You are never too old to reinvent yourself."

Steve Harvey

~~~114~~~

"You must believe that everything happens for a reason, and that
everything that's done with good grace will work out in the end."

~~~115~~~

"Don't believe everything you think.
Your depression is trying to trick you, remember?"

~~~116~~~

"Every day is a new beginning. Take a deep breath and start again."

~~~117~~~

"Remember:
It's perfectly OK to admit that you're not OK."

~~~118~~~

"A flower does not think of competing with the flower next to it. It just
blooms."

~~~119~~~

"Often in life, your situation will keep repeating itself until you learn
your lesson.
So, whenever something goes wrong, always try to figure out why, and
extract all the knowledge you can from it."

~~~120~~~

"Hey, you:
Don't give up, OK?"

~~~121~~~

"If someone doesn't respect you, appreciate you and value you, then they
don't deserve you."

~~~122~~~

"If you're going through a hard time right now, make sure you do
something today that makes you smile."

~~~123~~~

"It is during the hardest times of your life that you will get to see the true colours of the people who say they really care about you."

~~~124~~~

"In the context of mental health, courage can be defined as the strength to ask for help."

~~~125~~~

"I try to shift my focus away from what I'm suffering from and towards what I can do about it."

Elizabeth Geffers

~~~126~~~

"Starting today, stop keeping track of all the mistakes you've ever made. It's time to forgive yourself and start being your own best friend."

~~~127~~~

"Your present circumstances don't determine where you can go. They merely determine where you start."

~~~128~~~

"It's not selfish to love yourself, take care of yourself, and to make your happiness a priority. It's necessary."

Mandy Hale

~~~129~~~

"Remember: recovery is not a race.
Take your time to heal."

~~~130~~~

"Remind yourself that it's OK not to be perfect."

~~~131~~~

"Always look for something positive in each day . . . even if some days
you need to look a little harder than others."

~~~132~~~

"Things may seem gloomy ahead, and you may feel like giving up, but if
you don't keep going, then you will never know what is just around the
corner."

~~~133~~~

"Patience is the calm acceptance that things can happen in a different
order than the one you had in mind."

David G Allen

~~~134~~~

"Protect your spirit from contamination by limiting your time with
negative people."

Thema Davis

~~~135~~~

"If you don't love yourself, then you'll always be chasing after people who don't love you either."

Mandy Hale

~~~136~~~

"If you have a family that loves you, a few good friends, food on the table and a roof over your head, then you are in all likelihood much richer than you think."

~~~137~~~

"Gratitude is one of the sweet shortcuts to finding peace of mind and happiness inside. No matter what is going on outside us, there's always something we can be grateful for."

Barry Neil Kaufman

~~~138~~~

"The cost of not following your heart is spending the rest of your life wishing you had."

J Paulsen

~~~139~~~

"Admitting you need help is the start of the recovery process."

~~~140~~~

"Numbing the pain for a while will make it all the worse when you finally feel it."

Albus Dumbledore

~~~141~~~

"Small changes eventually add up to huge results, so every day, make sure you do something to try and recover from your depression."

~~~142~~~

"Spending time complaining about yesterday won't make today any better."

~~~143~~~

"Never lose yourself while trying to hold on to someone who doesn't care about losing you."

~~~144~~~

"When you feel like giving up, remember why you've held on for so long in the first place."

Hayley Williams

~~~145~~~

"You can't change how people treat you or what they say about you. All you can do is change how you react to it."

~~~146~~~

"Things don't go wrong and break your heart so you can become bitter and give up. They happen to break you down and build you up so that you can be all that you're capable of being."

Samuel Johnson

~~~147~~~

"Sometimes it's OK if the only thing you did today was breathe."

~~~148~~~

"You can't change what you refuse to confront."

~~~149~~~

"Never be ashamed of a scar. It simply means that you were stronger than whatever tried to hurt you."

~~~150~~~

"Don't allow your wounds to turn you into a person you're not."

~~~151~~~

"You are NOT your illness.
You have an individual story to tell.
You have a name, a history, a personality.
Staying yourself is part of the battle."

~~~152~~~

"Your past is just a story, and the sooner you realise it, the sooner you'll realise that it doesn't have to have any power over you."

~~~153~~~

"When you stop taking everything personally, you'll take a huge step forward in your quest to recover from depression."

~~~154~~~

"It is not weak to say,
I'm not OK, and I need help.
On the contrary, it is brave.
It is courageous.
And in the end, it could save your life."

~~~155~~~

"Being happy does not mean that everything is perfect. It means that you've decided to look beyond the imperfections."

Gerard Way

~~~156~~~

"The reason we struggle with insecurity is because we compare our behind-the-scenes with everyone else's highlight reel."

Steve Furtick

~~~157~~~

"Once you choose hope, anything is possible."

Christopher Reeve

~~~158~~~

"Be who you are and say what you feel, because those who mind don't matter and those who matter don't mind."

Dr Seuss

~~~159~~~

"Confidence is not thinking, 'they will like me'. Confidence is thinking, 'I'll be fine if they don't'."

~~~160~~~

"If you can't fly, then run.
If you can't run, then walk.
If you can't walk, then crawl.
But whatever you do, you have to keep moving forward."

Martin Luther King Jr

~~~161~~~

"Courage doesn't always roar. Sometimes courage is the quiet voice at the end of the day saying, 'I will try again tomorrow'."

Mary Anne Radmacher

~~~162~~~

"You don't protect your heart by acting like you don't have one."

~~~163~~~

"You can never cross the ocean unless you have the courage to lose sight of the shore."

~~~164~~~

"Whenever you find yourself doubting how far you can go, just remind yourself how far you have come. Remind yourself of everything you have faced, all the battles you have won, and all the fears you have overcome."

~~~165~~~

"Sometimes you don't always need a plan. Sometimes you just need to breathe, trust, let go, and see what happens."

Mandy Hale

~~~166~~~

"Don't make somebody a priority if they only make you an option."

Maya Angelou

~~~167~~~

"No matter who gives up on you, don't you ever give up on yourself."

~~~168~~~

"Waking up to who you are requires letting go of who you imagine yourself to be."

Alan Watts

~~~169~~~

"At the end of every day, ask yourself,
'what steps did I take today to recover from my mental illness?'
You should always be able to say something."

~~~170~~~

"Happiness is an inside job. Don't assign anyone else that much power over your life."

Mandy Hale

~~~171~~~

"You can do anything you want if you abandon the belief that you can't do it – and that includes recovering from depression."

~~~172~~~

"Being happy involves letting go of what you think your life is supposed to look like and celebrating it for everything that it is."

~~~173~~~

"Everything is going to be OK.
Maybe not today, but eventually."

~~~174~~~

"Don't carry your mistakes around with you. Instead, place them under your feet and use them as stepping stones."

~~~175~~~

"Suicide doesn't end the chance of life getting worse.
It just eliminates the possibility of life ever getting better."

~~~176~~~

"Rock bottom became the solid foundation on which I rebuilt my life."

J. K. Rowling

~~~177~~~

"A strong person is not the one who doesn't cry – it's the one who cries for a while but then wipes their tears away and keeps on fighting."

~~~178~~~

"It's not easy to detach from people who you've had close ties with, but sometimes, it's necessary in order to recover from depression."

~~~179~~~

"Don't waste words on people who deserve your silence. Sometimes, the most powerful thing you can say is nothing at all."

Mandy Hale

~~~180~~~

"You only fail when you stop trying."

~~~181~~~

"What you think of yourself is often much more important than what other people think of you."

~~~182~~~

"Be patient. After all, sometimes you have to go through the worst in order to get to the best."

Kevin Hart

~~~183~~~

"Even the darkest night will end and the sun will rise."

Victor Hugo

~~~184~~~

*"We cannot in a minute get rid of unhealthy habits we've been practising for a lifetime.
That's why it takes time for therapy to work."*

~~~185~~~

"When writing the story of your life, don't let anyone else hold the pen."

~~~186~~~

"Mental illness is nothing to be ashamed of – and neither is talking about it."

~~~187~~~

"Never stop doing your best just because someone doesn't give you credit for it."

~~~188~~~

"Don't ruin a good day by thinking about a bad yesterday. Instead, let it go."

Grant Cardone

~~~189~~~

"Sometimes the hardest part of the journey is believing you're worth the trip – but I'm here to tell you that you are."

~~~190~~~

"When you're going through hell, keep on going. Never, ever, ever give up."

Winston Churchill

~~~191~~~

"The art of being happy lies in the power of extracting happiness from common things."

Henry Ward Beecher

~~~192~~~

"If you can't figure out where you stand with someone, then it might be time to stop standing and start walking."

~~~193~~~

"Have you heard the expression that success is the sum of small efforts repeated day-in and day-out?
Well, so is recovering from depression."

~~~194~~~

"Close your eyes and imagine the best version of yourself possible. That's who you really are. Let go of any part of you that doesn't believe that."

C. Assaad

~~~195~~~

"Instead of wondering when your next vacation is, maybe you should set up a life you don't need to escape from."

Seth Godin

~~~196~~~

"Suicide is a permanent solution to a temporary problem."

~~~197~~~

"Our greatest glory is not in never falling, but in rising every time we do."

Confucius

~~~198~~~

"At any moment you have the power to say, 'this is not how my story is going to end'."

~~~199~~~

"Having a mental illness is nothing to be ashamed of.
And neither is seeking help for it."

~~~200~~~

"Pain doesn't show up in our lives for no reason. It's a sign that
something in our lives needs to change."

Mandy Hale

~~~201~~~

"Life is like a camera:
Focus on what's important, capture the good times, develop from the
negatives, and if things don't work out, take another shot."

~~~202~~~

"Money is a number, and numbers never end. If it takes money to be
happy, then your search for happiness will never end."

Bob Marley

~~~203~~~

"When you get to the end of your rope, tie a knot and hang on."

Franklin D Roosevelt

~~~204~~~

"No amount of guilt can solve the past, and no amount of anxiety can change the future."

Umar Ibn Al-Khattaab

~~~205~~~

"Your self-worth does not decrease based on someone's inability to see it or their refusal to acknowledge it."

Christi Paul

~~~206~~~

"Boundaries are a part of self-care. They are healthy, normal and necessary."

Doreen Virtue

~~~207~~~

"Whatever you do, never forget that you're human. It's OK to have a meltdown. Just don't unpack and live there. Cry it out and then refocus on where you are heading."

~~~208~~~

"When you have a mental illness, reaching out for help is not weak. Rather, it's a sign of strength."

~~~209~~~

"You don't have to be ready to recover from depression, but you do need to be willing."

~~~210~~~

"Not every person is going to understand you, and that's OK. They have a right to their opinion, and you have every right to ignore it."

Joel Osteen

~~~211~~~

"Acceptance doesn't mean resignation. It means understanding that something is what it is and that there's got to be a way through it."

Michael J. Fox

~~~212~~~

"Remember:
Your illness does not define you.
Your strength and your courage does."

~~~213~~~

"If we magnified our successes as much as we magnified our disappointments we'd all be much happier."

Abraham Lincoln

~~~214~~~

"If you never give up, then you will win. Maybe not straight away, but definitely in the end."

~~~215~~~

"No one is ever too broken, too scarred or too far-gone to recover. If you keep on fighting, then anything's possible."

~~~216~~~

"One day, you'll wake up and realise that the pain's still there but that it doesn't hurt quite as much as it used to. That's when you're on the road to healing."

~~~217~~~

"Getting over a painful experience is much like crossing the monkey bars – you have to let go at some point in order to move forward."

C.S. Lewis

~~~218~~~

"Sometimes when things are falling apart they may actually be falling into place."

~~~219~~~

"Why self compassion?
Because how has being mean to yourself worked out so far?"

~~~220~~~

"Be strong enough to stand alone, smart enough to realise when you need help, and brave enough to ask for it."

Ziad K. Abdelnour

~~~221~~~

"If you're searching for that one person who will change your life, then take a look in the mirror."

~~~222~~~

"Oh yes, the past can hurt. But the way I see it, you either run from it, or learn from it."

The Lion King

~~~223~~~

"Never let someone who doesn't know your value tell you how much you're worth."

~~~224~~~

"Sometimes you have to forget about what's gone, appreciate what still remains, and look forward to what's coming next."

~~~225~~~

"You'll never change your life until you change something you do daily. The secret of your success is found in your daily routine."

John C Maxwell

~~~226~~~

"Every minute you are angry you lose 60 seconds of happiness."

Ralph Waldo Emerson

~~~227~~~

"Never, ever forget that you are special, and that you touch more lives than you'll ever know."

~~~228~~~

"Just like there's always time for pain, there's always time for healing."

Jennifer Brown

~~~229~~~

"Unfortunately, the truth is that no one is coming to save you. This life is 100% your responsibility, and it's up to you to save yourself."

~~~230~~~

"There is no need to suffer silently and there is no shame in seeking help."

Joel S. Manuel

~~~231~~~

"Happy people are always evaluating and improving themselves. Unhappy people are always evaluating and judging others."

~~~232~~~

"Don't be discouraged. After all, it's often the last key in the bunch that opens the lock."

~~~233~~~

"When you focus on problems, you'll have more problems. When you focus on possibilities, you'll have more opportunities."

Kamari aka Lyrikal

~~~234~~~

"It's easy to think that you're struggling alone, but the person next to you could also be struggling and hiding it just like you are."

~~~235~~~

"The less you worry about what people think, the less complicated life becomes."

~~~236~~~

"The best way out is always through."

Robert Frost

~~~237~~~

"Comparison is the thief of joy."

Theodore Roosevelt

~~~238~~~

"The happiest people don't worry too much about whether life is fair or not – they just get on with it."

Andrew Matthews

~~~239~~~

"Maybe not today, tomorrow, or even in a year, but if you keep fighting and never give up, then things will eventually turn around, and you'll be able to look back with relief and shout, 'Yes! I made it!' "

~~~240~~~

"When the world says, 'Give up',
Hope whispers, 'Try one more time'."

~~~241~~~

"Don't let small minds convince you that your dreams are too big."

~~~242~~~

"When you face difficult times, just remember that challenges are not
sent to destroy you – they're sent to strengthen you."

~~~243~~~

"You will begin to heal when you let go of past hurts, forgive those who
have wronged you, and learn to forgive yourself for your mistakes."

~~~244~~~

"My therapist saved my life . . . and the right one can save yours, too."

Danny Baker

~~~245~~~

"I know the transformation is painful, but you're not falling apart;
you're just falling into something different, with a new capacity to be
beautiful."

Willian C. Hannan

~~~246~~~

"You, yourself, as much as anybody in the entire universe, deserves your love and affection."

Buddha

~~~247~~~

"Never forget that walking away from something unhealthy is a very brave thing to do – even if you stumble a little on your way out the door."

~~~248~~~

"Anger is an acid that can do more harm to the vessel in which it is stored than to anything on which it is poured."

Mark Twain

~~~249~~~

"Be who you are – not who the world wants you to be."

~~~250~~~

"Hardships often prepare ordinary people for an extraordinary destiny."

C. S. Lewis

~~~251~~~

"Depression is a war. Don't give up just because you lost a battle."

~~~252~~~

"Some days, life is all about your dreams, hopes and vision for the future. But on other days, all it's about is trying to put one foot in front of the other. And you know what? That's OK."

~~~253~~~

"You are imperfect, and permanently and inevitably floored. And you're still beautiful."

Amy Bloom

~~~254~~~

"Don't believe everything you think.
After all, depression is a LIAR.
It's trying to trick you to make you suffer."

~~~255~~~

"You're primary goal every single day should be to just be happy. That's really all you can do."

~~~256~~~

"Relationships are like glass – sometimes it's better to leave them broken than to hurt yourself trying to put them back together."

~~~257~~~

"Remember that just because you hit rock bottom doesn't mean you have to stay there."

Robert Downy Jr

~~~258~~~

"If you're a perfectionist, then remember that finished is better than perfect."

Sheryl Sandberg

~~~259~~~

"MYTH: You will be depressed forever.
FACT: With the right help, you can beat your depression and go on to live a happy, healthy, fulfilling life."

~~~260~~~

"Recovering from depression is difficult as hell – but it's not as difficult as living in pain for the rest of your life."

~~~261~~~

"Look at a stone cutter hammering away at his rock, perhaps a hundred times without as much as a crack showing in it. Yet at the hundred-and-first blow it will split in two, and I know it was not the last blow that did it, but all that had gone before."

Jacob A. Riis

~~~262~~~

"Stop beating yourself up. You are a work in progress, which means you get there a little at a time, not all at once."

~~~263~~~

"I will breathe. I will think of solutions. I will not let my worry control me. I will not let my stress level break me. I will simply breathe. And it will be OK, because I will not quit."

Shayne McClendon

~~~264~~~

"Someday, everything will make perfect sense. So for now, laugh at the confusion, smile through the tears, and keep reminding yourself that everything happens for a reason."

~~~265~~~

"I can't change the direction of the wind, but I can adjust my sails to always reach my destination."

Jimmy Dean

~~~266~~~

"Perseverance is the hard work you do after you get tired of doing the hard work you already did."

Newt Gingrich

~~~267~~~

"I need to learn how to be content with simply not knowing, and be at peace with the notion that everything does not need an explanation."

~~~268~~~

*"Don't let negative and toxic people rent space in your head.
Instead, kick 'em out."*

Robert Tew

~~~269~~~

*"Forgiveness is not something we do for other people – we do it for
ourselves to get well and move on."*

~~~270~~~

*"Don't compare your progress with that of others. After all, we all need
our own time to travel our own distance."*

~~~271~~~

*"When you accept yourself, you free yourself from the burden of needing
others to accept you."*

Dr Steve Maraboli

~~~272~~~

"What consumes your mind controls your life."

~~~273~~~

"It's hard to beat a person who never gives up."

Babe Ruth

~~~274~~~

"When someone asks 'how are you?', it's actually OK to say, 'the truth is, I'm struggling, and I'd really appreciate some help'."

~~~275~~~

"If you've ever had suicidal thoughts, then I'm glad you're still here. Keep holding on."

~~~276~~~

"Caring for yourself is not self-indulgent – rather, it's an act of survival."

Audre Londe

~~~277~~~

"Do not believe all the things you tell yourself late at night."

~~~278~~~

"Gratitude can transform common days into thanksgivings, turn routine jobs into joy, and change ordinary opportunities into blessings."

William A. Ward

~~~279~~~

"Not caring what other people think is the best decision you will ever make."

~~~280~~~

"The best revenge is living well."

~~~281~~~

*"A great attitude becomes a great day, which becomes a great month,
which becomes a great year, which becomes a great life."*

Mandy Hale

~~~282~~~

*'Don't change so people will like you.
Be yourself and the right people will love the real you."*

~~~283~~~

*"Waiting for someone to make you happy is a good way to make you sad.
When it comes to your happiness, take control of it yourself."*

~~~284~~~

*"Don't look back, because if you do, you might fall over what is in front
of you."*

~~~285~~~

*"Self-love requires you to be honest about your current choices and
thought patterns and undertake new patterns that reflect self-worth."*

Caroline Kirk

~~~286~~~

*"Sometimes, we must accept the end of something in order to begin to
build something new."*

~~~287~~~

"If you're thinking about giving up today, just live until tomorrow. And when you do, read this again."

~~~288~~~

"Patience is key, because when the right time comes, everything you're waiting for will be so, so worth it."

~~~289~~~

"Just because your path is different, it doesn't mean you're lost."

~~~290~~~

"Forget about your life situation and pay attention to your life. Your life situation exists in time. Your life is now. Your life situation is mind-stuff. Your life is real."

Eckhart Toll

~~~291~~~

"Given how expensive private therapy is, self-help books written by those same professionals who charge such high hourly rates are an immensely, immensely underutilised resource in almost everyone's quest to recover from depression."

~~~292~~~

"Don't be afraid of going slowly – only be afraid of standing still."

Chinese Proverb

~~~293~~~

"Staying positive will give you power over the darkness in your life."

Mark DenBraber

~~~294~~~

"Don't let the fear of the time it will take to accomplish something stand in the way of you actually doing it. The time will pass anyway – so you might as well put that passing time to the best possible use."

Earl Nightingale

~~~295~~~

"Unexpressed emotions will never die. They are buried alive and will come forth again in uglier ways."

Sigmund Freud

~~~296~~~

"Recovery often involves doing what you should do instead of what you want to do.
But in the end, it is so, so worth it."

~~~297~~~

"Every journey begins with one single step."

Maya Angelou

~~~298~~~

"Recovering from depression is not about not dying. Rather, it's about being able to live a rich, full and happy life."

~~~299~~~

"You may have to fight a battle more than once to win it, but if you never give up, you will get there eventually."

~~~300~~~

"Sometimes, you don't see all of the people who accept you for who you are. All you notice is the one person who doesn't."

~~~301~~~

"The past is like an anchor that holds you back. You have to be able to let go of who you were in order to become who you want to be."

~~~302~~~

"Happiness doesn't depend on what you have or who you are. It depends on what you think."

Buddha

~~~303~~~

"People inspire you or they drain you – pick them wisely."

Hans F Hanson

~~~304~~~

"When you find the courage to let go of what you can't change, you'll take a giant leap forward in your quest to recover from depression."

~~~305~~~

"The past is good to learn from but it's not good to live in."

~~~306~~~

"Recovering from depression and finding happiness again involves working out exactly what's triggering your depression, and then learning how to manage those triggers so that they no longer have the power to trigger you."

~~~307~~~

"Being yourself is the prettiest thing a person can be."

~~~308~~~

"Recovery from depression is the sum of small efforts, repeated day-in and day-out."

~~~309~~~

"Never confuse a single defeat with a final defeat."

F. Scott Fitzgerald

~~~310~~~

"Real transformation begins when you embrace your problems as agents for growth."

Michael A. Singer

~~~311~~~

"Some days are tougher than others, and many times your stresses can seem insurmountable. But hang in there, never give up, and always, always be proud of yourself."

John Cena

~~~312~~~

"Hating yourself will never, ever get you as far as loving yourself will."

~~~313~~~

"Beautiful things happen when you distance yourself from negativity."

~~~314~~~

"The world will not end if you do not figure everything out tonight, so stop pacing, stop sweating, and stop fretting. Instead, go to bed and start again tomorrow."

~~~315~~~

"One in four people suffer from a mental illness. I know it may feel like it, but you are NOT alone."

~~~316~~~

"Remember that sadness is always temporary, and that this, too, shall pass."

Chuck T. Falcon

~~~317~~~

"Keep your thoughts positive, because your thoughts become your words.
Keep your words positive, because your words become your behaviour.
Keep your behaviour positive, because your behaviour becomes your habits.
Keep your habits positive, because your habits become your values.
Keep your values positive, because your values become your destiny."

Mahatma Gandhi

~~~318~~~

"There comes a time when you have to stop crossing oceans for people who wouldn't jump puddles for you."

~~~319~~~

"I know it's hard, but if you don't ask for help, then how can anybody help you?"

~~~320~~~

"Change your thoughts and you'll change your world."

~~~321~~~

"Be a reflection of what you'd like to see in others.
If you want love, give love.
If you want honesty, give honesty.
If you want respect, give respect.
You get in return what you give out."

~~~322~~~

"Break-ups are painful, but not as painful as staying in a relationship
that makes you unhappy."

~~~323~~~

"When you focus on problems, you'll have more problems. When you
focus on possibilities, you'll have more opportunities."

~~~324~~~

"Good things come to those who believe, better things come to those who
are patient, and the best things come to those who never give up."

~~~325~~~

"One day, you will wake up and there won't be any time to do the things
you've always wanted. Do it now."

Paulo Coelho

~~~326~~~

"Your job is to maximise your own kindness, happiness, and health."

Martha Beck

~~~327~~~

"Don't limit yourself. Many people limit themselves to what they think they can do. You can go as far as your mind lets you. What you believe, remember, you can achieve."

Mary Kay Ash

~~~328~~~

"Accept – then act. Whatever the present moment contains, accept it as if you had chosen it. Always work with it, not against it . . . this will miraculously transform your life."

Eckhart Tolle

~~~329~~~

"I'm not in this world to live up to your expectations, and you're not in this world to live up to mine."

Bruce Lee

~~~330~~~

"Forget what hurt you, but never, ever forget what it taught you."

~~~331~~~

"No matter how far you've travelled down the wrong road, you can always turn around and get back on the right track."

~~~332~~~

"Never waste your time trying to explain yourself to people who are committed to misunderstanding you."

~~~333~~~

"Life is short. Cut out negativity, forget gossip, say goodbye to people who hurt you, and spend your days with people who are always there for you."

~~~334~~~

"I am not a victim. No matter what I've been through, I am still here. I have a history of victory."

Dr Steve Maraboli

~~~335~~~

"Worry about your character and not your reputation, because your character is who you are and your reputation is only what people think of you."

John Wooden

~~~336~~~

"Ask yourself: is what you've done this week getting you closer to recovering from depression? If the answer is no, then it's time to make some changes."

~~~337~~~

"No matter how you feel, get up, dress up, show up, and never give up."

Regina Brett

~~~338~~~

"One of the most dangerous myths surrounding depression is that it is a life sentence, when in reality, if you seek the right help and keep on fighting, you can recover, and live a happy, healthy, depression-free life."

~~~339~~~

"Don't compare your progress with that of others. We all need our own time to travel our own distance."

Jerry Corstens

~~~340~~~

"Always find time for things that make you happy to be alive."

~~~341~~~

"Be a winner.
Think 'I can';
'I am';
'I will'."

~~~342~~~

"Never let the things you want make you forget all the things you have."

~~~343~~~

"In the end, we only regret the chances we didn't take."

~~~344~~~

"When everything feels like an uphill struggle, just think of the view from the top."

~~~345~~~

"Nothing is permanent in this world – not even our troubles."

Charlie Chaplain

~~~346~~~

"Give thanks for what you are today and go on fighting for what you want tomorrow."

William Shakespeare

~~~347~~~

"Life has many chapters, and one bad one does not mean that it's the end of the book."

~~~348~~~

"Just because you're strong enough to handle the pain of depression, it doesn't mean that you should have to.
Please seek help.
You owe it to yourself."

~~~349~~~

"If you're feeling suicidal, write down your dreams.
Block everything else out and picture them coming true.
Use them as reasons to keep on fighting."

~~~350~~~

"I am not a product of my circumstances. I am a product of my decisions."

Steven Covey

~~~351~~~

"Eat like you love yourself, move like you love yourself, speak like you love yourself, and act like you love yourself."

~~~352~~~

"Don't let the shadows of your past darken the doorsteps of your future. Forgive and forget."

~~~353~~~

"The greatest risk to a person is not that he aims too high and misses, but that he aims too low and hits."

Michael Angelo

~~~354~~~

"Be kind to yourself, for your sorrows and wounds are healed only when you touch them with compassion."

~~~355~~~

"Never put off until tomorrow what you can do today."

Thomas Jefferson

~~~356~~~

"Things are as they are, and sometimes the only reason we're suffering is because we always imagined different."

~~~357~~~

"If you're depressed, anxious or sick over your weight, it can help to remember that sexy is not a size, every calorie is not a war, your body is not a battleground, and your value is not measured in pounds."

~~~358~~~

"Surround yourself with people who are good for your mental health."

~~~359~~~

"One of the simplest ways to stay happy is to let go of things that make you sad."

Daily Dose

~~~360~~~

"Remember how far you have come, not just how far you have to go. You are not where you want to be, but neither are you where you used to be."

Rick Warren

~~~361~~~

"Life is tough but so are you."

~~~362~~~

"Finding the right therapist is a bit like dating . . . sometimes you have to try a few before you find a good match."

~~~363~~~

"Sometimes the smallest step in the right direction ends up being the biggest step of your life. Tip toe if you must, but make sure you take the step."

~~~364~~~

"The most dangerous risk of all is spending your life not doing what you want on the bet that you can buy yourself the freedom to do it later."

~~~365~~~

"The way I think of it is that, I'm not suffering from depression per se – rather, I'm just learning how to be happy. I'm learning how to be happy because I'm learning how to understand myself better. I'm learning what triggers those plummets into despair. I'm learning, through therapy, how to pick myself back up again whenever I do take a plunge. And, I'm learning valuable lessons from my psychologist that I'll carry with me for the rest of my life. In that way, it's as if there's a fortress surrounding my brain that's there to protect me from getting depressed, and every time I learn a bit more about how to be happy, another armed guard gets posted outside it. Sure depression's army still gets through from time to time, but that just means that there aren't enough guards defending it yet. But if I keep learning how to be happy like I have been, then – combined with me diligently taking my medication, eating well, sleeping well and exercising frequently – I'll eventually have so many armed guards protecting me that depression's army will be shut out for good. It will have no way of getting through."

Danny Baker

Actually, I'm Not OK

Book #4 in the bestselling *Depression is a Liar* series

INTRODUCTION

As anyone who's ever suffered from depression knows, it can make us feel like we're living in a body that fights to survive, with a mind that tries to die.

It can make us feel scared, miserable, empty, numb, ashamed, embarrassed and unable to recognise the fun, happy person we used to be.

It can make it impossible to be able to construct or even envision a future.

It can make us feel so confused and mixed up that we can't see a single answer for any of the problems in our lives, and it can make us feel devastatedly helpless as a result.

It can be so overwhelming that it can feel as if we're fighting to keep our head above water when it's up to our nose, and the water keeps getting deeper, and we don't know how to swim, and there's no one around to save us, and no matter how much we kick and struggle and scream, we just keep sinking. And after a while, it can make us question, *what's the point? What's the point in continuing to fight a battle we don't think we can win?* And it can make us wonder if everything wouldn't be better if we just disappeared . . .

Under any circumstances, depression is a horribly difficult illness to deal with. However, what makes it all the more crippling is that due to the stigma surrounding it, many sufferers don't feel as if they can talk about it with their loved ones. Consequently, instead of receiving the care and support they need, they keep all their pain to themselves, and thus have that pain compounded by feeling isolated, alone, and misunderstood.

Unfortunately, I know exactly how this feels. When I was younger, I suffered from life-threatening bouts of depression that for four years led to alcoholism, drug abuse, medicine-induced psychosis and multiple hospitalisations – and when I was first afflicted by the illness, I had very few people to talk to about it. Like many others, I was too scared to tell my friends what I was going through, and on the rare occasions I tried to, the conversation would never go the way I'd want, and once again, I'd find myself feeling bereft of support. Yet over time, I realised that being able to talk about my condition was a skill like anything else, and as I continued to hone it, I started having a lot more of the open, honest, comfortable conversations that I wanted to have. And, thanks to this, in the latter months and years that I battled the black dog, I was able to cultivate a wonderful group of friends and family members that I could turn to for help.

Actually, I'm Not OK

In this book – the fourth one in the *Depression is a Liar* series – I'll show you how you can tell your loved ones that you suffer from depression in such a way that it leads to you having your own open, honest, comfortable conversations about your illness, and thus ultimately results in you developing that understanding network of supporters that you so richly deserve.

Here's a breakdown of exactly what this book will cover.

Chapter 1: Why it's a good idea to talk about our depression

If we're not sold on the benefits of opening up about our illness in the first place, then it's highly unlikely that we're going to actually do so. Accordingly, we're going to start by outlining the seven reasons why it's important to talk about our depression with the people closest to us.

Chapter 2: Addressing common worries associated with talking about our depression

Even if we're convinced that it's a good idea to talk about our illness, we may have a few fears, worries or misconceptions that are holding us back from doing so. In this chapter, we'll confront some of the most common concerns people have head on, including worrying that others will judge us, stressing out that they won't understand us, being scared of opening ourselves up and talking about something personal, worrying that we're burdening our loved ones, and feeling as if they just don't care.

Chapter 3: Preparing to have a conversation about our depression

In this chapter, we'll delve into how we can prepare to tell someone that we suffer from depression. Specifically, we'll talk all about getting in the right "mindset", and discuss how we can decide who to tell, how much to tell them, where to tell them, and when to tell them.

Chapter 4: Having the conversation

This chapter will deal with how best to start a conversation about our illness, how to handle our friend or family member's response, and how to resolve the conversation so that we get what we want out of it.

~~~

Now that you know exactly what we'll be covering, it's time to get started. I can't wait to go on this journey with you, and I wish you the very best of luck throughout it.

Much love,

Danny.

CHAPTER 1

Why it's a good idea to talk about our depression

Like we've said, if we're not convinced that it's worth talking about our illness, then it's highly unlikely that we'll actually be willing to do so in the first place. Accordingly, let's begin by discussing the seven reasons why it's beneficial to tell the people closest to us that we're suffering from depression.

Reason #1: To gain support

As you and I both know, depression is excruciatingly difficult to deal with under any circumstances, but it's even harder to cope with when we're trying to do so all by ourselves. For this reason, having people we can turn to for comfort and support when we're feeling low can make a world of difference.

Reason #2: To realise that we're not alone

Keeping our depression to ourselves usually goes hand-in-hand with feeling isolated and alone, which almost always serves to intensify our suffering. However, knowing that there are other people who understand us, who know what we're going through, and who are on our side in our fight against depression can be very, very comforting.

Reason #3: So that they can help us see the light at the end of the tunnel

Like we've said, one of the most important reasons to tell someone that we're suffering from depression is to gain their support. Similarly, another reason why it's critical to tell the people closest to us about our illness is so that on our worst days, those people can give us the hope and encouragement we so often need to be able to see the light at the end of the tunnel. After all, as you may have experienced, sometimes when we're suffering from depression it's possible to get so trapped in the fog of our misery that we can't see any way out. Consequently, it often takes someone else to point out to us that there will be better days ahead, and that even though we may not be able to see it right now, that it *is* possible to recover and be happy again.

Reason #4: To develop deeper relationships with our loved ones

One of the least talked about benefits of being open about our depression with our friends and family members is that it can often lead us to have deeper, more meaningful relationships with those people. Speaking from experience, I'd find that telling one of my friends that I suffered from depression would often induce them to share a trial or tribulation that they were going through or had been through previously. As a result, we'd end up having a really personal, meaningful conversation – one that would often lead to more personal and meaningful conversations in the future – and so our relationship would naturally deepen and the two of us would grow closer together.

Reason #5: To help our loved ones understand why we may be acting differently from usual

Another critically important reason why we should tell our loved ones that we're suffering from depression is so that they can understand why we may be acting differently from usual. For example, when we're depressed, we often prefer to stay at home rather than go out and socialise, and as a result, we may not see our friends or family for a number of days, weeks or even months. If they have no idea that we have depression, then they're likely to conclude that we're simply avoiding them – perhaps because we're angry or upset with them, or because we no longer value our relationship with them. However, if we take the time to explain that the reason we haven't seen them lately isn't in fact because of anything to do with them personally, but rather just because we've been battling depression and have needed some time to ourselves, then they're much more likely to understand as opposed to jump to false conclusions. The same goes for if we've been moody around our loved ones, irritable, quiet, unresponsive, detached, aggressive, angry, or if we've outwardly displayed any of depression's other unfortunate symptoms.

Reason #6: To help us understand what may be triggering our depression

As I discuss in *This Is How You Recover From Depression* – which is the second bestseller in the *Depression is a Liar* series – in order to recover from depression, we first need to figure out precisely what's triggering it. There are many ways to do this, but one helpful method is to talk to the people closest to us about our condition and see what they think may be triggering our despair. After all, our partner, for example, may notice that when we don't get a good night's sleep, we're really cranky and crabby the next day. Similarly, our kids might notice that we're tense and irritable if we don't exercise for a week.

Reason #7: To decrease the stigma surrounding depression

The more we all talk about our depression, then the more we all, gradually and collectively, eliminate the stigma surrounding the illness, and thus create a more understanding, compassionate world for ourselves and future depression sufferers.

Key takeaways from this chapter

There are seven reasons why it's beneficial to talk to our loved ones about our depression:

1/ To gain their support;

2/ To realise that we're not alone;

3/ So that they can help us see the light at the end of the tunnel;

4/ To develop deeper relationships with those people;

5/ To help them understand why we may be acting differently from usual;

6/ To help us understand what may be triggering our depression;

7/ To decrease the stigma surrounding depression.

CHAPTER 2

Addressing common worries associated with talking about our depression

Over the years, I've spoken to thousands of people who suffer from depression, and I've noticed that those who don't talk about their illness with their loved ones tend not to do so for two main reasons:

1/ Because they're not completely sold on the benefits of doing so;

2/ Because they're worried about how their friends or family members will react.

We dealt with the first reason in chapter one, so in this particular chapter, we're going to address the second.

Worry #1: That people will judge us

This is a fear that plagues nearly everyone who suffers from depression, including myself when I used to battle the black dog. However, in almost all cases, it's a trepidation that's largely unfounded. Personally speaking, I have told every single one of my friends and family members and countless other people about my depression; I've written nearly 30 articles about my experiences with mental illness for the Huffington Post and other publications that have been read by over 1,000,000 strangers; and of course, I've also written a tell-all memoir detailing my struggle and eventual recovery – and, aside from in a handful of cases, I have never felt judged for having suffered from depression. If that seems unbelievable, then let me remind you that the World Health Organisation estimates that 350 million people have depression worldwide. While it may not seem like it, depression is very, *very* common, which means that most people have been touched by it in some way or another – either because they've battled it themselves, or because someone close to them has. Accordingly, most people recognise depression as a legitimate illness, and will not judge you or think you're a "freak", a "loon" or "crazy" for suffering from it.

As regards the minute percentage of people who may judge you, then I'd like to share an idea with you that's always helped me:

Those who matter don't mind and those who mind don't matter.

In other words, the sort of people you want in your life are not going to judge or debase you for having depression, and if a few people do, then quite frankly, you're better off without them, because they're not the sort of people you'd be able to have a close relationship with anyway. This is a lesson I specifically remember my psychologist teaching me before I released my memoir *Depression is a Liar* in 2013.

'So Danny, how've you been feeling?' he asked when I arrived.

'Yeah, really good on the whole. But I've been a bit nervous lately about publishing my memoir. I mean, a lot of people don't know that I used to suffer from depression, so what are they going to say when they find out I did? And what are they going to say when they discover that it led to alcoholism, drug abuse, medicine-induced psychosis and multiple hospitalisations? What if some of my friends read my book, conclude that I'm a freak, and then decide they don't want to be friends with me anymore?'

'I don't think anyone is going to think that,' my psychologist said. 'But even if a few people do, then it doesn't really matter, does it?'

I was shocked.

'Huh? How can you say that it doesn't matter?'

My psychologist smiled at me gently.

'When you release your memoir, Danny, there are going to be a lot of people who find it inspiring, uplifting and encouraging – and dare I say it, I think there are going to be some people who find it life-saving. However, you may also get some people who can't deal with what you've been through, and who for that reason, may choose to distance themselves from you. But let me ask you this: if a person chooses to distance themselves from you because they don't like your past or because they think you're a "freak", as you put it, then do you think you'd ever be able to have a good relationship with someone so judgmental anyway?'

I thought about it for a few moments.

'No,' I eventually said. 'I guess not.'

'Would you even want to be friends with them?'

I considered that question for another few moments before shaking my head.

'No.'

'So then why would you care if a few people think like that after reading your memoir? Those who matter don't mind, and those who mind don't matter, remember?'

I really took that advice to heart, and ever since that conversation, I've never worried about what people might think of me when I tell them I've suffered from depression (but like I've said, almost everyone has been accepting of it, and in reality, I've only very, very rarely felt judged).

Worry #2: That people won't understand

While it's unlikely that many people will judge you for having depression, unfortunately I'd be lying if I told you that everyone will understand what you're going through. Sadly, because depression has only recently started to get media attention and be discussed more openly, a lot of people don't quite get it, and thus say things that can come across as derogatory or insensitive like:

- 'You just need to get over it.'
- 'But there are so many people who are worse off than you!'

- 'Everyone has bad days from time to time.'
- 'Stop feeling sorry for yourself.'
- 'You just need to get out of the house more.'
- 'What do you have to be depressed about? You've got a great life!'

While such comments can be incredibly frustrating, what I eventually came to realise is that in almost all cases, people aren't saying these things to be mean or because they don't care about us. In reality, they almost always *do* care, but because depression is very difficult to understand if you haven't been through it yourself, many non-sufferers unfortunately just don't know any better. Accordingly, if we take the time to address their misconceptions and help them understand depression more clearly, it's been my experience that they usually come around, and can often turn into very caring, compassionate supporters. We'll talk a lot more about how we can help other people understand depression better in chapter four, but for now, just know that the chance that someone may not quite get it initially is not a good reason to avoid telling them that you're afflicted with this illness.

Worry #3: That we're scared or embarrassed to open ourselves up about something so personal

Of course, being open about our depression can seem like a very scary, confronting and nerve-wracking thing to do. After all, it's much easier to fake a smile and mumble "I'm fine" than it is to be vulnerable and open ourselves up. But if we find ourselves in this position, then we need to do the following to overcome this fear:

1/ Remind ourselves that having depression is nothing to be ashamed of

Depression, as we've said, is an illness, and in the same way we wouldn't feel ashamed of having a broken leg or a physical illness like cancer or diabetes, we have no reason to be ashamed of having depression, either. Absolutely none whatsoever.

2/ Remind ourselves how common depression is

Like we've said, the World Health Organisation estimates that 350 million people suffer from depression worldwide, and for this reason, the majority of people – whether directly or indirectly – have been touched by depression in some way. Accordingly, most people accept it as being the illness that it is, and are unlikely to judge us for suffering from it.

3/ Ask ourselves, "how would I react if one of my loved ones told me something similarly personal about themselves?"

If one of your loved ones told you something similarly personal about themselves, would you judge them? Would you freak out? Would you think they're weird or strange? Would you think it was a "really big deal"? On the contrary, chances are you would just listen and do your best to help them. For this reason, if you're scared of opening up to your friend or family member about something personal like your depression, then it helps to remind yourself that in the same way you wouldn't judge them, freak out, find them strange or think of their problem as a "really big deal", that they're similarly unlikely to judge *you*, freak out, find *you* strange, or think of *your* problems as a "really big deal". After all, suffering is part of the human condition. In our own way, we're all battling something, so when we open up about our difficulties, people are often far more receptive than we might originally anticipate.

4/ Remind ourselves of all the reasons why it's beneficial to talk about our depression

Remembering all the reasons why it's a good idea to talk about our illness won't necessarily make us any less scared of doing so, but it can help give us the strength we need to be able to face that fear.

Worry #4: That we're burdening our loved ones with our problems

This is another concern that a lot of us have, particularly when it comes to talking about our illness with our lover or people in our family. However, it's important to remember that our loved ones are our loved ones for a reason. While it may be difficult for them to come to terms with the fact that we have depression, the people who truly care about us would still prefer to know, because they'd want to try and help us through it, and because they'd hate for us to suffer in silence.

If you're not convinced, then try to imagine the shoe being on the other foot. Ask yourself, *if someone I loved had depression, would I want to know about it so that I could try to support them? Or, would I rather them suffer in silence all by themselves?*

In the same way you'd want to know so that you could lend a helping hand, they would too. Not only that, but like we said in chapter one, one of the most important reasons to tell our loved ones that we suffer from depression is to explain away any uncharacteristic behaviour that we may be exhibiting, so that those people know not to take that uncharacteristic behaviour personally. For this reason, opening up to our loved ones about our depression actually *improves* – not compromises – our relationship with them.

Worry #5: That nobody will care

One of the cruellest traits of clinical depression is that it can cause us to hate ourselves, and thus convince us that everyone else in our life – including our friends and family – also hate us as well (or at the very least, couldn't care less about us). If you feel this way, then please know that this is just the illness talking. After all, this is what depression does – it tries to convince you that you're not as good as everyone else, that nobody likes you, that you'll never recover, and that the world is better off without you.

But depression is a *liar*.

You *are* as good as everyone else.

You *can* recover.

The world is *not* better off without you.

And people *do* care about you.

And, the sooner you tell someone what you're going through, the sooner you'll be able to see this for yourself.

Key takeaways from this chapter

There are several worries that often prevent us from being open about our depression, including:

1/ Worrying that people will judge us;

2/ Worrying that people won't understand;

3/ Being scared or embarrassed to share something so personal;

4/ Worrying that we'll burden our loved ones with our problems;

5/ Worrying that nobody will care.

We can overcome these worries by:

1/ Reminding ourselves that because depression is so widespread and common these days, that it's unlikely that anyone is going to judge us;

2/ Reminding ourselves that even if people don't immediately understand exactly what we're going through, that we can help them understand over time, and that as a result, they can turn into wonderfully caring supporters.

3/ Reminding ourselves that:

    a) In the same way we probably wouldn't think it's a big deal if someone told us something personal about themselves, that someone else probably won't think it's a big deal if we tell them something personal about ourselves;

    b) That all the benefits that come from talking about our depression make it worth stepping out of our comfort zones and being open and vulnerable to another person.

4/ Reminding ourselves that the people who care about us would much rather know about our problems and do what they can to help, as opposed to having us suffer in silence all by ourselves.

5/ Reminding ourselves that depression is a liar, and that while the illness may sometimes make us feel as if no one cares about us, that that's simply not true.

CHAPTER 3

Preparing to have a conversation about our depression

If we want to feel comfortable telling our loved ones about our depression, then it's helpful for us to do some preparation beforehand. Specifically, we want to try and get in the "right mindset", and also carefully consider who to tell, how much to tell them, where to tell them, and when to tell them. We'll turn our attention to each of these issues now.

Getting in the right mindset

Like I said at the start of this book, it was a while before I was able to have open, honest, fruitful conversations about my depression. Initially, they tended to be awkward and uncomfortable, and rarely concluded with me getting what I wanted out of them. I used to wonder why that was so, and in time, what I discovered was that the reason why those early conversations wouldn't go as smoothly as they could have was because I myself wasn't in a mindset that allowed me to come across as comfortable, confident and secure in that fact that I had depression.

Let me explain. You see, because depression is so minimally discussed, a lot of people don't know very much about it. Consequently, when we tell someone about our illness, they are often going to feel the same way about it as we do – for the precise reason that we tend to be swayed by the opinions of others on topics we ourselves don't know very much about.

For example, if we don't know very much about NBA basketball but we know that our friend watches it every single day, then we'll probably believe them when they tell us that the Golden State Warriors are going to smash the Philadelphia 76ers when they play in 2016.

If we don't know much about economics, then chances are we're going to believe an economist when they tell us that a fall in the interest rate is likely to cause the currency to depreciate.

If we don't know much about surf safety, then we're likely to believe the lifeguard when he tells us that the current is too strong for us to go for a swim.

Similarly, then like we've said, because a lot of people don't know a great deal about depression, they are likely to feel the same way about our illness as we do, because we – by virtue of suffering from depression – are going to be perceived as "experts" on the topic – just like our basketball-watching friend, the economist, and the lifeguard were in our examples. Consequently, if we give off the vibe that we think we're "neurotic", "strange", "abnormal" or "crazy" because we suffer from depression, then chances are that we'll influence the person we're talking to into feeling that way about ourselves and our illness too. Not only that, but if we're uncomfortable with the fact that we suffer from depression because we think it means that we're "neurotic", "strange", "abnormal" or "crazy", then we're almost certainly going to find talking about our illness very uncomfortable, and in a social setting, discomfort is contagious. After all, the more awkward and uncomfortable we appear to be, the more awkward and uncomfortable the person who we're talking to is likely to be as well. And, under such circumstances, it's almost impossible to have a calm, authentic chat about our illness.

Let me show you how this works in practice. Below is an example of the way a typical conversation about my depression would usually go with someone when I was first diagnosed – a time when I found talking about my condition extremely anxiety-provoking because I'd (very wrongly) concluded that having depression meant that I was "weird" and "inferior to everyone else".

Me: 'I have something I really need to talk to you about.'
Friend: 'Oh, OK. What's that?'

> **Me:** 'Look, um, it's pretty serious. It's pretty crazy. Are you sure you're ready for me to drop this bombshell on you?'
>
> **Friend:** (Fidgeting uncomfortably) 'Ah . . . yeah. I think so?'
>
> **Me:** (Looking away) 'I just got diagnosed with depression. How messed up is that?'
>
> **Friend:** (Fidgeting even more uncomfortably) 'Oh, um . . . yeah. I guess that is pretty messed up.'
>
> **Me:** (Still looking away) 'Yeah . . .'
>
> (Awkward silence)

As you can see, because I'd project the sentiment that having depression meant that I was "messed up", then the person who I'd be talking to – usually not knowing any better and thus taking their cue from me – would similarly conclude that I was "messed up" for having depression also. Not only that, but because I'd be so awkward and uncomfortable talking about my illness, they would feel very awkward and uncomfortable talking about it too. As a result, the conversation would quickly fizzle out, and I'd never end up getting what I'd want to get out of it.

On the other hand, when we project the notion that depression is "just an illness that we're dealing with" and "nothing to be ashamed of", then the person who we're talking to – once again taking their cue from us – is likely to gravitate towards that notion also. Similarly, the more comfortable we appear to be when talking about our illness, the more comfortable they are likely to be too, and the much more probable it is that we'll end up having that candid, genuine and easy-going conversation about our condition that we wish to have. This is what started happening after several months for me, when I finally realised that having depression didn't mean that I was "weird" or "inferior to everybody else" – as you can see from the transcript below.

> **Friend:** 'Hey Danny, how come you missed Bill's party the other night?'
>
> **Me:** 'Mate to be honest, I just wasn't in the right headspace for it. I've actually been going through a pretty rough time lately – in fact, earlier in the year I was diagnosed with clinical depression – and on that particular night, I just needed a bit of time to myself.'

Friend: 'Oh, OK. I didn't know you had depression.'

Me: 'Yeah, I've had it for about a year now. I'm getting help for it, so I am getting better, but there are some days where I get really low and I don't feel like doing anything.'

Friend: 'I'm sorry to hear that, but I'm glad you're getting better.'

Me: 'Yeah thanks mate, I'm definitely on the mend.'

Friend: 'You know, now that I think about it, you're not the only person I know who has problems with depression. I'm pretty sure another one of my mates has it as well.'

Me: 'Yeah, it's actually a really common illness. Not everyone knows this, but it's estimated that about 350 million people suffer from depression worldwide.'

Friend: 'Wow, I never realised how prevalent it is.'

Me: 'Neither did I until I was diagnosed.'

Friend: 'It's surprising that something so widespread is talked about so little.'

Me: 'Tell me about it, but it's good that lately . . .'

And that's kind of how the conversation would go. Because I'd project the image that depression is "just an illness that I manage" – instead of something that meant that I was "weird" or "inferior to everyone else" – the person who I'd be speaking to would tend to accept it as such as well. Not only that, but because I'd come across as being very comfortable talking about my condition, the person listening would usually feel comfortable talking about it too. As a result, it became much easier for me to have calm, candid chats about my depression, and thus develop a supportive network of friends and family members who I could turn to for support.

Another type of conversation that's more applicable to me these days is the one that often occurs as soon as I meet someone. Since being an author is my job, and my five books – *I Will Not Kill Myself, Olivia; Depression is a Liar; This Is How You Recover From Depression; Hold On, Pain Ends;* and *Actually, I'm Not OK* – are all centred around mental illness, then whenever someone I've just met asks me what I do for a living, the topic of depression inevitably comes up. You'd probably think it would be really awkward to talk about mental health with someone I've just been introduced to, but in reality, because I'm at peace with what I've been through and I'm comfortable discussing it, it's really not awkward at all. In fact, the conversation usually goes something as follows:

> **Person I've just met:** 'So Danny, what do you do?'
> **Me:** 'I'm an author.'
> **Person I've just met:** 'That's awesome! What books have you written!'
> **Me:** 'A fictional story called *I Will Not Kill Myself, Olivia* and a four part non-fiction series called *Depression is a Liar*.'
> **Person I've just met:** 'Oh, OK. So I take it that you've had some experience with depression, then?'
> **Me:** 'Yeah mate, when I was a little younger. I was in a pretty bad way for a few years there, but these days I'm very happy and healthy, so I wrote a memoir and a few other books to try and give current sufferers hope, and to try and pass on some of the things I learned in the course of my recovery.'
> **Person I've just met:** 'That's really great that you can use your experiences to help other people.'
> **Me:** 'Yeah, it is. In a way, it sort of makes everything I went through seem worth it. Almost as if it all happened for a reason.'
> **Person I've just met:** 'Yeah, that's really cool. My brother actually suffers from it as well, and . . .'

You see, because I'd be so comfortable, confident and secure talking about my depression, then the person listening would usually feel comfortable talking about it too.

But how do we become more comfortable talking about our depression?

At this point, I know what you might be thinking:

I understand that because many people don't know very much about depression, that the sentiment I project about my illness is often going to be the sentiment that they pay heed to; and, I understand that the more comfortable I am talking about my illness, then the more comfortable the person listening to me is likely to be as well. But, I feel very uncomfortable talking about my depression – so what can I do to feel more relaxed discussing it?

If this is how you feel, then my guess – based on communicating with thousands of people who've battled the black dog – is that you're uncomfortable talking about your condition because you fall into one or both of the following categories:

1/ You're uncomfortable talking about your depression because you're worried about what people are going to say, how they're going to act, or what they're going to think.

2/ You're uncomfortable talking about your depression because right now, you yourself are uncomfortable with the fact that you suffer from this illness (for example, because you think that having depression means that you're a "freak", a "loser", "strange", "abnormal", or "not as good as everyone else").

If it's the first category of people you fall into, then I encourage you to take some time to re-read the second chapter, and refresh your memory on why so many of the worries we have with regards to being open about our illness are unfounded. On the other hand, if it's the second category of people that you can relate to, then it helps to remember the following:

1/ Depression is an illness, and you have nothing to be ashamed of. We've mentioned this already, but whenever you feel like a "freak" or a "crazy person" or anything like that for suffering from depression, remind yourself that depression is an illness. And, just like you wouldn't feel ashamed of having a physical illness, there's no reason to feel ashamed of having a mental one.

2/ You are not alone. We've mentioned this before as well, but please take solace in the fact that you are not the only one in the world who suffers from depression. Just like you, there are millions of other people who feel overwhelmed. There are millions of other people who struggle to get out of bed some days. There are millions of other people who feel exhausted for no reason at all. And, there are millions of other people who think about ending their life sometimes. All of these people understand your pain and feel the same things you do, and together, you all form a 350 million person fraternity that's represented by every age, gender, nationality, colour, creed and profession in the world. You are not alone. You are not "crazy". You are not a "freak". And you have nothing to be ashamed of. You just happen to suffer from one of the most common illnesses in the world, that's all.

3/ Remember that you are so much more than just your illness. When I was first diagnosed with depression, I thought of myself as a "depressed person". But in time, I came to realise that while I did suffer from depression, there was also so much more to me than just my illness. I was a son, a brother, a grandson and a friend. I was a writer. I was a basketball player. I was someone who loved to read. I was someone who loved to travel. I was someone who loved to go to the beach. I was someone who loved to follow the NBA. I was someone who loved to do charity work, and someone who always tried to help people less fortunate than myself. I was someone who loved to think about the deep things in life, someone who loved to laugh about the silly things, someone who was always there for a friend in need, and someone who never minded so much what I was doing so long as I was doing it with the people I loved. I could go on and on, but my point is that I – just like you, just like anyone with depression – am so much more than just my illness. And once we all realise that our depression is just one part of us, and realise that deep down, we're still the same good, decent people that we've always been, then our depression becomes much easier to talk about, because thinking about our illness in this way allows us to retain our self-confidence, self-worth and self-respect.

Before we move on to the next section and discuss who in particular we should talk to about our depression, I'd just like to close this one by saying that as with anything, practice makes perfect. The more you talk about your illness with your loved ones, the more comfortable you are going to feel, and the easier you are going to find it. It will in all likelihood be difficult at first – even if you apply everything that's discussed in this book – but it *will* start to feel more and more natural over time, and all the benefits that come from talking about your depression are well and truly worth taking those initial steps out of your comfort zone.

Who in particular should we talk to about our depression?

Once we feel as if we can talk about our illness relatively comfortably, then it's time to carefully consider who we're going to open up to about it.

To start with, it's almost always in our best interests to tell the people closest to us – such as our spouse, our parents, and anyone else we interact with on a regular basis. The reasons for this are threefold:

1/ Firstly and most obviously, our closest circle of friends and family members are the ones who are most likely to support us.

2/ Secondly, like we mentioned in the first chapter, sometimes our depression can cause us to act in ways that are out of character – for example, by being overly angry, aggressive or irritable; or by being reclusive and avoiding almost everyone we know. Since it's the people closest to us who are most likely to experience this side of ourselves, it's important that we tell them what we're going through so that they can understand, and thus not take our uncharacteristic behaviour personally.

3/ Thirdly, like we also mentioned in the first chapter, the people closest to us can often give us insight into what may be triggering our depression.

Of course, telling friends and family members who we're somewhat less close with than our "inner circle" can also be very beneficial too – after all, the more support we have, the better! However, when it comes to this group of people, we may choose to be a little more picky about who we decide to talk to about our illness. While we're mulling such decisions over, it's important to bear in mind that the "best" people to open up to will have the following characteristics:

- **They will be caring.** The more caring they are, the more likely it is that they'll be willing to support us.
- **They won't be judgmental.** The less judgmental they are, the more likely they will be to try and understand us.
- **They will be trustworthy.** We obviously need to feel confident that anything private we tell that person won't be repeated to others without our permission.
- **They will be a good listener.** This is key to us having an open, honest conversation about our depression.
- **They will be comfortable discussing something serious and personal.** Not everyone has this capacity, but it's essential that anyone who we choose to talk to about our depression does.
- **They will be someone who we feel comfortable around.** The more comfortable we are with someone, the easier it will be for us to talk to them about our illness.

Additionally, it helps if the person has also had some experience with depression – either because they've battled it themselves, or because someone close to them has. However, there's usually no way to tell whether someone has any such experience, and regardless, it is certainly not a necessary prerequisite to them being a caring, understanding, supportive person to talk to about our condition.

Should we tell anyone at work or someone who we've just started dating?

These are questions I get asked all the time, so before we move on to talking about how much of our depression we ought to share with a particular person, let's first address each of these issues in turn.

When it comes to our employer, we need to carefully weigh the pros and cons of telling them about our illness. Generally speaking, the main benefit of doing so is that they may be able to accommodate us in some way – perhaps by giving us a bit of extra time off here and there when we're going through a rough patch, or by making our work commitments a bit more flexible so that our depression is easier to deal with. On the other hand, the main drawback is that our employer may, even unintentionally, "hold our depression against us" – perhaps by not giving us a promotion or by not placing us on a new and important project, because they're worried that we won't be able to cope with any additional workload or stress.

When it comes to weighing these pros and cons, we all need to judge our own situations on a case-by-case basis, and do whatever we feel is best for us. However, if it was me – and there are many doctors who agree with me – I would avoid telling my employer if I could help it, because I wouldn't want them to "hold it against me". My reason for feeling this way stems from a long way back, when I injured my knee a couple of weeks before a state basketball trial. I wasn't 100% going into it, so I thought it would be a good idea to tell the selectors this. However, my coach told me not to.

'This is a very competitive try-out,' he said, 'and there are a lot of people worthy of making the team. You're definitely one of them, but if you tell the selectors that you have an injury, then they're going to think, *what if Danny has to miss some games because of his knee? What if he can't get back to 100%? What if his body's not really that reliable? Can we really justify putting our trust in him?* And when it comes to choosing between you and another player who's of a similar skillset, then they'll probably use your injury to break the tie and go with him, because he'll be considered a "less risky" option. So no matter what you do, make sure you keep your injury a secret.'

This logic is prevalent in the professional leagues as well, where players with a history of injury always, *always* get paid less than they would if they'd customarily been healthy. Accordingly, they generally tend to downplay their injuries or keep them as quiet as possible, and if you have depression, then I'd suggest you at least think about doing the same with your employer – particularly if you work in a highly competitive environment, or if your workplace doesn't have a culture that encourages being open about such issues. You may think it's unfair for people to "hold our illnesses or injuries against us" like so, but it's just the way the world currently works, and in this particular instance, I believe it's in our own best interests to play by its rules.

Moving on, when it comes to telling someone we've just started dating about our depression, most people's fears are centred around telling that person too soon and thus scaring them off. While this is a valid concern, it's been my experience once again that if you're comfortable with the fact that you have depression, and if you're able to talk about your depression in a relaxed, confident and secure way, then the person listening is likely to feel comfortable talking about your illness too. For this reason, I recommend telling someone you've started dating at whatever point in time you feel comfortable enough to do so. If that's on the tenth date, then that's OK. If that's on the fifth date, then so be it. If that's on the first date, then I personally think that that's OK too. After all, like we've said, if you're comfortable telling someone that you have depression, then they're probably going to feel comfortable hearing it. And, if they do in fact have an issue with it, then wouldn't you want to find out sooner rather than later?

Once we decide who to tell, how do we decide how much to tell them?

Many people believe that talking to someone about their depression necessarily entails telling them *everything* about their illness. However, it's important to remember that our thoughts, feelings and emotions are our own, and how many or how much of those thoughts, feelings or emotions we choose to divulge to any particular person is completely up to us. For example, if we want to tell someone that we suffer from depression, but we don't want them to know that we've thought about killing ourselves, then we don't have to share that with them. If we don't want to tell them that we've self-harmed before, then we don't have to do that either. If we don't want them to know that we cry ourselves to sleep some nights, then that's another thing we can choose to hold back. We only have to tell them as much – or as little – as we feel comfortable with.

In saying that, however, this advice comes with a couple of caveats:

1/ We need to tell our doctors and our medical team *absolutely* everything. While it's perfectly OK to hold back certain aspects of our illness from our loved ones, we cannot keep secrets from our doctor, psychologist, psychiatrist, counsellor, or anyone else on our medical team. Doing so can drastically impact the treatment we receive, and in order for that treatment to be the most effective it can be, our medical team need to know exactly what we've been thinking and feeling.

2/ Remember that everybody's reaction to us telling them that we suffer from depression – including the level of sympathy and support they provide – is dependent upon what we actually tell them about our depression. Accordingly, if we're feeling suicidal for example, then while we have every right to keep that information to ourselves when we tell someone about our illness, it's not then fair for us to turn around and feel angry at that person for not offering the level of care, sympathy or support that we believe should be offered to a suicidal person. After all, if we didn't tell them that we're feeling suicidal, then how are they supposed to know? This isn't a caveat per se to the notion that we should only tell someone as much as we feel comfortable with, but it is something important to bear in mind.

Where's the best place to tell someone that we suffer from depression?

Once we've decided who we're going to talk to about our illness and how much we're going to tell them, we have to choose a place to have the conversation. While there's no one perfect location that will suit everybody, the spot we choose should ideally satisfy the following requirements:

1/ It should be somewhere where we feel at our most comfortable. Like we've said, the more comfortable we are talking about our depression, then the more comfortable the person listening is likely to be as well, and the greater the chance that the conversation will go the way we want it to. For this reason, it's important that we pick a location where we feel as comfortable as possible, whether that be at our house; at our favourite bar, café or restaurant; or somewhere else.

2/ It should be somewhere relatively quiet. We hardly want to be trying to have a deep, meaningful conversation over loud music at a nightclub, so in addition to picking a place we feel comfortable at, we need to pick one where it's quiet enough to have a proper conversation.

3/ It should be somewhere that's private. We're unlikely to feel at our most comfortable when there are people sitting a foot away who can hear everything we're saying, or when we're being interrupted every few minutes. So, we need to choose a spot where we have some privacy.

Is it OK to tell someone over the phone or via email or Facebook?

In my humble opinion, it's best to tell someone in person, because that's generally the most effective way to have an open, honest, authentic conversation about something important like our depression. However, if you just can't bring yourself to talk about your illness face-to-face, then doing so over the phone or via email or Facebook is always another option. After all, the most important thing is that you tell someone – regardless of what medium you choose to do so through.

When is the right time to tell someone that we're suffering from depression?

Just like when it comes to choosing the "right location", there's no such thing as a "right time" that will work for everybody. Rather, choosing when we're going to tell someone about our condition involves taking into account the following factors that are unique to our own particular situations:

1/ **How in need we are of support.** The more severe our depression and the more in need we are of support, the sooner we need to tell someone about our illness – and, if we're feeling suicidal and we think we might attempt to take our own life, then we need to tell a doctor, a therapist, Lifeline, a friend or a family member immediately. However, if our depression is less severe than that and we're not in urgent need of help from our loved ones, then we can afford to take our time a bit more if we so choose.

2/ When we feel "ready". As we've intimated, there can be a bit of preparation that goes into telling someone that we have depression, so unless we're in urgent need of assistance, it can often be best to wait until we feel as prepared as can be.

3/ When we have enough time to have a proper conversation. Five minutes before their train is due to arrive is not a good time for us to tell our friend that we suffer from depression. Instead, it's best to wait until there's time to have a proper conversation that won't feel rushed.

Key takeaways from this chapter

1/ Because depression is so minimally discussed, a lot of people don't know very much about it. Consequently, when we tell someone about our illness, they are often going to feel the same way about it as we do. As a result, if we give off the vibe that we think we're "neurotic", "strange", "abnormal" or "crazy" because we suffer from depression, then chances are that we'll influence the person we're talking to to feel that way about ourselves and our illness, too. However, if we project the notion that depression is "just an illness that we're dealing with" and "nothing to be ashamed of", then the person listening – once again taking their cue from us – is likely to adopt that view as well.

2/ The more comfortable we appear to be talking about our illness, the more comfortable the person we're talking to is likely to be as well, and the much more likely it is that we'll end up having that candid, genuine and easy-going conversation about our depression that we wish to have.

3/ We tend to feel uncomfortable talking about our depression because we are:

a) Worried about how people are going to react; or

b) Because we believe that having depression means that we're a "freak", "strange", "abnormal", or "not as good as everyone else".

    i. If it's the first category of people we fall into, then we need to remind ourselves why so many of the worries we have with regards to opening up about our depression are unfounded (see chapter 2).

    ii. If it's the second category of people we fall into, then we need to remember that we have nothing to be ashamed of for suffering from depression, that we are not alone, and that we are so much more than just our illness.

4/ It's important to tell our closest circle of friends and family about our depression because:

a) They are the people who are most likely to support us;

b) So that they understand why we may be acting out of character, and thus know not to take any uncharacteristic behaviour that we may be exhibiting personally;

c) So that they can give us some insight into what may be triggering our depression.

5/ When considering which, if any, people outside of our closest circle to talk to about our illness, we need to bear in mind that the "best" people to open up to will be:

a) Caring;

b) Non-judgmental;

c) Trustworthy;

d) Good listeners;

e) Comfortable discussing something serious and personal;

f) Someone who we feel comfortable around.

6/ When it comes to telling our employer about our illness, we need to carefully weigh the pros and cons of doing so. However, it's my personal opinion that it's best not to tell anyone at work, because unfortunately it's something that can be held against us (particularly if we work in a highly competitive environment, or if our workplace doesn't have a culture that encourages being open about such issues).

7/ When it comes to telling someone we've started dating about our illness, it's best to open up to them at whatever time we feel comfortable doing so.

8/ When deciding how much to tell a particular person about our depression, it's important to remember that we are the owner of our thoughts, feelings and emotions, and that for this reason, we only need to tell that person as much – or as little – as we feel comfortable with. However, it's also important to remember that we need to tell our medical team *absolutely everything,* and that everybody's reaction to us telling them that we suffer from depression – including the level of sympathy and support they provide – is dependent upon what we actually tell them about our illness.

9/ The location at which we choose to tell someone about our depression should ideally be:

a) Somewhere where we feel at our most comfortable;

b) Somewhere that's quiet;

c) Somewhere that's private.

10/ When deciding when to tell someone about our depression, we need to consider how urgently in need of support we are, and how ready we feel to have a conversation about our illness. Additionally, we also need to make sure that whenever we choose to do it, that there's enough time available to have a proper chat.

CHAPTER 4

Having a conversation about our depression

Once we're convinced that it's beneficial to talk about our illness; addressed all our fears and worries that are associated with doing so; gotten into the right mindset; and decided who to tell, how much to tell them, where to tell them and when to tell them, it will (finally!) be time to go ahead and have that all-important conversation about our depression. In this chapter, we'll start by covering the different ways we can begin a conversation about our condition, and then move on to addressing how we can handle another person's response to what we've told them, and how we can resolve the conversation to get what we want out of it.

How can we begin a conversation about our depression?

Broadly speaking, there are two main ways we can start a conversation about our illness:

1/ By raising it within the natural flow of conversation;

2/ By making a special point of bringing it up.

Raising it within the natural flow of conversation

This is my preferred method, because it tends to come across as casual and laid back – and, like we've said, the more relaxed we appear to be when talking about our illness, the more comfortable the person listening to us is likely to be as well. Here are a few examples of how I might've slipped my depression into a conversation in the past.

Example #1

Friend: 'So Danny, how've you been lately?'
Me: 'Not too good unfortunately, mate. I've actually been going through a pretty rough time, and to tell you the truth, I've been diagnosed with depression.'

Example #2

Friend: 'Hey buddy, you going to Cassie and Jake's housewarming on the weekend?'
Me: 'Nah, don't think so mate.'
Friend: 'How come?'
Me: 'I'm just not quite feeling up to it, I'm afraid. To be honest, I've been going through a pretty rough time lately – in fact, I've actually been diagnosed as suffering from depression – and some days, I just need some time to myself.'

Example #3

Me: 'What are you up to tomorrow, mate?'
Friend: 'Nothing much, why?'
Me: 'Just wondering if you wanted to go down to the park and play some basketball with me.'
Friend: 'Yeah sure, sounds good brother.'

Me: 'Sweet.'

Friend: 'You've been playing a lot lately, haven't you?'

Me: 'Sure have been, yeah.'

Friend: 'You training for a big tournament or something?'

Me: 'Nah, just need the exercise, mate. To be honest, I've actually been going through a really difficult time lately – a doctor even diagnosed me as suffering from depression – and I find that exercising a lot and being really active just helps me deal with it.'

Making a special point of bringing it up

Alternatively, rather than raising our depression in the natural flow of conversation, we may prefer to make a special point of mentioning it. For example, by saying something like:

'I've been feeling really down lately. Would you mind if we talked a little bit about it?'

Or:

'I haven't told many people this, but I've actually been struggling with depression lately. If it's OK with you, then I'd really like to talk to you about it now.'

Again, I personally prefer naturally weaving it into conversation, because it tends to come across as laid back and relaxed. In saying that, however, if you don't have much experience talking about your illness, then it can be difficult to know how and when to raise it organically, and for this reason, you may prefer to make a special point of mentioning it. Either way, it's your choice – just do whatever you feel most comfortable with.

How to handle another person's reaction when we tell them that we have depression

Of course, we always hope that whenever we tell someone that we're suffering from depression, that they're going to be supportive and caring right off the bat. For example, perhaps by saying something like:

a) I love you.

b) I'm here for you.

c) Is there anything I can do to make you feel better?

d) Would you like to talk about what you're going through?

e) I've suffered through depression myself.

f) I'm sorry you're in pain.

g) This must be very hard for you, but you're going to get through it.

h) Is there something we can do to take your mind off it?

i) I don't quite understand what you're going through, but I'm here to support you anyway.

Each of these responses is warm and supportive, and should make it relatively easy for us to open up about our illness. However, I'd be lying if I said that everyone is likely to respond in this way. Unfortunately, some people may initially make annoying comments like 'you just have to think positive!', because they don't realise how debilitating of an illness depression really is. Alternatively, some people may immediately try to pinpoint why we might be depressed and offer what's usually overgeneralised, simplistic advice about what we can do to feel better, whereas others may not know how to respond and thus be relatively silent. For this reason, prior to telling someone that we're struggling with depression, it's useful to think about the different ways they might react, and about how we can respond to those different reactions. In fact, this is such a helpful exercise that we're going to turn our attention to it right now.

What if someone says something irritating that clearly shows that they don't know very much about depression?

Unfortunately, when we tell someone that we're battling depression, it's possible they'll respond in a way that comes across as insensitive, uncaring or dismissive of our illness. This of course can be incredibly frustrating, but like we said in chapter two, usually the reason someone makes a comment like "you just need to get over it" or something along those lines is not because they're a jerk who doesn't care about us – rather, it's because they don't properly understand how depression affects a person, and/or they don't appreciate how debilitating of an illness it can actually be. And for us, this is good news, because we can help them understand depression and thus help turn them into loyal, caring supporters.

Accordingly, if someone says something that comes across as insensitive, uncaring or dismissive of our illness, it's important that we *do not* get our backs up and start deriding them for not knowing more about depression. Instead, what we want to do is calmly and collectedly explain to that person why what they're saying isn't quite true, and offer them an alternative viewpoint that will help them understand depression – and thus ourselves – much better than they do at present.

Below is a list of common insensitive, uncaring or dismissive comments people might make about your illness, and what I suggest you say in response.

Comment: 'You just need to get over it.'
Response: 'I wish I could, but unfortunately, it's not nearly that simple. Not everyone knows this, but depression is an illness, and because it's an illness, people can't just "get over it" – in the same way no one can just "get over" diabetes, cancer, or any other illness or injury.'

Comment: 'We all have bad days now and then.'
Response: 'That's true, but unfortunately, depression is much, much more than just a bad day. People with depression often feel miserable for days, weeks, months or even years on end. And the intensity of their despair is usually far greater than that experienced by a non-depressed person. Some people with clinical depression hate themselves. Some self-harm. Some kill themselves. Clinical depression is an illness, and it can be very serious.'

Comment: 'You can't be depressed, because there are so many people in the world who are worse off than you.'
Response: 'Yes, there are people in the world who are worse off than me, but that doesn't mean that it's not possible for me to suffer from depression. After all, depression is an illness, and the fact that there are people in the world who are less fortunate than me doesn't mean I'm immune from getting it – just like I'm not immune to getting diabetes, cancer, or any other illness or injury.'

Comment: 'Just think positive.'
Response: 'I'm trying my best to, but unfortunately, that doesn't mean I can automatically be cured of my depression. Not everyone knows this, but depression is an illness, and in the same way that positive thinking can't magically cure a broken leg, heart disease or any other illness or injury, it can't magically cure someone's depression, either.'

Comment: 'You're just looking for attention.'
Response: 'It's really quite the opposite, mate. If you want to know the truth, I've actually been suffering from depression for X

weeks/months/years, but every day, I fake a smile and pretend I'm fine, because I'm scared to tell anyone how I'm really feeling. On the rare occasions I do tell someone like yourself, I feel uncomfortable, and scared, and nervous, and it takes all the courage I can muster to bring myself to do it. Believe me, the last thing I want is attention – but, I do need your support, which I why I've reached out to you today to tell you what I'm going through.'

Comment: "I thought you were stronger than that."
Response: "I am strong, but I'm also sick. Not everyone knows this, but depression is actually an illness, and in the same way strong people can fall victim to cancer, diabetes or any other physical illness or injury, they can also fall victim to depression as well.'

Comment: 'But you don't look depressed.'
Response: 'You're right, I don't – but that's only because due to the stigma surrounding mental illness, I fake a smile and pretend I'm fine. The truth though is that this is a very difficult time for me. I'm really, really struggling, and I'd really appreciate your help.'

Comment: 'But look how lucky you are.'
Response: 'You're right, I am really lucky, but that doesn't mean that it's not possible for me to suffer from depression. After all, depression is an illness, and just like lucky people are not immune from getting cancer, diabetes or another physical illness or injury, they're not immune from getting depression, either.'

It's been my experience that if we respond in a calm way like so that gently points out the fallacy in someone's ignorant remark, then that person will often listen to what we're saying and do their best to understand where we're coming from – and, as a result, they can end up becoming one of our most caring supporters. However, if we take the time to try and enlighten them and it's clear that they're not really listening, then it's generally best to leave it for a while and have another crack a bit later on – after all, it's possible that, given a bit more time, they may come around. If we try to talk to them a few more times after that though and it's just more of the same, then sadly, they're probably not someone who we're going to want to turn to when we're going through a rough patch. While this is unfortunate, it helps to remember that there are plenty more fish in the sea, and that for every one of those unsupportive people, there'll in all likelihood be a handful who will happily be there for us.

What about when someone starts trying to "fix" us?

Sometimes when we tell someone that we're afflicted with depression, they'll respond straight away with something like:

- 'You just need to do more of X.'
- 'You'll feel better if you stop doing Y.'
- 'It's only because of Z – sort that out and you'll be fine.'

It's a bit difficult for me to advise you on how to respond to such remarks, because hearing a variation of the above can affect different people in different ways. For example, some sufferers may appreciate the suggestions, and from there may want to explore with that person the different things they may be able to do to alleviate their depression. If that's you, then by all means run with the conversation and see where it takes you. However, many people feel one or both of the following emotions whenever someone tries to "fix" them like so:

- **Annoyed** – because often the suggestions are overly simplistic and imply that depression is a piece of cake to fix.
- **Unsatisfied** – because often when someone plucks up their courage to tell their loved one that they're suffering from depression, what they're after is to be supported and listened to – as opposed to being bombarded with solutions.

If you can relate, then here's how you can respond to someone who's trying to "fix" you:

- **If you feel irritated:** 'I appreciate you trying to help, but unfortunately, depression is a lot more complicated than that. It is a serious mental illness that afflicts 350 million people worldwide, and while I wish I could fix it by just doing X, Y or Z, unfortunately it's nowhere near that simple.'
- **If you feel unsatisfied:** 'I appreciate you trying to help me find solutions to my depression, but I'm working to overcome my illness with my doctor/psychologist/psychiatrist/counsellor, and we're making good progress. From you, what I really need is someone who'll listen to me when I need to get something off my chest, and someone who'll be there to support me when I'm feeling low. Do you think you could do that for me?'

Again, it's important for us to remember to stay calm and in control of our emotions. While it can certainly be irritating when someone tries to "fix" us with overgeneralised suggestions, we need to remember that that person does care about us and that their heart is in the right place (after all, if they didn't care for us, then they wouldn't bother trying to "fix" us in the first place!). Like we've said, such comments merely stem from the fact that depression is minimally spoken about, and thus minimally understood by people who haven't experienced it themselves. However, the more that we as people with lived experience of depression talk about our illness, the more we will collectively break down these barriers, and help create a world that understands and supports people who suffer from depression.

What about when someone responds by just being silent or by changing the subject?

Unfortunately, this is how some people may respond when we try to tell them about our depression – usually because they're just caught off guard, or because they don't really know what to say. When this happened to me, I used to let it slide on that particular occasion, but then raise it again at the next available opportunity. When that time came, instead of trying to slip the subject of my depression into the conversation like I usually would, I would make a special point of bringing it up, and ask that person point blank if we could talk about it together. Sometimes that would work and we'd have a good chat, but unfortunately, other times they'd be similarly evasive the second time around. If the latter happened, then I'd usually conclude that for whatever reason, that person just wasn't comfortable discussing a serious subject like depression, and moving forward, I'd focus on talking to some of my other loved ones about my illness. While this is a disappointing conclusion to have to reach, it's important to remember that that person still does care about us, and no doubt wishes us all the best in our recovery – it's just that for whatever reason, they're not capable of talking about our condition with us.

How to resolve the conversation so we get what we want out of it

While we're having a conversation about our illness, it's important to keep in mind what we want to get out of it. For example, is it to have someone to talk to when we're feeling low? Is it to have someone to come to the doctor with us? Is it to have someone to call and check up on us from time to time? Is it someone to play a game of squash with us every Tuesday so that we can get more exercise? Whatever it is, it's important that we communicate our needs to our loved one at some point during the conversation. If they voluntarily offer to provide the kind of support we need, then that's great – but it's a mistake to expect this to happen and then be disappointed when it doesn't. After all, our loved ones are not mind-readers, so how are they supposed to know exactly what we want unless we tell them? Not only that, but like we've said, depression is a very difficult illness to understand if you haven't experienced it yourself, and for this reason in particular, it's up to us to take the lead with our friends and family and communicate exactly what we need from them.

Key takeaways from this chapter

1/ There are two main ways we can begin a conversation about our depression:

a) By raising it within the natural flow of conversation (my preferred method because it comes across as casual and relaxed);

b) By making a special point of bringing it up (this method is less laid back, but some people may find it easier).

2/ If someone, after telling them that we suffer from depression, responds in a way that comes across as insensitive, uncaring or dismissive of our illness, it's important that we *do not* get our backs up and start deriding them. Instead, what we want to do is remain calm, do our best to explain to that person why what they're saying isn't true, and offer them an alternative viewpoint that will help them understand depression – and thus ourselves – better than they do at present.

3/ If someone, after telling them that we suffer from depression, tries to instantaneously "fix" us with suggestions of how we can alleviate our despair, then:

a) If we're receptive to their suggestions, we can run with the conversation and see where it takes us;

b) If we feel annoyed because their advice is overly simplistic, then we can explain to them how serious of an illness depression is, and how complicated it is to solve;

c) If we feel unsatisfied because, as opposed to wanting advice from that person, what we really need is moral support from them, then we can make a point of communicating this need to them.

4/ If someone, after telling them that we suffer from depression, responds by either being silent or by changing the subject, then we can try to broach the subject again on future occasions when they may be more receptive to discussing it.

5/ While we're having a conversation about our illness, it's important to keep in mind what we want to get out of it, and, before the conversation comes to a close, ensure that we communicate those needs to our loved one in question.

CLOSING THOUGHTS

So that's it – we've covered the seven reasons why it's beneficial to talk about our depression; addressed the most common worries associated with doing so; analysed how to get into the right mindset to have a conversation about our illness; discussed who we ought to tell, how much we ought to tell them, where we ought to tell them and when we ought to tell them; and talked about how to start a conversation about our condition, how to respond to other people's reactions when we broach the subject of our illness, and how to resolve the conversation so that we get what we want out of it. By now, I hope you feel much better prepared to have a talk with your loved ones about your depression, and I truly hope that those conversations lead to you developing a supportive network of friends and family members who you can turn to when you need them.

Before we finish up though, I'd just like to say that talking about your illness is something that will get easier with time. After all, it is a skill, and like any skill, practice makes perfect – so even if you find it difficult at first, rest assured that if you keep on pushing yourself to give it a go, then it will gradually become something that comes a lot more naturally to you.

On a somewhat different note, the last thing I'd like to stress is the fact that even though it may appear inconceivable at times, it *is* possible to recover from depression and find happiness again. To prove my point, I'd like to share with you an excerpt from my #1 international mental health bestseller *Depression is a Liar*, which is a memoir about my struggle and eventual triumph over depression.

April, 2010

The days dragged along. This was the worst I'd ever felt. Period. There was no relief from the ceaseless dread. I could barely function. Paying attention in class was almost impossible. Studying was too overwhelming. I'd fallen absurdly behind. I hadn't touched my book [that I was writing] in days. I'd quit my [part-time] job at the law firm, too – needed all my free time to try and catch up on uni. But there was never enough time. I was constantly exhausted. Drained of life. Depression sucked at my soul. My spirit withered. My goal for the day got broken down even further: just survive the next six hours, *I'd tell myself.* The next four hours. Hold off killing yourself until then. *[At which point, I'd tell myself the same thing over again.]*

I'd previously thought I'd get better. I'd always thought it true that hope and depression were bitter rivals until one inevitably defeated the other, and I'd always thought that hope would win out in the end. But for the first time in my life, I was void of hope. I honestly believed that being depressed was just the way I was, and that being depressed was just the way I'd be, for the rest of my life. And because I was so convinced that I'd never get better, there seemed no point in fighting my illness. Instead of willing myself to "hang in there" because I believed that my suffering was temporary and that everything would be better one day, I comforted myself with the knowledge that human beings are not immortal. That I would die, one day. One special, glorious day. Then I could spend the rest of eternity moulding in a grave, free from pain. You might be wondering why I didn't just kill myself if I wholeheartedly believed that my future consisted of nothing more than excruciating misery. Well, first of all, I still was not a quitter. But more importantly, I didn't want to hurt the people that loved me.

It's not fair to commit suicide and ruin their lives, *I thought.* So I have to hold on. No matter how much it hurts me I have to hold on.

Hence why I drew comfort from the thought that one day I'd die and finally be free.

When you're that depressed, that insanely and utterly depressed that you genuinely believe you'll suffer that acutely for the rest of your days, life seems to lack all purpose.

After all, *I remember thinking,* what's the point in working, fighting, striving for a better life if I'm sentenced to one of chronic anguish and despair? There is no better life. There is no life outside of pain. So what's the point in doing anything but waiting until death finally arrives on my doorstep and whisks me away to the Promised Land?

I was still studying, and I still planned on finishing my novel and trying to get it published, but it was more out of force of habit than anything else. My passion had been drained. My zest for life asphyxiated. I was like a ghost, just drifting through the ghastly days.

'Shit! What's wrong, mate?' an old friend once said when I ran into him at uni. 'Perk up, brother!'

I was shocked. One of the most well-known attributes of depression is that it is entirely possible – and very common – to suffer horrifically without anybody knowing. But somehow without realising it, I'd crossed the line from a place where I was able to put on a front and fool people into thinking I wasn't depressed to a place where I was so sick that it was obvious to people I hadn't even seen for a year. When I got home I looked in the bathroom mirror, and realised that I was staring back at a man whose eyes were exhausted slits, whose whole face shrieked of agonising misery. I was staring back at a man whose spirit had been broken, whose soul had been destroyed. I was staring back at a man who, for all intents and purposes, was already dead.

As you can see, I was so convinced I'd never get better. I was 100% sure of it. But after a while, one of the multiple medications I tried started to work, and I saw a terrific therapist who helped me understand that recovering from depression could be broken down into the three straightforward steps detailed in my second mental health bestseller *This Is How You Recover From Depression.* I followed those steps assiduously, and by the start of 2012, I'd kicked my depression for good. Ever since then, I've been feeling great.

And I'm hardly the only person who's recovered from depression. I'm just one of thousands – tens of thousands – probably millions.

Depression is a maestro at suffocating your hope, but countless people have proved that depression is a liar. Recovery *is* possible – even if you don't believe it right now.

Wishing you lots of luck in your journey towards happiness,

Danny.

Bonus Content

Thank-you so much for reading the *Depression is a Liar* series. I hope you enjoyed reading it as much as I enjoyed writing it, and I really hope it's helped you in your fight against depression.

Even though you've finished this series, I'd love to continue trying to help you by emailing you a supportive, uplifting quote each morning to help you through your day. If you'd like to join all the other readers who receive my quotes, then please visit www.dannybakerwrites.com/quotes.

Printed in Great Britain
by Amazon